People and Chips

The Human Implications of Information Technology

THIRD EDITION

Christopher Rowe and Jane Thompson

THE McGRAW-HILL COMPANIES

London · New York · St Louis · San Francisco · Auckland
Bogotá · Caracas · Lisbon · Madrid · Mexico
Milan · Montreal · New Delhi · Panama · Paris · San Juan
São Paulo · Singapore · Sydney · Tokyo · Toronto

Published by McGraw-Hill Publishing Company
Shoppenhangers Road, Maidenhead, Berkshire, SL6 2QL, England
Telephone 01628 23432
Fax 01628 770224

British Library Cataloguing in Publication Data
The CIP data of this title is available from the British Library

    ISBN 0–07–709345–3

Library of Congress Cataloging-in-Publication Data
The CIP data of this title is available from the Library of Congress,
Washington DC, USA

McGraw-Hill

A Division of The McGraw·Hill Companies

The right of Christopher Rowe and Jane Thompson to be identified as the
authors of this work has been asserted by them in accordance with the
Copyright, Designs and Patents Act, 1988.

12345   CL   99876

Typeset by Ian Kingston Editorial Services, Nottingham
and printed and bound in Great Britain by Biddles Ltd, Guildford, Surrey.

Printed on permanent paper in compliance with ISO Standard 9706

Contents

Preface to Third Edition

It is now ten years since *People and Chips* first appeared, and in that time we have been struck by the number of people who, on discovering we have written a book on information technology, respond with something like: 'Oh, that's interesting. Tell me, what's this new technology going to do to us?'. At this point we respond by pointing out that the key concern is not what the technology will do *to* us, but rather, what we will do *with* the technology. For we are faced with *choices* – choices over why, when and how we use the new technology – and it is how we exercise these choices that matters. In saying this, however, we should also note that there are *levels* of choices, for the options we face are largely determined by the decisions of others (i.e. those more powerful than ourselves) and we need to understand these to realize our own opportunities. How wide and deep are our choices? This will vary from person to person, but the important point is to appreciate that they exist. The central argument of the book, therefore, remains the same: the bones have not altered, it is the flesh that has changed. The thread that runs through the whole work is still a division between 'optimists' and 'pessimists' – between those who welcome the new technology and those who view it with apprehension – and apart from an additional chapter on networks we have retained the former structure.

The pace of technological change, and the applications this has spawned, continues unabated (and shows no sign of slowing), but what is striking as one reviews the situation a decade on is that so many current outpourings and utterances have a familiar ring to them and echo the concerns first expressed in the early 1980s. Many of the most interesting and significant contributions were made at this time, which is why we still refer to them. While the technology may have changed out of all recognition, the striking thing is that people's aspirations, hopes, fears and prejudices are much the same.

There have been a multitude of reports and studies on information technology and, although we refer to many of them, we have not attempted to include all in the bibliography; however, the major ones are recorded. We have taken a similar approach with the glossary of abbreviations: we do not claim that all are there, but certainly the main ones are.

We are grateful to the many students, colleagues and industrial contacts who have contributed in various ways to the rewriting of this book and in particular for the material we received from the BMA, TUC, CBI, Data Protection Registrar, Det. Sup. Ken Bates of Humberside Police and Bankside Engineering, Hull. Acknowledgements are also gratefully given to the authors whose work is quoted, and to their publishers for granting permission to reproduce this material.

Christopher Rowe
Jane Thompson

Acknowledgements

The authors and publisher are grateful to those cited for permission to reproduce the following material:

Extract from Berg, A. (1995) A gendered socio-technical construction: the smart house, in Heap *et al.* (eds) *Information Technology and Society*, published by Sage in association with the OU, London.

Extract from Cooley, M. (1984) Computers, politics and unemployment, in Sieghart (ed.) *Microchips with Everything*, published by Comedia, London.

Extracts from Jenkins, C. and Sherman, B. (1979) *The Collapse of Work*, published by Methuen, London.

Extract from Masuda, Y. (1981) The information society as post-industrial society. Reprinted from *The Futurist*, published by the World Future Society, 4916 St Elmo Avenue, Bethesda, MD 20814.

Figure from Parker, S. (1983) *Leisure and Work*, reproduced by permission of George Allen & Unwin, London.

Figure from Rowan, T. (1986) *Managing with Computers*, reproduced by permission of Pan Books, London.

Extracts from Taylor, F. W. (1980) *The Principles of Scientific Management*, published by W. W. Norton, London.

Figure from Watson, T. J. (1987) *Sociology, Work and Industry*, reproduced by permission of the publishers, Routledge & Kegan Paul, London.

Illustration from Zorkoczy, P. and Heap, N. (1995) *Information Technology: An Introduction* (4th edn), reprinted by permission of Pitman Publishing Ltd, London.

Glossary of Abbreviations

ACARD	Advisory Council for Applied Research and Development
ACTT	Association of Cinematograph, Television and Allied Technicians
AEEU	Amalgamated Engineering and Electrical Union
AOL	America Online
APEX	Association of Professional, Executive, Clerical and Computer Staffs
ASTMS	Association of Scientific, Technical and Managerial Staffs (now MSF)
BAe	British Aerospace
BBC	British Broadcasting Corporation
BIFU	Banking, Insurance and Finance Union
BMA	British Medical Association
BPR	Business process re-engineering
BSB	British Satellite Broadcasting
BSkyB	British Sky Broadcasting
BT	British Telecom
CAD	Computer-aided design
CAE	Computer-aided engineering
CAM	Computer-aided manufacture
CBI	Confederation of British Industry
CCTV	Closed Circuit Television
CD	Compact disc
CIM	Computer-integrated manufacture
CNC	Computer numerical control
CPIS	Computerized personnel information systems

CSC	Computer Sciences Corporation
CSE	Conference of Socialist Economists
DBS	Direct broadcasting by satellite
DEP	Department of Employment and Productivity
DES	Department of Education and Science
DoE	Department of Employment
DTI	Department of Trade and Industry
EU	European Union
EETPU	Electrical, Electronic, Telecommunication and Plumbing Union
EPOS	Electronic point of sale
ESPRIT	European Strategic Programmes for Research and Development in Information Technologies
EUREKA	European Research Coordination Agency
FLAG	Fibreoptic Link Around the Globe
FMS	Flexible manufacturing systems
FTP	File transfer protocol
GDP	Gross domestic product
GNP	Gross national product
GPMU	Graphical, Paper and Media Union
HOLMES	Home Office large major enquiry service
IBA	Independent Broadcasting Authority
IBM	International Business Machines
IC	Information centre
ICTs	Information and communication technologies
IHS	Interactive home systems
ILF	Internet Liberation Front
IT	Information technology
ITAP	Information Technology Advisory Panel
ITC	Independent Television Commission
ITEC	Information Technology Centre
ITV	Independent Television
JIT	Just-in-time
LAN	Local area network
MAP	Manufacturing automation protocol
MEP	Microelectronics Education Programme
MITI	Japanese Ministry for Industry and Technology
MSF	Manufacture, Science and Finance Union
MSN	Microsoft Network
NAFIS	National Automatic Fingerprint Identification System

NC	Network computer
NCCL	National Council for Civil Liberties
NCIS	National Criminal Intelligence System
NCU	National Communications Union
NDIU	National Drugs Intelligence Unit
NEDC	National Economic Development Council
NFIU	National Football Intelligence Unit
NGA	National Graphical Association
NHS	National Health Service
NIB	National Identification Bureau
NSPIS	National Strategy Police Information Systems
NTA	New technology agreement
NUJ	National Union of Journalists
OCR	Optical character recognition
PC	Personal computer
PHOENIX	Police and Home Office Extended Names Index
PIN	Personal identification number
PNC	Police national computer
PR	Proportional Representation
RACE	Research into Advanced Communications in Europe
R&D	Research and Development
RSI	Repetitive strain injury
SDP	Social Democratic Party
SOGAT	Society of Graphical and Allied Trades
TGWU	Transport and General Workers' Union
TOP	Technical and office protocol
TUC	Trades Union Congress
UK	United Kingdom
UPI	Universal personal identifier
USA	United States of America
VDU	Visual display unit
VLSI	Very large-scale integration
WAN	Wide area network
WP	Word processing
WRULD	Work-related upper limb disorders
WWW	World-Wide Web

CHAPTER ONE

Introduction

It is a sobering thought that, by the time you read this book, much of the technology it discusses will have already altered. This is not to suggest that you should stop reading – on the contrary, a major theme is that the issues raised are irresolvable and ongoing, and will be as alive in the next century as they are today – but merely to acknowledge the astonishing pace of technological change.

Most of this change stems from that burgeoning branch of science known as information technology, and in particular the development of a device no bigger than a thumbnail, no thicker than a leaf, which is popularly known as the 'chip'. This contains extremely complex electronic circuitry which can be used as the central processing unit or memory of a computer. It was on Friday, 31 March 1978, that the BBC showed a *Horizon* programme called 'Now the chips are down', which is generally acknowledged as the moment when Britain first became aware of the chip. Since then we have been inundated with books, TV programmes, government reports and a host of other pontifications as to whether – to paraphrase the marriage service – this will be for better or worse, for richer or poorer, or even whether it will lead to sickness or health. We are told that every aspect of life will be affected, and so vast and varied have been the outpourings that it has seemed impossible at times – particularly with regard to the human effects – to disentangle and make sense of them. This book attempts to rectify that situation.

To start with, chips were made from silicon, but now they are also made with other materials, such as plastic and gallium arsenide, which can offer processing speeds over ten times as fast as their silicon rival. The constant aim is ever greater miniaturization, power and capacity through organic materials replacing silicon. Capacity could be multiplied one million times, i.e. a billion times smaller and more powerful than the silicon chip. In 1978 chips were made that held 64 000 bits of information, and this was thought extraordinary, but chips can now hold over 20 million bits of information – the equivalent of all the words from half-a-dozen issues of *The Times* on a fingernail. In 1996, IBM's 'Deep Blue' – a 32-node, 256 chip machine which can consider 200 million moves a second – became the first computer to win a game of chess against a world champion under tournament rules when it defeated Gary Kasparov, though the champion did recover to win the six-game series. It seems only a matter of time before an unbeatable computer is devised.

Millions of chips are now in use. In the home they are found in cookers and refrigerators, telephones and cars, watches and TV games; in the factory they control assembly lines, machine tools and paint sprays; in offices they are contained in personal computers (PCs) and photocopying machines; in supermarkets, banks and garages they are found in computerized tills, automatic teller machines and petrol pumps. Hotel and theatre bookings, banking, news-gathering, weather forecasting, medical analysis – you name it: all are being continuously transformed by new technology.

However, this is not a book about the technology itself – how it works and what it does – so much as a discussion of the possible effects it is having upon people. Some have predicted it will usher in a totally new and better form of society, while others fear it will exacerbate many of the less desirable features of present-day living. We shall consider people: first as consumers (the effects on patterns of expenditure, changes in lifestyle and developments in leisure patterns); secondly as citizens (the impact on democracy and privacy); and finally as workers (the effects on employment, industrial relations and occupational skills). We consider these issues by drawing on sociology, psychology, economics, law and politics to explore the central question of the human effects of new technology.

Consequently we shall not say a great deal on definitions and terminology. We shall refer to microelectronics to identify that wide field of technological development that incorporates and applies electronic components or circuits made to very small dimensions, but recognize that it is when this is linked with other new developments – especially in computing and telecommunications – that it becomes particularly significant. It is this convergence – relating to the creation, transmission, manipulation and presentation of data – that has spawned such labels as 'information technology', 'microtechnology', 'new technology', or even the well-established abbreviation, IT. None of these can be precisely defined – the pace of change and range of applications make this impossible – and we hope that we may be excused for using them interchangeably and not spending time distinguishing between them.

Our task is to consider ways in which life is being – and will continue to be – affected, whether at work or in the home, and in doing this we are less concerned with providing solutions than raising issues. There are no clear-cut answers regarding the human effects of information technology, for what we expect from IT is very much determined by the way we look at it. In short, we do not suggest what *will* happen, but rather consider what *might* or *could* happen. Our aim is not to preach a particular 'line' but to examine the various lines being preached. We shall particularly focus upon work, partly because this is where much of the debate has centred, but also because it is here that our special interests lie. In a short book such as this we cannot hope to cover every human aspect, and work is given special prominence. Finally, though IT is now a world-wide phenomenon, we focus much of our discussion on developments in Britain.

INFORMATION TECHNOLOGY

Why should so many claim that the microchip is revolutionary and is transforming human society as we know it? After all, scores of new technological developments have resulted in new products, industries, extended markets and greater prosperity, but these were not all labelled 'revolutionary'. Moreover, the functions that the chip performs are essentially no different from those of earlier computers, and all that has happened is that scientists have been able to incorporate increasing numbers of components on ever smaller pieces of silicon. Why should this be regarded as 'new'? The chip's distinctiveness, and why many regard it as a 'breakthrough technology', can be summarized under six simple headings.

Size
With the continuing trend towards miniaturization it is now possible to contain millions of components on a chip one centimetre square, and it is thought this might eventually reach a billion components. A one-inch optical disk can hold the same amount of information as hundreds of thousands of A4 sheets and the fact that microelectronics allows small, light computing power to be installed in an increasing range of products

and applications offers enormous gains in terms of space. Complete microprocessor computers, capable of handling 10 million instructions a second, can now be put on one chip, and the next step is to construct cooperative arrays of such computers to work in parallel on enormously complex problems.

In 1989, Bell Labs in the USA announced a molecular breakthrough whereby 'plastic bags' holding semiconducting clusters of 100 to 100 000 atoms are grown inside microscopic water droplets and then sealed, which could, by (say) 2020, provide computers too small to be seen, yet more powerful than any machine today. In 1996, American scientists produced a silicon engine a millimetre square which will lead to miniature robots operating inside us – 'patrolling' human arteries, clearing up cholesterol, repairing torn ligaments, sorting out kidney problems, checking for heart disease etc. These 'micromotors' will also be used in such varied applications as car design, military systems and pest control. In the same year, Texas Instruments announced a thumbnail-sized chip with electrical connections as thin as 0.18 microns wide – less than one six-hundredth the diameter of a human hair – and the processing power of 20 PCs. With 125 million transistors packed on to a single chip this will lead to lighter and more powerful digital telephones, portable computers with significantly longer battery lives, and domestic computers capable of speech recognition.

Cost

Since the 1970s the power of computers has increased over 10 000 times, while the cost of each unit of performance has fallen over 100 000 times. Information technology costs continue to fall by over 25% a year; experts predict that the cost of telephone calls could be removed altogether; and we can expect to 'wear' IT equipment that is powered by body heat. Research efforts are now focused on 'jumbo chips'. While microchips are made separately – by the hundred on silicon wafers, from which they are cut out and mounted individually, and then wired up by the hundred again to work as computers – jumbo chips make the wafer itself a single computing machine. Everything can be done in one stage, and if chips are linked within the silicon wafer then electrons can work without the uncertainty of wired connections. Such a development further reduces costs dramatically.

Finally, the substitution of microelectronic components in various products reduces their cost, not only because the products themselves are cheap to make, but also because they make possible massive savings in energy consumption, maintenance, testing, floor-space and backup facilities.

Reliability

Whereas a computer in the 1960s required tens of thousands of hand-made connections, all capable of failure, a large-scale integrated circuit in the 1980s required only ten separate elements. The coming of jumbo chips reduces this further and leads to great gains in reliability. The microchip is thousands of times more reliable than the electronic components of the 1950s, and this has dramatically affected the manufacture of many products, e.g. calculators and watches. Digital watches, costing £40 in the mid-1970s, were down to a few pounds by the 1980s, and captured 50% of the market in ten years because of their greater reliability. Similarly, in the field of robotics, increased reliability means that microprocessor-controlled robots can now work in environments hostile to human beings, such as sewers, coal mines, paint spray shops and oil rigs. The quality of chip production, both silicon and gallium arsenide, has greatly increased, and this seems certain to continue.

Capacity

The power and performance of computers continues to increase, and experts predict that, by 2010, the computer will equal the human mind in terms of information storage and computational abilities. This is why IT is a 'heartland technology': it affects *all* sectors – industry, commerce, education, the home – as chips are used in robots, data banks, telephone exchanges, domestic appliances, and many other operations. Advances in networking also increase capacity, for, irrespective of where data is stored or the format it takes, it can more easily be accessed and shared.

Between 1986 and 1989 Risc (reduced instruction set computer) chips increased in power from 4 mips (millions of instructions per second) to 150 mips. This seemed remarkable, but the American manufacturers Intel then announced the I860 microprocessor, with over a million transistors, capable of carrying out 80 million operations (consisting of several individual instructions) per second, and, as we noted earlier, by 1996 chips had been developed with 125 million transistors.

Speed

By the mid-1980s memory chips were available which could provide information at a rate of more than one bit of basic information every 30 billionth of a second. In 1985, a team at Glasgow University came up with a device that could 'read' five Bibles in eight seconds, and in 1987 IBM produced the blueprint for an optical microchip that could read 40 encyclopaedias in a second. In 1988, Southampton University built what was then the world's largest supercomputer (based on 1260 transputers) capable of handling 10 000 million operations a second, and with the potential to increase that tenfold. Transputers promise a new generation of computing equipment around 200 times faster than conventional microcomputers. In 1995, British scientists developed a method of making silicon emit light: optical computers, running on light, will be far faster than their electric forebears, will carry much more information, and will never overheat. By 1996 Intel had launched the Pentium Pro, employing 5.5 million transistors and running at double the speed of previous Pentium chips. Development work is now being done on gallium arsenide chips, many times faster than silicon, which can do calculations in hundreds of picoseconds (1 picosecond is 1 million-millionth of a second).

Flexibility

All the various features we have considered can be combined under a final heading – flexibility. Information technology can be applied to virtually every human field: it can direct a guided missile, monitor fish stocks, permit sophisticated surveillance systems, operate a coffee dispenser, regulate the use of petrol in a car, control an industrial production line, provide computerized maps and a host of other things. Even the human body can be used to transmit data, because it can hold an electromagnetic field. Tests have been done whereby one person can shake hands with another and transmit data from a business card to the other person's computer.

An area of growing importance is neural networks: artificial networks of processors that mimic the structure of neurons in the human brain and which can process large amounts of imprecise data according to certain patterns. Neural computers can learn, judge, infer and draw conclusions about new situations. Research results have exceeded expectations and networks are already being used for developing robot vision, matching fingerprints, analysing fluctuations in stock market prices and predicting weather patterns. Some American programmes are now investigating the use of biological chips that would change their structure to solve new problems. Such developments would provide a flexibility in applications unheard of hitherto.

The situation can be summed up with a comparative example: if the motor industry had developed at the same speed as the computer industry, then a Rolls-Royce would now cost under a pound, it would do millions of miles to the gallon, its speed would be invisible to the human eye, and one could handle dozens of them. Similarly, if the aerospace industry had developed at the same pace, a Boeing aircraft would cost a few pounds and could circle the Earth on a couple of gallons of fuel, while Concorde would have been flying nine months after the Wright brothers took off.

Forms of application

The range of applications is of course enormous, but they can be conveniently grouped within four general categories. They can:

- serve as the basis for new products, e.g. digital watches, electronic games, video recorders, calculators and personal computers
- replace conventional circuitry in existing products, e.g. car components, TV components and wrist watches
- change the production process itself, e.g. robotics
- affect basic information systems, e.g. networks, telecommunications systems and surveillance systems.

Over recent decades we have become increasingly familiar with the first two applications, but it is with regard to the latter two that the greater long-term effects can be expected. In his seminal book, *The Mighty Micro*, Christopher Evans (1979) distinguished between three periods: the short-term future (1980–82), the middle-term future (1983–90) and the long-term future (1990–2000). He predicted that in the short term we would simply become aware of microtechnology – start to play computer games, wear digital wristwatches and replace our pencils with calculators – which is very much what happened. But after this he expected a rapid acceleration to take place. Whether it happened as he predicted remains debatable, but we have certainly witnessed remarkable developments. Chips now allow scientists to devise machines that can 'talk' to the deaf, translate written sentences from one language to another, and replace workers on assembly lines. Robots can now 'see' to pick up a thrown dice and put it in an appropriate box, or dig up samples on other planets; satellites can resolve disputes over fishing boundaries; and people can watch TV on a wristwatch. In a remarkable 'world first' in 1996, Dr Luc van der Heyden performed a hernia operation from Belgium on a patient 144 miles away in Holland by using a robot and telephone line. The field of artificial intelligence allows us to create machines with 'knowledge' that can increasingly supplant human brain power as well as muscle power. No area of human activity seems likely to remain unaffected, particularly as the various forms of new technology increasingly converge.

In considering the pervasiveness of microtechnology, one can perhaps draw useful parallels from the first industrial revolution. The steam engine – generally considered one of the key inventions – was initially used solely for pumping water out of mines, and this it did most effectively for half a century. Only when it was linked with other technologies, however, did it become a true heartland technology: fitted to a wagon it created a locomotive; added to a loom it provided a power loom. Similarly today, it is when the microchip is linked to other (mainly 20th century) technologies that its significance becomes fully apparent: when linked with a typewriter, telephone and television screen we obtain a networked PC; when added to a machine we create a robot.

It is the elements of pervasiveness and technological convergence that we wish to stress, and to consider in relation to social and industrial life. It is not just in the field of *information* that effects are being felt (with the introduction of microcomputers etc.), but equally important are developments with regard to *production* (e.g. robotics, computer-aided design (CAD), computer-aided manufacture (CAM), lasers) and *communication* (e.g. cable systems, satellites, telecommunications). This can be represented as a 'micro explosion', affecting all areas of human existence (Fig. 1.1).

While we have experienced change before, Evans believes that the social repercussions from the chip will be of such magnitude as to totally alter our society and present way of living. Social institutions, work patterns, beliefs and attitudes, political structures – all will be transformed out of recognition.

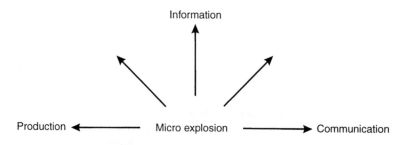

Figure 1.1   The micro explosion.

TECHNOLOGY AND SOCIETY

There is no doubt that technology can greatly affect society: we only have to think of the impact of the motor car or television on our own age to see this. But the danger with Evans's approach, and those who similarly laud the potential of information technology, is that they rather present the technology as though it operates in a vacuum, apart from political and economic forces. The relationship is not monocausal; for just as technology affects society, so, in its turn, society influences technology, both in terms of its research and development, and in relation to its application and control. We need to pause for a moment to consider this.

When we think of technological breakthroughs we tend to envisage the process starting with a research idea – 'the eureka moment' – which then leads to applications and products. At this point – when the technology is applied to the market – inventions become innovations, and diffusion occurs as new technologies replace old (e.g. transistors replacing valves). This, however, rather suggests that technological development is an 'independent variable', operating in isolation from social forces, and transforming society the moment it becomes available. In reality, this is not the case, for technology is also a 'social product', largely determined by those who hold and administer power at a given time. Technology now becomes the 'dependent variable', and innovation more significant than invention. One can illustrate this with reference to the great 'inventions' of the first industrial revolution. In a sense they were not inventions at all, but rather applications – innovations when the economic situation was ripe – by practical business people. The theoretical, scientific knowledge on which many machines were based had been available for over a century, and there are countless examples where societies do not innovate technologically even though the knowledge exists. Braverman (1974), for instance, notes how artificial dyes based on coal tar were developed in Germany but not Britain because the latter could import dyes from the colonies. It is true that the distinction has become increasingly blurred as large companies now employ research and development staff to both invent and innovate, but it is analytically useful for our purposes.

The distinction is important in the work of Nikolai Kondratiev (1925), the Russian economist who argued that economic development always proceeds in 'long waves', and the key to technological innovation is not some inspired moment of invention so much as the current level of economic activity, innovations being more likely in periods of economic recession. He observed that it took the world economy about 50 years to move through a boom-to-slump-to-boom cycle. According to his theory, the Western world was due for a downturn during the 1970s – precisely what happened – and we are unlikely to return to substantial growth before the end of the 1990s. He would maintain we have come through the fourth 'wave' – having experienced considerable technological innovation at a time of economic recession – and moved into a fifth during the mid-1990s. It is the entrepreneurs (the innovators) rather than the scientists (the inventors) who therefore provide the fuse for new technological applications, investment, growth and employment.

This suggests that it might be dangerous to imply that a particular technology *causes* a certain type of society; for while it is true that any technology contains societal implications, its actual introduction, and therefore the resulting socio-economic effects, also to a considerable extent *reflect* the nature of that society. Technology does not just 'happen', but is largely dependent on governmental and corporate action in making funds available for scientific research. It is therefore very much a social product.

For example, the reason we have experienced silicon chips over the past two decades is not simply because someone chanced to discover that silicon (one of the world's most available resources) could be used as a semiconductive material, but also because the US government, desperate to maintain its defences and stay in the space race with the Soviet Union, invested enormous sums toward providing smaller, lighter computers for spacecraft and weapon systems. Had the same research effort gone in other directions, we might today have a cure for cancer.

TECHNOLOGY AND CHOICE, OR WHATEVER

A new technology is therefore to a considerable extent a social product, but, more than this, once it comes into existence its actual application can proceed in very different directions. For example, electricity may be used to provide people with light and heating or to execute them; the American space programme not only placed men on the Moon but gave us non-stick frying pans and improved hearing aids; and at the present time, lasers are being developed which can be deployed in 'Star Wars' defence programmes, applied to medical surgery (such as the removal of brain tumours) or used in the coding of manufactured products.

Technology, with regards to its application, is therefore also a matter for human choice. One cannot say technology is 'good' or 'bad'; this all depends on what we as human beings choose to do with it. The extent to which technology determines society, or how much it is a social product, and whether we as individuals can affect the outcome, therefore provides a 'three-cornered' arena (see Fig. 2.2) for debate. The danger with Evans is that he rather implies that particular developments will happen, while others fear that the uses of technology will be totally controlled by those holding economic and political power. Both views rather play down the element of choice, which we suggest is important, for the more we as people are aware of the alternatives, the more effectively – both collectively and individually – we can influence the outcome. The aim of this book is to increase that awareness.

In the work sphere for instance, there is no doubt that manufacturing and commerce can be increasingly mechanized and automated by microelectronic devices, but this is no more than a technological capability which could be realized in many different ways. Work can be reskilled or deskilled; expanded or destroyed. What is technologically *possible* should not be confused with what is *probable*, for the actual human and social consequences of new technology remain uncertain. We may know what technology can do, but how it will be applied remains contentious: a matter for debate, a matter of choice.

Finally, even when we focus upon a particular application, we cannot make objective judgements as to the effects of the technology. For instance, has the motor car been of benefit to society? Clearly, on one side, it has greatly assisted transport and communication and enabled people to visit parts of the world that would otherwise have remained inaccessible to them; but, on the other hand, it has resulted in traffic jams on overcrowded motorways, new forms of crime, polluted air and serious accidents. Despite increased technological sophistication, the average car now travels through central London at a slower speed than at the start of the century. Progress? Many now question this. While the 1960s represented a period of 'technological optimism' – with people eventually reaching the Moon – the 1990s reflect a mood of profound pessimism. Technology now seems to raise as many problems as it solves, and those who preach the 'new millennium' are increasingly viewed with suspicion. More now see technology as a 'mixed blessing', conceding that there are both pluses and minuses. How one sees this 'mix' is therefore a highly personal, subjective matter. To take the most obvious (and fearful) example of modern technology, nuclear weaponry: whether one views this as a danger or a benefit depends on one's own particular standpoint. It is a technology that no one actually wants to use, but if you see nuclear weapons as a threat to the survival of our entire planet then you see them as a 'bad thing', whereas if you consider that they provide a deterrent to political adversaries who threaten a form of society you hold dear, and make war less likely because they provide a power balance, then you see them as necessary, justified and beneficial.

There is no uniform approach to new technology. Our response is increasingly uncertain: hopes and expectations mixed with doubts and misgivings. It creates responsibilities and moral dilemmas which we feel ill-equipped to handle even though we possess greater knowledge and control over nature than ever before. It is as though we have created an awesome monster we feel unable to contain. Thanks to technology, we can live longer (and more healthily) in a fuller, richer life, but we can also burn up in a few decades the oil created over millions of years. We can expand our travel and leisure facilities but at the same time pollute rivers, gravely endanger rare animal species and destroy rain forests. We can provide the world with sophisticated drugs and chemicals yet suffer the kind of human disaster that occurred at the Union Carbide chemical plant in Bhopal, India, in 1984, when over 3000 people were killed and 500 000 injured following a gas leak at the factory. Or the accident at Chernobyl in the Soviet Union in 1986, when a leakage at a nuclear power station created radiation levels at least 100 000 times higher than usual. Over 30 people were killed, 135 000 evacuated, and many thousands are expected, in the long term, to die from related cancers. Technological progress?

Or take the threat of a 'scorched earth' due to damage to the ozone layer. Considerable fears are being expressed over the rise in skin cancers as many parts of the world are now experiencing hotter, drier summers. Scientists confirm that various pollutants – in industry, agriculture and energy – have produced a 'greenhouse effect', with the 'greenhouse gases' letting sunlight through but preventing the heat of the rays from escaping back into space. Estimates are that, over the next half century, world temperatures will rise by anything from one to four degrees Celsius – and an increase of two degrees represents a significant change. The 1990s, therefore, have seen technological issues become increasingly prevalent – witness the rise of the Green movement – as people have posed vital questions. Is technology necessarily beneficial? Are we responsible in handling it? Do we need to devise new forms of living that rely less on technological development?

These sorts of question will recur continually throughout the book, for they focus on our central concern, which is the interface between society and technology – especially information technology – and the choices we make. Clearly, the matter is subjective and highly contentious. It shows why there is an irreconcilable debate as to whether technologies such as microelectronics represent a 'revolution' or merely a further 'evolutionary' stage in technological and social development: something radically new or simply 'more of the same'. Will this technology create a fresh form of society, or does it rather provide further tools for those who presently hold economic and political power to entrench their position? Does it enhance the quality of human existence or merely augment the less desirable features of industrial life? Moreover, is technology (in whatever form) something we simply have to accept, or can we exercise choice in the matter? If so, how much and in what form? And, most important, if this is inadequate, what do we propose to do about it?

Clearly, we shall experience significant change, but far less certain are the precise form and direction it will take; the rate at which it will occur; and the effects it will have. These issues are debatable, and we cannot say one view is right and another wrong, for they represent different *perspectives* – different ways of looking at technology and society. Technology – like beauty – is clearly very much in the eye of the beholder; a subjective rather than an objective matter. To paraphrase Marx: what we see does not determine our perspective; on the contrary, it is our perspective that determines what we see. This explains the diversity of views from those who prophesy a 'Utopian tomorrow' to those who warn of 'Orwellian totalitarianism'. The key question of perspectives is considered further in the next chapter and provides a framework for the remainder of the book.

CHAPTER TWO

Contrasting Perspectives

A common theme since 1978 – when people in Britain first began to talk about microelectronics – is that 'western society is experiencing a series of technological revolutions which is changing our society and our economy as profoundly as did the Industrial Revolution' (Stonier, 1979). Just as people's working lives were transformed by the invention of the spinning-jenny, the steam engine, electricity generation and the internal combustion engine, so it is argued that the microchip will have an equivalent impact. Writing in 1978, Tom Forester suggested that 'the invention of the chip represents a quantum leap in technology far more important than the clumsy great computers of the 1950s, and it could be as important as the discovery of electricity itself'. Other writers have similarly maintained that the industrialized world is on the brink of economic and structural upheaval and that the microchip will create a new society which has variously been described as post-industrial society (Bell, 1974, 1979), the third wave (Toffler, 1981), the information society (Masuda, 1982), the network society (Castells, 1996) and cybersociety (Jones, 1994; Featherstone and Burrows, 1996).

Many find such predictions premature and overblown. One view – which we reject – argues that the chip is simply a further stage in technological advancement and that society will adjust as it always has in the past. Put simply, this view cannot see what all the fuss is about. We would label this the 'complacency view', for it totally underestimates the chip's potential and the degree of change we might expect. An alternative, and more subtle, response is one that acknowledges the chip as an astonishing device (for it possesses an 'intelligence' function), and accepts that change will occur, but questions whether this necessarily means wholesale social transformation. Are we justified in talking of a micro *revolution*, or any other kind of revolution for that matter? We need to consider the word revolution carefully, for it can be applied in various forms – technological, industrial, social, political – and though these are invariably intertwined we may experience one apart from the others, or one form may clearly precede another. The fact that the chip is small, cheap and highly reliable could mean that it is revolutionary in a technological sense – but no more than this – and it might perhaps be better seen as merely a further (if important) stage of scientific advancement.

THE FIRST INDUSTRIAL REVOLUTION

The industrial revolution is the term used to describe the changes that occurred – first in Britain between the mid-18th and 19th centuries and then in other parts of the world – to mark the transition from agricultural production to manufacturing. Britain changed from an agricultural country, with a small population, a low standard of living, a hierarchical social structure and a ruling aristocratic oligarchy, to a nation dependent on manufacturing and extractive industries, with a large population, growing urban centres, increasing social mobility, greater political democracy and vastly increased wealth. Virtually no English institution or aspect of life remained untouched by these changes; and not only was more produced, but work was done in new ways.

When writing of the first industrial revolution, Phyllis Deane (1980) identifies a series of fundamental changes which she suggests characterized the period. She argues that these interrelated changes, if they develop together and to a sufficient degree, constitute an industrial revolution. It is not just changing technology that is important, but the fact that it brings forth fresh ways of living. Deane lists seven main features that characterize an industrial revolution:

- Widespread and systematic application of science and knowledge to the process of production for the market

The first industrial revolution was dramatically affected by certain key inventions, which allowed for massive increases in output and created spin-off effects throughout the rest of the economy.

- Specialization of economic activity for wide markets

Manufacturers began to mass-produce goods for the market which could then be sold at a profit to provide for further capital investment.

- Movement of population

In 1780, England's population was 9.7 million people, and nearly 80% lived and worked in the countryside. By 1830 there were 14 English towns of over 50 000 people, and Britain became rapidly urbanized.

- The movement of labour between employment sectors

Agricultural employment fell from 75% of the total labour force in 1688 to 50% by 1780, 25% by 1840, and 3% by 1980, even though production increased nearly seventy-fold thanks to new technology. The agricultural revolution thereby stimulated the industrial revolution, which in turn stimulated a service revolution, fresh labour being released in each instance.

- The growth of new units of production and patterns of work

Small-scale, domestic production was replaced by large-scale, factory production. A switch occurred from 'natural power' (water, animals, wind etc.) to inanimate, calculable power, based first on steam and later on electricity and atomic energy. Changing work patterns also demanded a disciplined, time-conscious workforce. Workers had to develop new attitudes to time, morals, drink, thrift etc., as work became governed by the clock rather than the sun and the seasons.

- Intensive and extensive use of capital resources

Capital became a substitute for, and complement to, human effort. This stimulated the development of technology, which resulted in intensified mechanization, automation and the subdivision of workers' tasks.

- The emergence of new social and occupational classes

Industrial capitalism was a fresh mode of production which threw up new social classes: the bourgeoisie and proletariat. The former's power rested on its ownership of capital in the form of property, machinery, raw materials etc. Labour power became bought and sold as a commodity, and profit determined work relations and the development and utilization of technology.

The first industrial revolution therefore involved not only significant technological change but also dramatic *social* transformation. In the light of present-day developments, are we justified in talking of a 'new industrial revolution' and can we expect changes of similar magnitude? In particular, can we expect these changes to occur as a direct result of the application of new forms of technology?

A NEW INDUSTRIAL REVOLUTION?

One writer who believes we are experiencing change on a similar scale to that of the first industrial revolution is Daniel Bell, who argues that, just as we moved from pre-industrial to industrial society, so now we are moving into a new form of society that is best termed 'post-industrial'. He argues that knowledge (and especially scientific knowledge) has acquired a centrality in society that it previously did not have and that authority (based on knowledge) is now more important than ownership of property. 'Technocrats' are the dominant elite, rather than the bourgeoisie, and developments in microelectronics and 'intellectual technology' are encouraging this process. The imperatives of technology, not the forces of ideology, now determine the shape of society.

If we revert to Deane's seven characteristics, Bell would argue that they apply as much today as they did two centuries ago.

- Widespread and systematic application of science and knowledge to the process of production for the market

Scientific knowledge and its application now become important as decisions are increasingly taken by technocrats who base their judgements on scientific expertise rather than entrepreneurial flair. More decisions can be programmed as computers are used for decision-making, and forecasts made by universities, research units, professionals etc. increasingly override the views of politicians, the business community and others. Knowledge becomes the guide to action.

- Specialization of economic activity for wide markets

Economic activity encourages even greater specialization as new products are developed and sold in ever-widening markets. The activity takes on a new form in that, instead of imperial powers exploiting their colonies for raw materials and markets, trade now occurs within large economic units (e.g. the European Union) and products are manufactured and sold by multinational companies the world over.

- Movement of population

While people previously moved from the countryside into the towns, they now switch from the inner-city areas to the suburbs, as new work patterns emerge. People also move between regions, and just as the north of England experienced population growth during the first industrial revolution, so expansion can now be expected elsewhere.

- The movement of labour between employment sectors

As people moved from the primary to the secondary manufacturing sector, so now increasingly they transfer to the service or tertiary sector. Bell even argues that with two-thirds in service employment, this sector can itself be usefully subdivided – between those who provide services based on the transfer of information and those who do not. Stonier predicts that by the turn of the century 40% could work in what he terms 'the knowledge industry', and Jones (1982) suggests that this will represent a further 'post-service' stage (Fig. 2.1).

- The growth of new units of production and patterns of work

Mundane factory and office tasks are taken over by technology, and workers freed from the constraints of industrial work patterns. They no longer need to assemble together at the same time and place, and more will work from home. The new technologies will provide our basic needs

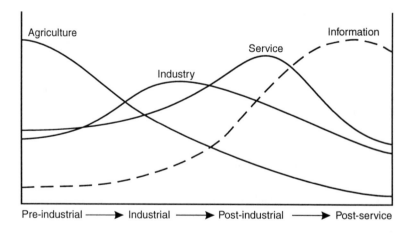

Figure 2.1   Towards a post-service society.

and allow greater time for education, travel, sport and other leisure activities.

- Intensive and extensive use of capital resources

Capital investment again plays a crucial role in stimulating new technological development, but now it takes a different form. Whereas in the 18th century investment came principally from entrepreneurial business people – 'talented tinkerers', as Bell terms them – investment in the post-industrial economy comes overwhelmingly from national governments, multinational corporations and large-scale research organizations. This is due to the considerable cost and complexity of modern technological research.

- The emergence of new social and occupational classes

Finally, as work organizations grow in size and complexity, so control becomes concentrated in the hands of the technocrats and specialist managers, while ownership is diluted due to the growth of joint stock companies. The managers are more 'socially responsible' than the exploiting bourgeoisie, developing a 'corporate conscience' and remaining neutral between capital and labour. The growth of managers, professionals and white collar workers makes obsolete the Marxist view of society polarized between bourgeoisie and proletariat. This is replaced by a more open, fluid, meritocratic and pluralist society. Expertise becomes dispersed, with specialists in one functional area providing checks and balances on those in another.

Bell suggests that we are experiencing a new industrial revolution in that Deane's seven characteristics apply as much today as they did in the 18th century. Microelectronics represents such a leap in technological advancement, and its influence is so widespread, that we are leaving the industrial age and entering post-industrial society. This view is shared by Alvin Toffler, who believes that human experience has gone through 'three waves' – agricultural, industrial and post-industrial – and that while the first covered thousands of years, and the second 300, the third (which began around 1955) will 'sweep across history and complete itself in a few decades'. Thus we are at the clashing of the waves, with the third hitting the second before, in many parts of the world, the first has even spent its force. Toffler argues that the industrial revolution created a chain of societies based on mass production, mass consumption, mass education, mass communication, mass entertainment and mass political movements, and that today, instead of becoming more 'massifying', many of these societies are 'demassifying' – breaking up the masses into smaller and more valued groupings. His argument is that we are no longer becoming more uniform, but on the contrary, more heterogeneous, and we see this in production, distribution, communication and family life. Just as the industrial revolution led to the overthrow of the political institutions of feudal agriculture, so the rise of the 'third wave' makes present political arrangements obsolete. In similar vein, Masuda talks of 'Computopia' – a new information-based society.

All these writers tend to see technological development as a virtually autonomous force which compels society to adapt to it – what critics would call 'technological determinism'. According to this model, societies are classified by the stage of technological development they have reached, and we in effect do this when we refer to the Stone Age, Bronze Age, Steam Age, Nuclear Age, Computer Age, and so on. A dominant technology is taken as the overriding influence on a given historical epoch. Moreover, as society is determined by the nature of its technology, it is assumed that societies at parallel stages of technological development will be similar in other respects, and that this will encourage greater harmony between them.

AN OPTIMISTIC VIEWPOINT

These writers adopt a highly *optimistic* standpoint: they view technological change as 'progressive' – leading to a 'better' society in terms of material benefits, work satisfaction, enhanced freedoms, greater consensus, more leisure time etc. Nowhere is this more apparent than in the work of Kerr *et al.* (1973, 1984) who argue that convergence is occurring not just in the technological realm, but in a broader, social sense. The essence of their 'convergence thesis' is that industrialism – and the technological advances it implies – have brought with them certain inevitable changes in social life and imposed common patterns of social behaviour, i.e. societies that have industrialized have 'converged' and become increasingly similar. Put simply, the suggestion is that whether one is in London, Los Angeles or Moscow, cities now look ever more alike, with skyscraper blocks, supermarkets, cars, television etc., and this is primarily the result of universal technology. Microelectronics is intensifying this. The 'internal logic of industrialism' has been disseminated from Britain to Europe, the

USA, Russia and Japan by the pressures of world-wide military technology and trade, and this will eventually embrace the whole world. Certain key characteristics are now found in all industrialized countries, including large-scale mechanized factory production; high levels of technical skill and professional competence; considerable social, occupational and geographical mobility; universal education that stresses science and technology; 'large-scale society' based on mass production, large cities, big government, large bureaucracies etc.; a reduction of national cultural differences and an impetus towards consensus on values; a central role for government in the development of transport, welfare and broadcasting; and the universal development of industrialism which should lead to a reduction in world conflict. Thus a distinctive consensus develops within free pluralist societies which relates individuals and groups to each other and provides an integrated framework of ideas, ideologies and values. Technological advances such as microelectronics further these developments, and allow post-industrial society to become a world-wide phenomenon.

This viewpoint was expressed in a speech from arch-optimist Ronald Reagan, which he gave at the Guildhall, London, shortly after vacating the US presidency. In it he maintained that the 'information explosion' brought about by new technology would bring the inevitable end of totalitarianism. He argued that:

> The biggest of Big Brothers is increasingly helpless against communications technology. Information is the oxygen of the modern age. It seeps through the walls topped by barbed wire, it wafts across the electrified, booby-trapped borders. The Iron Curtain of Churchill's day is the Maginot Line to the microchip.... The centrally-controlled societies are in a quandary. To enter the information age, which is the direction their economies must head, they must allow the flow of information. But to allow the flow of information undermines central authority.

He would no doubt cite the break-up of communism in Eastern Europe to justify his argument.

Modern telecommunications further illustrates the point. Whereas the British government did not know of the American Declaration of Independence in 1776 until a sailing ship had crossed the Atlantic to tell them, Billy Graham was able, in 1996, to preach via satellite to more than 2.5 billion people in over 200 countries. Indeed, the assassination attempt on Reagan himself was seen on TV by millions across the world before many Americans even knew it had happened. (It took over a week for news of President Lincoln's assassination to reach London!) World-wide extravaganzas are now commonplace – royal weddings, Sports Aid, Moonie mass marriage ceremonies, Nelson Mandela's 70th birthday concert – and seem certain to continue.

But satellites are not merely transmitting rock concerts, sports events, religious services and birthday parties. More significantly, as Reagan pointed out, they are transgressing political and national boundaries. For instance, a country like Hungary (because of its geographical position) can receive a multitude of satellite TV channels and broadcasts itself to Romania, Austria and Russia. Technology thus provides a convergence that supersedes political frontiers; what has been termed a 'global village'.

There may still be differences between societies but these are now less important, Kerr argues, than the things that bind them together. Similarly, there may still be social differences *within* societies, but these will increasingly fade with growing affluence, and as conflict becomes contained within agreed rules and norms. The two overriding implications of the convergence thesis are that we can expect less divisiveness thanks to new technology, and therefore less developed countries should be encouraged and assisted to follow the same path, through industrialization, to post-industrial society.

Bill Gates (1995), co-founder of Microsoft, talks of wallet-sized PCs, telecommuting, video-conferencing, home shopping, electronic security, the information superhighway and surfing in cyberspace: 'I think this is a wonderful time to be alive', he says. 'There have never been so many opportunities to do things that were impossible before. It's the best time ever to start new companies and advance sciences such as medicine that improve the quality of life.'

Put simply, all these writers depict a Utopian tomorrow. They *like* the new technology: they marvel at its potential; welcome its introduction; and are confident of the social benefits. So vast will be the change that they think it realistic to speak of a new industrial revolution and to expect a fresh social order. The chip will free people from the toils of labour and domestic chores; release them from the fears of war and crime; allow superior services in health and education; permit greater democratic participation; and generally provide a higher quality of life. The technology is presented as liberating and positive. In that such writers are generally uncritical of existing society, and highly supportive of the material benefits that could accrue from technological advancement, their viewpoint gains considerable support from the political right.

THE PESSIMISTIC VIEWPOINT

In contrast, there are many who are far less exuberant about the coming of new technology. This distinction – between 'optimists' and 'pessimists' – has already been touched on by various writers (Burns, 1981; Forester, 1980; Jones, 1980; Francis, 1986), usually in connection with labour displacement, but it has not been discussed in depth or widely applied. We shall adopt these labels to present contrasting perspectives, though, as we indicate, they must be used with care, as writers vary in their degrees of optimism/pessimism, and some are optimistic in one sense but pessimistic in another. No writer *wholly* subscribes to either position, and one should not think of two separate, mutually opposed camps so much as a continuum ranging from one extreme to the other, containing various viewpoints in-between (rather like the left/right divide in politics or the urban/rural distinction in geography). This provides us with a useful 'conceptual clothes line' on which to peg the wide range of contributions to the new technology debate, and for further clarification we shall introduce additional labels as different issues are discussed.

With regard to the pessimists, it must be stressed at the outset that their pessimism can take different forms, and for convenience we subdivide them into various groups. The central concerns of each are somewhat different, and we need to consider them at descending levels. The extreme pessimistic position would presumably be one that totally rejects any human use of technology, and no one seriously subscribes to this, though some believe we have allowed our world to become too 'technology-oriented' and reject the general notion that technological advancement is somehow synonymous with progress. Their attacks, however, would be directed less at information technology (which is not directly atmospherically polluting or a great guzzler of natural resources) than at other forms (e.g. nuclear power) and, consequently, our discussion is not over-concerned with this first level. Of greater importance for our purposes are those writers who concentrate, not so much on the technology itself – indeed, they are not particularly opposed to the technology – but are wary as to how it will be applied and controlled in a capitalist economy where private commercial interests predominate. IBM, for instance, still dominates the world computer market (though to a lesser extent than it once did) while Microsoft has become a similar force with regard to operating systems. Thomas (1995) finds it difficult to see how information technology is helping to create a more egalitarian society. IT is often presented as liberating – as are public libraries and public broadcasting

– but if the *information* is privately owned and distributed and its costs privately determined then these liberating characteristics become somewhat muted.

Pessimists in this group focus more at the societal than the global level. They see the diffusion of microtechnology as part of the continuing process of rationalization and the industrial revolution, and would include those of a Marxist persuasion (e.g. Braverman) who are critical of industrial capitalism, and see information technology as a further exploiting tool for the ruling bourgeoisie class. They view the process as deterministic – i.e. social controls are bound to increase and will result in a progressive degradation of work – and such a situation can only be rectified by total transformation of the existing social and economic order.

Within the confines of capitalism, this viewpoint remains highly pessimistic. A deviation on this, however, is a view that holds that while the capitalist system has to maintain this rationalization process, the technology itself is neutral, and thus through conscious political and institutional action (e.g. through trade unions) people can shape its effects. This group of writers (e.g. Cooley, 1980; Jenkins and Sherman, 1979; Benson and Lloyd, 1983) may be equally disenchanted with many facets of capitalism, but they allow for an element of choice, and offer some degree of optimism within their overall pessimistic scenario. Consequently, they are slightly further to the centre of our continuum. They look at various factors (political, social, industrial, cultural, economic etc.) and note how these *shape* technologies, arguing that users have an important role to play in negotiating technological change. This approach has been variously described as 'socio-technical' (Trist and Bamforth, 1951), 'social shaping' (Noble, 1985; MacKenzie and Wajcman 1985), and 'social constructionist' (Bijker *et al.*, 1987). There are sharp divisions between these perspectives, but essentially they all examine the way boundaries between the 'social' and 'technical' are negotiated, rather than accepting them as given. For example, Noble looked at the automatic control of machine tools and identified various paths that the technology *could* have followed (e.g. numerical control, record playback) He claims, however, that it was the industrial relations issues and career interests of engineers that determined how the technology developed.

Another group of writers adopt a feminist perspective. Downing (1980), for example, looks at how technology is gendered and pessimistically predicts that it will lead to further deskilling. Others focus on technological design and implementation, which they maintain are male-dominated (Cockburn and Ormrod, 1993; Grint and Gill, 1995). Berg (1995) considers the development of smart (or 'intelligent') houses in Norway and shows how the home has traditionally been the domain of women while technology has been the preserve of men. She examines how technologies are used (and whether they are adopted to make housework easier), but concludes that the whole area of housework is virtually ignored in these futuristic homes. Instead of technology being used to *lighten* workloads, there is greater preoccupation with lighting levels, humidity, surveillance and the appropriateness of appliances. In one type of house the technology announces that your microwave dinner is ready, activates music in the dining room, lowers the lights, and sends a robutler (drinks machine) to pour a red wine – all very clever, but the tray still has to be physically put in place. Berg concludes that 'the men (and it is men) producing prototypes of the intelligent house of the future and designing its key technologies have failed to visualize... the user/customer.... They have ignored the fact that the home is a place of work (women's housework) and overlook women, whose domain they are in effect transforming, as a target consumer group'.

Moving further along our continuum, there are other writers who, while not necessarily opposed to the technology (or even to capitalism), are pessimistic as to the outcome if certain political policies are adopted. These writers place even greater emphasis on choice, for they stress the considerable variation between societies and show how technology can be applied in many different ways. This level of pessimism therefore suggests that more acceptable outcomes *can* be achieved within existing institutional arrangements, and would include those who are critical of certain policies, such as those of the Conservative government in Britain.

This subdividing process can of course be extended further. For instance, one might be pessimistic over how new technology is being introduced into a particular firm (or even by a particular manager) while remaining optimistic in other respects. A growing number of writers believe that it is here, at the micro-organizational level, that analysis should concentrate, for they are wary of suggestions that new technology has particular universal effects – either for good or for bad. They too focus more on strategies than the technology itself – how the technology is actually *implemented* – and advocate a case study-based, 'contingency approach' (e.g. Child, 1988; Piercy *et al.*, 1984). Willcocks and Mason (1987), Checkland (1981) and Mumford (1983) talk of 'soft systems' – a model for introducing change that involves participants – as opposed to hard systems models where the emphasis is traditionally on the hardware and users are rarely considered. These writers can be located at the centre of our continuum, for they reject a wholly optimistic or pessimistic position; argue that every application is unique; focus at the organizational level; stress the neutrality of technology; and emphasize human choice.

As we have discussed these different forms of pessimism and moved towards the centre of our continuum, so it should be noted that the level of analysis has descended (from the global to the particular); the element of optimism has increased; and greater emphasis has been placed on human choice. This allows us to extend our continuum somewhat, and the conceptual framework the reader should keep in mind is shown in Fig. 2.2.

We would not wish to overstate this model, or suggest that all contributions can be neatly fitted into it, for the continuum is not made up of straight lines so much as messy squiggles – blurred here, sharp there – but it does provide a useful, general framework for classifying the different viewpoints. It also reminds us that a particular writer might be optimistic in one sense but pessimistic in another, and we must be clear as to the level and in which context a label is being applied.

Discussion of the broad question over whether we should reappraise our whole attitude to work, and our uses of technology, is deferred until Chapter 11. In the other chapters, most of the debate centres at the 'middle levels of pessimism' – i.e. with those commentators who are critical of our existing capitalist order or towards certain policies that are being introduced. Consideration of the British context is particularly strong in Chapters 3, 8, 9 and 10.

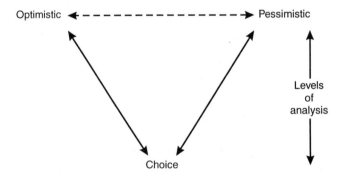

Figure 2.2   The optimistic/pessimistic continuum.

Technology as a social product

Whereas the optimists start with technology, the pessimists start with society and its power structures, and consider technology more as a social product. They see technology principally as the *dependent* variable, resulting from various social, political and economic forces. Their overriding fear is that technology will be allowed to develop on terms dictated by power-holders – big business, governments, multinational companies – to the detriment and exclusion of the mass of the population. To varying degrees, they fear greater control and surveillance (by particular countries, companies and social groups); mass unemployment; the misuse of valuable natural resources; growing inequalities in wealth and power; and further depersonalization of life and work.

Those writers who are critical of industrial capitalism particularly reject the convergence writers' suggestion that technology somehow 'spontaneously emerges' to determine independently the form a particular society takes. On the contrary, they argue that technologies are found because they are sought; and are adopted, designed, released, applied and controlled by those trying to protect their own interests. Technology is not snatched from thin air, but reflects the way we live and work, and if we lived and worked differently, then technology would reflect it. Dickson (1974) and Reinecke (1984) expound this view, which holds that we live in a capitalist (as opposed to an industrial) society, one based on exploitation and conflict rather than convergence and consensus, and divided between those who hold economic and political power and those who do not.

Braverman, too, when writing on the workplace, argues that under capitalism, labour power is geared to the creation of profit rather than the satisfaction of people's needs, and technology is used to enhance this. The division of labour takes on a particular form, and far from allowing workers to *choose* to subdivide tasks among themselves (the social division of labour) it is now used to assign workers to specific tasks (the manufacturing division of labour). This means workers become incapable of carrying out a complete production process and that through the increased use of technology, jobs are simplified (deskilled) and cheapened so that capitalists can employ unskilled as opposed to skilled labour, and use machines to replace human strength and skill. Instead of justifying the division of labour in terms of 'preserving scarce skills' – as Bell would claim in the case of his skilled technocrats – Braverman argues that its main appeal is to provide cheap labour for unskilled jobs. In that this view is critical of the *status quo* and apprehensive as to how new technology might be used, it tends to find favour on the political left.

Taylorism

A key factor in this process, along with scientific and technological development, is the application of the scientific management principles of Frederick Taylor (1980) which he advocated in the USA at the start of the century. The essence of scientific management, or Taylorism, was that managers should study jobs 'scientifically' – in terms of operations, tools, speed etc. – to determine and impose one 'best' method for each task which then replaces all others. As Taylor himself explained, 'In my system, the workman is told minutely what he is to do and how he is to do it, and any improvement he makes upon the instructions given to him is fatal to success'.

The gains, according to Taylor, would be that management and workforce could each concentrate on what suited them best; problems of worker slacking and managerial incompetence could be overcome; and all would benefit financially through higher wages or profits. As Taylor put it, 'The principal object of management should be to secure the maximum prosperity for the employer, coupled with the maximum prosperity of each employee'. He called for a 'mental revolution' in which 'Both sides should take their eyes off the division of the surplus as the all important matter and together turn their attention towards increasing the size of the surplus'.

The application of Taylor's principles certainly produced far greater output and wealth, but Braverman argues that it also permitted managers to monopolize all existing knowledge and dissociate the labour process from the skills of the workers. Workers are now paid to work, not to think, and the conception and execution of work become divorced from each other. Workers no longer use their initiative; are forbidden from 'conceiving' the job to be undertaken; and merely execute the task in the swiftest possible manner according to set instructions. Work is deskilled in terms of knowledge, responsibility and discretion.

The impetus is thus for employers to make jobs as simple and precise as possible, and this is assisted by the installation of machines designed to incorporate the manual and mental skills previously held by workers. This also had implications for factory organization, and the likes of Henry Ford extended Taylor's ideas through the development of assembly-line production. Tasks now required very few skills, as workers became mere appendages to machines – machines which ultimately might totally replace workers and deny them the opportunity to work at all.

Stages of technological development

This view of technological development proceeds through certain stages in which those who apply the technology aim to replace human skill, effort and control with mechanical devices.

We can classify this process as follows:

1. Mechanized manual production, in which tools and machines are used by skilled workers to perform tasks.
2. Mechanized production, in which work is performed by machines partly operated by workers.
3. Integrated mechanized production, in which the whole production cycle is performed by machines, controlled and regulated by workers.
4. Automated production, in which tasks are performed by machines that are checked by workers.
5. Integrated automated production, in which the production process is totally automated and human intervention is not required.

Seen through this model, the assembly line is a transitional technology which can now be replaced through microelectronics with the fully automated factory. Technology becomes increasingly reliable and incorporates automatic monitoring and fault-correcting devices which dispose of virtually all human skills.

In a sense, therefore, Braverman envisages a society similar to Bell – in which technology performs our various tasks and provides for our basic needs – but the means of achieving this end are totally different. He rejects the notion that there is some evolutionary 'logic of industrialism' that results in a particular form of society and, while he would agree that in a society based on cooperation and trust new technology could have a liberating rather than a degrading effect, he sees little sign of this happening under capitalism. For Braverman, the nature of work and production technology are still the products of class relations: capitalism remains very much intact, and without fundamental changes new technology will simply reinforce the *status quo*.

CONCLUSION

We have presented different perspectives on the technology–society interface and shall shortly relate these to a more detailed discussion of information technology. For purposes of clarification, the different em-

Table 2.1   Characteristics of the contrasting perspectives.

	Optimistic view	Pessimistic view
Society	Industrial	Capitalist
Technology	Neutral product	Social product
Technological focus	Invention	Innovation
Technological change	Revolutionary	Evolutionary
Social structure	Elite (meritocratic technocrats)	Class (economic owners)
Changes to social structure	Convergence	Polarization
Social relations	Consensus	Conflict
Nature of work	Reskilling	Deskilling
State	Pluralist	Unitary
Political orientation	Conservative	Radical

phases of the two main camps – both of which acknowledge considerable change – are summarized in Table 2.1.

In order to point up the differences in the perspectives, our discussion has, necessarily, been broad and simplified. We repeat that we are not talking of monocausal relationships: this is never the case, and no writer subscribes to a simple-minded determinism. Our models are 'ideal type abstractions', which hopefully will assist our appreciation of the various viewpoints that range in-between.

In concluding this chapter, we should add that on some occasions the two camps seem to be talking past each other, for they tend to focus on separate issues; adopt different time-scales; and sometimes use the same labels to mean different things. For instance, though Bell talks of 'revolution', many would criticize his use of the word, for he applies it in a narrow, largely *technological* sense. If we consider the *means* by which the 'end' of his post-industrial society comes about, his approach is not 'revolutionary' at all, but strongly 'evolutionary'. Critics would question why, when the first industrial revolution clearly involved so much upheaval and class conflict, this present revolution should provide increasing harmony and consensus. They would particularly question whether new social and occupational classes have emerged, the last of Deane's features. Even if technocrats are more important, pessimists would claim that the capitalists are still very much in control, and society characterized by exploitation and conflict. Critics would insist that any true revolution has to involve a change in the mode of economic production and a shift in the make-up of the ruling class. New technology may be revolutionary in terms of what it can do, but it is a product of existing society rather than a catalyst for change. Thus a term like 'micro revolution' is acceptable to both camps, but the pessimists would question a 'new industrial revolution'.

There is also an important difference with regard to time-scale. Those who question whether new technology will itself fundamentally enhance the nature of work in capitalist society (i.e. the pessimists) tend to restrict their remarks to the short term, and in most instances prefer to focus at lower levels of analysis. The optimistic convergence writers, on the other hand, seem happy to indulge in long-term global speculation.

Having established the different perspectives, we shall now apply them to a discussion of the human effects of information technology, particularly in relation to employment, the workplace, citizenship and the home.

CHAPTER THREE

Employment Patterns

The issue in the new technology debate that has aroused most controversy – certainly during the 1980s when unemployment figures in Britain regularly topped three million – is probably that of labour displacement. Unemployment became a major problem for most industrialized nations, and government critics claim that, in Britain, the figure would have been far higher had the methods of counting not been altered on around 30 occasions. Labour politicians and trade unionists continually claimed that the true figure was over four million. Either way, this represented more than a fivefold increase since the mid-1970s, and led many to question the extent to which information technology was the cause of this and whether we should expect unemployment figures to increase still further. Interestingly, this discussion was more widespread in Britain and Europe than, say, Japan and the USA (perhaps because we experienced greater unemployment) and, consequently, this chapter will largely concentrate on the British experience.

What is interesting, however, is that as we moved into the 1990s, labour displacement became a less contentious issue. Official jobless figures dropped – the figure has been nearer two million in Britain for most of the 1990s, though critics would still maintain they are 'massaged' – and attention has turned from the *destruction* of jobs to whether or not IT encourages new *patterns* of working (e.g. part-time employment, short-term contracts, teleworking) This chapter, therefore, looks first at the central issue of labour displacement, and then focuses on the changing work patterns that seem to be emerging.

LABOUR DISPLACEMENT

Is the microchip the great 'job-killer' or alternatively, as some would claim, is it providing a much-needed stimulus for our economy, to carry us out of recession? It has at the same time been presented as the panacea for all our industrial troubles and as a force that will destroy work as we know it and divisively polarize society between those in regular, highly skilled employment and those with no work at all.

We can immediately divide between optimists and pessimists, and apply our continuum to consider the range of views. Towards one extreme are the 'ultra-pessimists' – for instance, Marxist writers who see new technology inevitably leading to higher unemployment, for this is a recurring feature of capitalism. Technology has always been used to replace labour power; microelectronics is no different, and many more will be unemployed in an increasingly polarized society. Optimists, on the other hand, argue that labour-saving technology is nothing new; that it has never by itself increased unemployment in the long term; that we have survived structural change before; and that microelectronics will create wealth and boost jobs.

This is to simplify and set the debate in broad terms. In one sense, everyone is a pessimist, for there is little dispute that information technology will displace *certain* tasks – the European Union in a 1994 Green Paper claimed that 10% of jobs were rendered superfluous each year because of expanding technology – but the argument hinges on whether it will also revitalize the economy to the extent that it creates new areas of work and higher employment levels overall. The pessimists concentrate on job *loss*, while the optimists stress job *creation*. We are therefore dealing with two separate issues: whether technology *causes* labour displacement, and whether, in the long term, it *results* in it. Though related, the two are not the same thing, and one can accept the first while rejecting the second. In other words, we first need to establish the existing sectors most likely to be affected by new technology and, secondly, to consider whether the effects of the technology itself could be such as to stimulate fresh jobs in new areas. This is a distinction between 'process innovation', where old tasks are done in new ways, and 'product innovation', where new markets, goods and services, and thereby jobs, are created. The first of these is far easier to determine and, as we shall see, there is general agreement that jobs in certain sectors are at risk. However, this need not mean that society experiences unemployment in *aggregate* terms, and this is the main issue for debate.

THE PRESENT CLIMATE

Any discussion of the effects of information technology on employment must be set in a broad context. Firstly, it must be stressed that IT has emerged against a backcloth of world recession, and in Britain within the framework of ostensibly monetarist government policies. If employment was high, then we probably wouldn't spend much time worrying about the effects of new technology, but then if it was high we presumably would not (if Kondratiev is correct) be thinking of installing new technology anyway. The context therefore colours the position that different people adopt. The pessimists are generally critical of government policies, which they believe have intensified unemployment; they insist that the continuance of such policies will only exacerbate the situation; and they believe that new technology could play an important role in this process. The optimists, on the other hand, believe that unemployment has been an international problem; that the government is right in trying to hold down inflation; that this is the only way of providing secure jobs in the long term; and that new technology can assist rather than hinder this process. Each side therefore approaches the issue from a totally different set of premises, which in turn means they reach very different conclusions. Secondly, new technology is merely one factor among many that may affect employment patterns. While technological change invariably creates transitional unemployment, this will vary considerably according to the underlying growth rate of a country's economy, its international competitiveness, the global energy situation, government policies, changes in the labour force etc., and consequently the same technology can have very different effects in different countries. Moreover, these various factors become so intertwined that it is impossible to extrapolate one as an independent variable and measure its precise impact. To talk of the effect of new technology in isolation from other influences is rather like talking about the impact of a new centre-forward on a football team without any reference to the other players in the team.

Nor should it be thought that a rise in unemployment necessarily means a fall in employment. A key factor in Britain over recent decades has been the growth in the labour force due to the facts that: (a) more women have sought work, (b) the baby boom of the 1950s and 1960s created more school-leavers, and (c) fewer people were retiring as fewer were born during the First World War. We now have a higher proportion of women in the labour force (along with Denmark) than any other EU country, and as many women now *expect* to work, they register as unemployed if made redundant, thus boosting the figures. Whereas women only made up 23% of Europe's unemployed in 1970, the figure was 50% by the mid-1990s. This helps explain why unemployment continued to rise during this period, despite the arrival of new jobs: Britain actually created new jobs better than most European economies – boasting a labour force of around 30 million by the mid-1990s – but unemployment remained persistently high throughout.

The unemployment problem has been most intense in manufacturing industry: 8.4 million worked in manufacturing in 1966, but this had fallen to 5 million by 1994. However, during the 1980s the service industries grew substantially, so that, by 1994, there were over 15 million workers in the service sector. By the mid-1990s, therefore, nearly three-quarters of the workforce were in the service sector, while only one-fifth were in manufacturing. This explains how, during the 1980s, the overall workforce *increased* even though, in 1986, 13 000 manufacturing jobs were being lost every month. This was because many more (especially women) were employed in the service sector and part-time work; there was a fall in male employment, a gain in full-time female employment and a *massive* increase in part-time female employment. Whereas part-time workers accounted for only 15% of the workforce in 1971, this had almost doubled by 1994 to 28%. By the year 2000, it is estimated that 45% of the labour force will be female – some 12.9 million.

Economists on the political right – who we can label 'monetarist' – argued in the 1980s that British employment legislation played a big part in increasing unemployment in that it made it too difficult for employers to 'hire and fire'. Unlike the American system, where income support is granted for only a few months, after which it runs out, our flat-rate system was seen as providing a minimum out-of-work income available indefinitely even to people not seriously looking for a job. By the mid-1990s the British government had moved more towards the American approach – income support became less accessible and the unemployed were required to undertake various community programmes – and our unemployment figures became noticeably lower than those of Germany or France. This provided a more fluid labour market, but the price was greater job insecurity and the new work patterns we discuss later in this chapter.

The monetarist argument is that 'effective demand' should regulate employment, and that if there is an over-supply of labour then wages should fall, thus making it profitable for employers to hire more workers. In other words, we should encourage perfect markets in which employers can offer jobs 'at the right price' and people are encouraged to go in search of them. Such an approach contrasts with those on the political left, who advocate more education and training to produce a 'high-wage, high-skill' economy, combined with a minimum wage and more secure working conditions. Monetarists insist that such demands merely keep wages artificially high, result in inflation and ultimately provide fewer jobs for others.

THE IMPACT OF INFORMATION TECHNOLOGY

The chip therefore further compounds an already highly complex and contentious situation. As we have stressed, it is impossible to determine the precise amount of labour displacement attributable to IT, particularly in Britain, where initial take-up was relatively slow, and when economists adopt contrasting perspectives. There is a wide gulf between those who expect unemployment to rise by many more millions and those who predict an eventual increase in jobs. Just as economists vary in their emphasis on particular causal factors, and how they collate and interpret statistics, so they divide over their predictions of future work patterns.

It is understandable that IT has aroused concern in Britain, for we have experienced a serious unemployment problem, and fears have been intensified by the astonishing development of microelectronics, which makes people wary of suggestions that this is 'just another technology'. It is hardly surprising that by the late 1970s a 'pessimistic viewpoint' was already emerging over the employment effects of microelectronics.

The pessimistic view

This view argues that the net effect of new technology will be to create an overall decline in job opportunities and thus lead to large-scale and possibly permanent unemployment problems. Information technology is seen as qualitatively different from earlier forms, for it significantly replaces work by brain as well as by hand. While, in the first industrial revolution, workers displaced from the land could move into the fast-growing towns, in the present situation, those displaced from factories and offices seem likely to have nowhere to go, as any new industries will be highly automated and only employ minimal workforces. In the short term, lack of innovation and investment may hold back the effects, but in time they will become significant. The scale of these effects will of course be influenced by governmental policies – and, it is argued, they will be far greater if monetarist policies are pursued than if public investment is expanded – but overall the outcome will be one of substantial job loss.

This pessimistic view first gained momentum in the late 1970s through the likes of Clive Jenkins' and Barrie Sherman's much-publicized book *The Collapse of Work*, in which they argued that Britain was faced with 'Hobson's choice' over information technology:

> Remain as we are, reject the new technologies, and we face unemployment of up to 5.5 million by the end of the century. Embrace the new technologies, accept the challenge, and we end up with unemployment of about 5 million.

They suggested that if we did not embrace new technology we would suffer unemployment, for we would cease to remain competitive as an industrialized nation, but similarly, if we did embrace it we would still experience job losses, for microelectronics would perform our necessary tasks – hence 'work collapses'. They argued that of these alternatives the latter was preferable, for it allowed us to remain a wealthy, advanced nation. Their work involved an industry-by-industry analysis of likely job effects, and they suggested that occupations could be divided into three basic groups:

(a) Occupations that would hardly be affected at all: farm labourers, trawlermen, general labourers, top management, leisure employees.
(b) Occupations that would be minimally affected: security and protection specialists, professional staffs, catering, hairdressing and other personal services, education, health and welfare services, construction and mining.
(c) Occupations that would be considerably affected: handling and storing, clerical work, manufacturing workers, repair workers, middle management, supervisors, financial staff and 'information' employees.

Among manpower economists, the Institute of Manpower Studies at Sussex University predicted 'jobless growth' in manufacturing industry (i.e. greater output but fewer jobs) and only a slight employment rise (3%) in the service sector. In the study (based on the plans of half Britain's employers) Rajan and Pearson (1986) predicted that new jobs would emerge in wholesale distribution, business services, contract cleaning, research and development, finance and hotels and catering, but this would not compensate for the losses in manufacturing. The job gainers would be female, skilled, young and in the south; the losers would be male, unskilled, elderly and in the north. As a result, they feared a dangerous polarization between (a) a large underclass of unemployable labour and (b) a small group of highly skilled and highly paid workers in employment.

At Cambridge University, in work less specifically directed at new technology, the Economic Policy Group were also predicting that unemployment could reach anything from four to seven million by the 1990s, depending on government policies. Due to the unprecedented combination of demographic factors, they expected the workforce to rise significantly up to 1990, but the situation would go into reverse after that, and 300 000 new jobs would be needed to prevent unemployment rising. This would require a growth rate in excess of 5% per annum, a tall order given the post-war performance of the British economy.

Leach and Wagstaff (1986) likewise reject the assumption that renewed economic activity will in itself bring lower levels of unemployment: job loss from industry is the common experience of western industrialized countries, and there is no automatic employment growth from the service sector. Information technology will not produce the necessary number or diversity of jobs, nor will public expenditure or the use of economic planning make more than a modest contribution. Even on the most optimistic assumptions, they argue, orthodox economic policies will leave most industrialized nations with unemployment at unacceptably high levels, which will necessitate major changes in our tax and benefits systems.

This depressing (some would say alarmist) outlook has even received support from the National Economic Development Council (NEDC) which supposedly reflects the collective views of government, industrial management and the trade unions. In 1982, their policy for the UK electronics industry suggested that people could well lose jobs to new machines, and they rejected the notion of mass unemployment being 'temporary' as 'dangerously false'. They questioned political cant about restoring employment and suggested that, at best, employment would do no more than remain stable.

Support for the pessimistic viewpoint has also come (perhaps surprisingly) from Ronnie Gilbert (1989), a former member of the Conservative research department. He questions whether the market-place and prudent economic management can ever deliver jobs on a sufficient scale. He rejects the notion that service industries offer the potential for expansion, and maintains that the best prospects still lie in the production sector –

cars, microwaves, computers etc. – which can themselves provide services conveniently and efficiently. He believes new technology will allow more people to do *their own* car servicing, gardening, DIY tasks etc., and that more jobs will, therefore, be made available in the manufacture of tools and machines rather than in the provision of services. He proposes an improved NEDC (on the lines of Japan's MITI) to plan national developments, chaired by the Prime Minister and including the Opposition.

The pessimistic viewpoint is, therefore, still very much alive. While optimists would claim that recent falls in unemployment levels show the dire predictions of the early 1980s to have been misplaced, pessimists would simply reply that the true figures have been camouflaged (by counting methods) and that the long-term outlook for jobs still remains bleak.

Case studies

There is a vast amount of case study material from both the manufacturing and office sectors to support the pessimists' claims, though we repeat that it is hard to disentangle the effects of automation from those of recession. In traditional manufacturing, many companies have drastically cut labour and there seems little indication that this sector will provide the springboard for new jobs in the future. At Rolls-Royce, Derby, three workers per shift can produce what once required 30; Plessey reduced their Liverpool workforce by 825 over two years as they expanded production of digital telephone exchanges; Austin Rover cut their workforce by 20 000 and invested heavily in automation; GKN reduced their UK workforce by 35 000 in five years, and so on. The high-technology industries themselves are generating many new jobs, but whether this will prove sufficient to replace those that are lost seems doubtful, as there is every indication that they will prove capital-intensive, rather than labour-intensive.

In the office sphere – identified by Jenkins and Sherman as a key sector – the effects have been equally alarming. Bradford City Council reduced its staff in one sector from 44 to 22 with the introduction of nine word processors, providing a productivity increase of 20% and an estimated annual saving of some £60 000. At the Provident Financial, when three IBM machines were introduced into the central typing pool the full-time staff was cut from 27 to 17, and part-time staff from 13 to three. The expanding Halifax Building Society moved from automatic typewriters to 16 IBM word processors, trebled its workload, but took on no extra staff. Littlewoods, the mail order firm, introduced a computer and cut

600 jobs. And so one could go on. Ursula Huws (1982) found in her study of 40 workplaces in West Yorkshire that new technology was particularly likely to hit women's jobs. While 60% of the workplaces employed more men, only in 17% of cases were more men's jobs affected.

Jenkins and Sherman have certainly been proved right in their predictions for workers in the financial sector. In banking – once considered a 'job for life' – around 100 000 jobs were lost between 1990 and 1996 as 3000 branches were closed. The Banking, Insurance and Finance Union (BIFU), like other white-collar unions, predicted in 1996 that another 100 000 redundancies could occur by the turn of the century as multimedia kiosks – which are touch-screen-based and can connect clients direct to bank employees over a video-conferencing link – increasingly replace high street branches. The banks do not contest the predictions: 20% of bank employees can expect to lose their jobs before 2000. Ironically perhaps, jobs losses have, during the 1990s, been heaviest in the service sector – local and central government, offices, shops and banks – and in the south of England, where the sector is largest.

The optimistic view

In the light of such depressing forecasts, it may seem surprising that others should have taken a totally opposite line – but they have. The optimists concede that new technology may cause some temporary dislocation, unemployment and hardship, for this has always been the consequence of technological innovation, but they reject the idea that it will *result* in higher unemployment overall. They advocate what Francis terms 'compensation theory' – that the level of employment in the economy is, in the long run, determined only by the overall level of demand, and that if demand is kept constant then savings made by productivity gains through the use of new technology in one sector will feed through into other sectors through lower prices, increased wages and higher profits. Unemployment is, therefore, not the result of new technology but rather global forces such as world recession, demographic changes, energy crises, trade unions or economic management. In short, the argument is that, unless money is stored in socks, its circulation *must* boost employment, and that 'the leisure society' only arrives when people choose extra leisure in preference to extra income. Francis believes there is little evidence that people have, in general, reached this point in our society.

They began to present their case in the early 1980s, largely as a response to the pessimists, and this was hardly surprising, for without the promulgations of Jenkins and Sherman and others, they would have seen no need to raise the matter at all. Being optimists, they see little cause for concern regarding new technology: technological change is a continuous feature of industrial development, and there is as much reason to suppose that it stimulates employment opportunities as depresses them. Employment in the railways, chemicals and metal manufacture all rose significantly following technological innovation, and there were actually more professional musicians, not less, after the arrival of the domestic record player! To say that we are moving into a world in which there will not be enough to do because technology carries out our basic tasks is, to the optimists, to consider employment solely in terms of producing the goods and services we *presently* need. These are not fixed, and though displacement may occur in some areas, fresh opportunities should emerge in others. Optimists therefore incline to the view that the effect on jobs will ultimately be qualitative rather than quantitative. Employment patterns will certainly change as new jobs replace old, but this should be slow, giving the economy time to readjust.

This viewpoint gained support at a microelectronics conference in Tokyo in 1985, sponsored by Japan's Ministry of Labour. Over 500 representatives attended from 29 countries, and the main conclusions were that automation did not appear to remove jobs; IT created new jobs; and all employees needed to be given IT skills. The conference report concluded that

> There is no indication that microelectronics leads to increased unemployment... the number of employees engaging in research and development, information processing and servicing increases while the number of workers engaging in production and office work decreases.

Japan is, of course, continually quoted as the shining example to disprove the pessimists' foreboding. Though that society has invested massively in information technology, unemployment has been kept to around 3%, and five times as many people are now employed in areas such as marketing and production planning. Just as the Luddites were misguided in 1811 when they smashed up the machines they feared would destroy their jobs, and the 'prophets of doom' in the 1950s were proved wrong when they claimed the first mainframe computers would result in unemployment so, it is argued, pessimists overstate the likely effects of microelectronics.

One of the best-known optimists is Patrick Minford (1984), who rejects the view that new technology destroys jobs and maintains that the long-term outlook for employment can be bright if government helps rather than hinders fluidity in the labour market. He suggests that unemployment will fall (as it did before) as we come through recession, and dismisses the idea that unemployment is becoming a permanent feature of industrial society as 'rubbish'. Just as in the past new jobs were created when technology displaced old ones, so the same thing will happen again. As a 'market-oriented' economist, he views technology as uniform and dismisses the suggestion that particular forms may have special effects. He believes that market forces can deal with unemployment and that these work best if not interfered with by government. This school of thought believes that recession cures itself. Workers will accept lower pay, shops will charge lower prices and that will stimulate demand for goods. In time the economy will grow again. Minford accepts some degree of frictional unemployment as inevitable, but argues that *cyclical* unemployment is largely determined by global economic forces and will only fall as we come through recession. His Liverpool University macroeconomic forecasting group have predicted a cloudless horizon of continuing growth, falling unemployment and declining inflation. They conclude that 'the UK picture is as encouraging as ever'.

The argument of the optimists is that if human wants remain to be satisfied, then higher demand will call forth the production of new goods and services. Yesterday's luxuries become today's necessities, and people's expectations rise. In the 1930s many people demanded little more than a waterproof home, protection from major diseases, sufficient food and a steady job: there was no demand for television performers as the technology did not exist.

This optimistic line appeared in many early reports from various government advisory bodies. For instance, in its report to the Cabinet in 1980, the Advisory Council for Applied Research and Development (ACARD) advocated the necessity for immediately embracing microelectronics and rejected the notion that this would lead to increasing unemployment. Presenting the traditional argument that economic growth leads to greater employment, it adopted an optimistic standpoint and suggested that:

> If new technology leads to an increase in market share, there is generally an increase in employment opportunities. The labour resources made available by reductions in employment in some manufacturing sectors will provide the opportunity for rapid expansion in quite different sectors.

Likewise, in its 1979 report, the Department of Employment (DEP) Manpower Study Group concluded that

> ...the overall employment effect is virtually impossible to gauge. However, past empirical work suggests that, in the long run, technological change has been beneficial to both output and employment... the employment implications in quantitative terms are likely to be insignificant. (Sleigh *et al.*, 1979)

This 'compensatory argument' continued to appear in various government reports and, perhaps not surprisingly, was embraced by the Confederation of British Industry (CBI). Just as many trade unions adopted a pessimistic line, so the CBI took an optimistic stance and, from its 1980 report onwards, maintained that the only permanent solution to unemployment was to create viable jobs in new and expanding industries, and that microelectronics could help in this process. It sees the impact of new technology on unemployment as being uneven, and while some sectors could decline, fresh areas for work should emerge.

The Nobel prize-winning economist Wassily Leontief (1986) of New York University has suggested that far from microtechnology displacing workers, it is more likely that there will not be enough workers to operate all the machines we will want. In that he believes job creation will overshadow job loss, Leontief might be termed a 'super-optimist'. He concedes that there will be a dramatic fall in office workers (but not production workers) and argues that this will be compensated for by a rise in craft workers, labourers, operatives, service workers and, in particular, professionals (Table 3.1).

Blue-collar workers may lose their present jobs, but they will be rehired in growing industries producing equipment for the technological revolution. As regards America, his projections suggest that *too many* jobs will be generated by 2000 for what is likely to be the size of the labour force. If unemployment does stay high, he suggests it will be for reasons other than technology, such as the deflationary response of government to pay claims. There are differences, of course, between the USA and Britain (e.g. the USA has more farmers), but Leontief believes that the same broad changes will occur in all industrialized economies. His overriding message is that the faster we adapt ourselves to the new technology, the sooner we will be able to experience high living standards and low unemployment.

Table 3.1   Predicted make-up of the United States labour force, 2000.

	1978(%)	2000(%)
Farmers	3.2	3.4
Labourers	4.9	5.5
Sales workers	6.6	6.5
Managers	9.5	7.2
Professionals	15.6	19.8
Operatives	15.7	16.5
Craft workers	13.3	15.0
Service workers	12.4	14.7
Clerical workers	17.8	11.4
Miscellaneous	1.0	0.0
	100.0	100.0

The long-term optimistic view

In-between the two views we have considered so far is a third group of writers who we shall label long-term optimists (or, if you prefer, short-term pessimists) who are located closer to the centre of our continuum. This includes those who adopt a Keynesian view; favour a 'mixed economy'; and believe government should play a key role through public investment in stimulating economic activity. They are optimistic over long-term job creation and believe that employment consequences are manageable within present institutional arrangements – if, of course, appropriate policies are adopted. Their pessimism is therefore more short term and relates to the specific policies being pursued by the present government, i.e. they are 'lower level' pessimists. Their scenario suggests that new technology will cause considerable displacement in certain sectors, but this should prove temporary, and though the rate of change will greatly depend on interrelated factors, such as government policies, energy costs and bank interest rates, there is every reason to expect that, long term, overall employment levels will rise.

This view is well represented in the work of Tom Stonier (1983, 1984) who maintains that jobs in traditional manufacturing industries will be removed by new technology and that the new hi-tech industries will not provide new ones in sufficient numbers to balance the displacement. He predicts that by the turn of the century only 10% of the labour force will be needed to provide our material needs. Of the remainder (if they are not unemployed), 10% will be in finance and commerce, 5–10% in leisure industries, 25–30% in health, police and other social services, and 40% in what he terms the 'knowledge industry'. (He would no doubt point to the fact that during the 1980s, when unemployment remained consistently high, there was a continuous surplus of IT jobs.) This is close to Daniel Bell, who suggests that people-to-machine jobs, in both factory and office, will decline, to be replaced by people-to-people jobs. Information now becomes a more important resource than land, labour or capital, and just as technology allowed people to move from the land to the factory, so now it allows them to move from the factory to the new service sectors.

To Jenkins and Sherman, these 'information' jobs are equally ripe for automation; but Stonier shares Minford's optimism that they could help create fresh employment opportunities. Where they differ, however, is over the particular policies they believe will bring this about. Stonier is Keynesian in that he advocates a major *governmental* role in job creation, not just in infrastructure projects but also in 'human capital' through the expansion of such areas as education and health care. The 'caring industries' could be improved by decreasing the client/staff ratio, and rather than destroying employment, should have an almost infinite capacity, Stonier argues, for providing work. This 'social policy response', as he terms it, would encourage projects that had a clearly positive impact on the country's productivity and would yield revenue to the government either directly or indirectly. Government's role would therefore be to help the private sector produce wealth, and also expand public sector employment.

POLITICAL RESPONSES

During the 1980s the Thatcher governments pursued essentially 'monetarist' policies – controlling the money supply and raising interest rates to contain inflation – which, though criticized by many economists, were hailed by supporters as creating an 'economic miracle'. Inflation was significantly reduced, unemployment fell during the late 1980s and, by 1990, productivity was rising faster than in most other European countries, but critics viewed this as no more than a recovery from earlier disasters. By the 1990s GDP growth still remained at only 2%; investment was barely back to its 1979 level; unemployment was nearly double what it was in 1979; and the UK had a serious balance of payments problem.

Despite such criticisms, however, the view of the government (with regard to IT and unemployment) remained defiantly optimistic throughout.

In 1987 Margaret Thatcher predicted that mass unemployment would not last forever and justified her confidence with reference to the mill owners of the early 19th century.

> The opportunities of the industrial revolution eliminated jobs to start with but afterwards they led to massive numbers of new jobs. I believe that will happen again.

In this clear statement of compensation theory she forecast that technology would bring a return to full employment as new inventions and processes would lead to an initial fall in the workforce followed by massive job gains. As far as industry was concerned, it was not automation, but the *failure* to automate, that put jobs at risk: it was a case of 'automate or liquidate'. This has remained the government's position through the 1990s.

The Labour Party, on the other hand, seems to correspond more to the position of Stonier. The party is not 'anti-new technology', and does not believe that it will necessarily result in long-term labour displacement. In a 1995 report the party claimed that:

> ...Over time the new information society has the potential to change things for the better. The information industries will represent one of the main wealth-creating sectors of the economy in the coming decades... and they can lead to the generation of many thousands of jobs.

But the report also insists that this will only come about if the government plays a leading role.

> ...Labour believes that government must play a much more proactive role in order to ensure that the development of the infrastructure happens as rapidly as possible, and that the best possible uses are made of it thereafter. Innovation in technology should be leading to innovative ideas for public policy.

Britain should invest in the national infrastructure – roads, railways, sewers, water services etc. – and develop the necessary facilities – fibre-optic cable, satellites, home terminals, appropriate workplaces etc. – to accommodate the new technology. Secondly, government should invest in the labour-intensive, welfare industries – as Stonier suggests – to provide new jobs as well as to improve the quality of the services themselves.

The Liberal Democrats set up a commission to look at the future of employment and concluded that Britain had no choice but to embrace technological development. This requires creating greater access to venture capital, a better qualified workforce, a suitably educated school population, improved information regarding IT, an increase in resources and better liaison between education and industry. Support for such policies (albeit to a lesser extent) has also come from the ranks of the government's own supporters, the CBI and other industrialists.

The common theme in this argument is that the government should be prepared to borrow in order to invest in the national infrastructure to provide new jobs and equip society for technological change. This is so vital that it cannot solely be left to the private sector and, as in other countries, government must play a dominant role. The Conservative government's reply is that we have been down this road many times before and it always leads to inflation.

Ultimately, the whole issue depends on one's view of how efficiently and quickly markets work. If they work perfectly (or could be made to work perfectly), then unemployment cannot persist for any great length of time, irrespective of any 'shocks' to the system such as microelectronics, oil crises or whatever. If, on the other hand, prices and wages are inflexible, and supplies and demands only respond to changes slowly (as appears to be the case in Britain), then imbalances such as unemployment can persist. Once again, therefore, we come back to perspectives and to reminding ourselves that how we look at something largely determines what we see. The monetarists approximate more closely to the view that the government should disengage itself from direct economic activity and allow market systems to work, while Keynesians insist they will never work effectively without governmental stimulus.

RECONCILING THE DIFFERENT APPROACHES

We have collated the wide range of contributions to the employment debate into three main camps: the pessimists, optimists and long-term optimists. All agree that displacement in certain sectors (e.g. the office, banking etc.) is virtually certain, but while the pessimists believe that this will result in greater job losses overall, the long-term optimists maintain it should only be for the short term, while the optimists claim that new jobs will replace old. (The super-optimists even believe we shall eventually create more jobs that we can fill.)

To the lay person – who up to now might have had some faith in economics – much of this must seem puzzling. With such disparity between those who predict unemployment possibly rising to seven million and those who expect greater employment as a result of microelectronics, one can see why economics is termed the 'dismal science'.

All is not lost, however, for one could claim that the different schools are not so far apart as they might appear. In the first place, because the various contributors adopt different perspectives, they also employ very different methodological approaches. The pessimists base most of their work on macro-economic models which, critics claim, insufficiently allow for the wide range of extraneous variables. Suggestions that microelectronics can cause X million unemployed can, by themselves, be very misleading, for, as we have seen, regional variations, female employment and population trends are just some of the secondary factors that must be taken into account. Pessimists can easily overstate the potential of new technology, implying that it will be adopted overnight, and confusing what is possible with what is probable. In Britain the take-up has been generally slow – due, many would say, to the fact that we are a relatively low-wage economy which provides little incentive for firms to invest in new, expensive techniques. Finally, critics maintain that some pessimists wish to use new technology to prove something they already believe, i.e. that capitalism is doomed and the British economy is in irreversible decline.

As to the optimists, because they are suspicious of large-scale economic models, they prefer to employ a more 'micro' approach and focus on individual workplaces, but this too has its limitations. Those firms that have invested significantly in new technology tend to be more progressive and successful, and labour displacement has been avoided through increases in market share. (At a national level, this in effect is what has happened in Japan.) In Britain they still represent a minority and should not be taken as representative in terms of labour displacement effects. As we saw earlier, one can easily quote workplace examples that argue the opposite outcome. Consequently, because of the methods they adopt, pessimists run the risk of overstating, and the optimists understating, the likely displacement figures.

Another factor we have to consider is work time. This is not fixed, and while during the industrial revolution the average working week was over sixty hours, this has now fallen to under forty and could fall further. Clearly, changes to the working week, longer holidays and earlier retirement could significantly alter the situation. Jenkins and Sherman certainly expect such developments in view of the displacement they predict, and talk not just of a 'shorter working week' but a 'shorter working lifetime'.

They envisage far greater flexibility in working hours, sabbaticals, job changes, earlier retirement etc. But Stonier too foresees people working far shorter hours, and this view is shared by politicians of all persuasions.

If this is so, are the various camps really that far apart from each other? After all, to say that everyone will be in work but will only work four days a week and 40 weeks a year (and possibly retire at 50) is surely not so different from saying that unemployment (with conditions unchanged) will rise to five million. The difference is simply in terms of how the available work is spread. Therefore, if one delves beneath the differences in emphasis – and rhetoric – one starts to identify a broad scenario that many would subscribe to. It goes something like this. Britain must adopt new technology if we wish to remain as a competitive, western industrialized nation, but this will certainly lead to labour displacement in certain areas. New areas of work will emerge as new products and services are provided and fresh demands arise. These will provide new wealth, but are unlikely to create sufficient jobs to balance the displacement, so what is available must be shared if those who desire work are to obtain some. This will demand new working arrangements.

CHANGING WORK PATTERNS

The labour displacement debate has, perhaps, ground to something of a stalemate, but what cannot be denied is the fact that, as a result of new technology, the *nature* of work has changed significantly over the past two decades and, as a consequence, we have witnessed shifts in employment patterns. We shall examine these in the remainder of this chapter and then, in Chapter 4, consider the technological changes in more detail.

For the major part of this century the western industrialized world has been dominated by mass production. This involves the mass manufacture of standardized products in mechanized production plants where work is planned according to assembly line principles (i.e. Taylorism). Large numbers of (predominantly male) low-skilled workers are employed, and considerable economies of scale are achieved. Moreover, this is often accompanied by considerable state support – as was certainly the case in the immediate post-war period – through public investment, policies for high employment and the creation of an affluent working population with mass purchasing power. Factory production produced a concentrated,

urbanized, relatively homogeneous, male, affluent, full-time manual working class. Everything was 'massified': mass production led to mass advertising and mass consumption.

From the early 1970s, however, this situation became increasingly
undermined by inflation, mass market saturation, recession, and the
increasing power of the multinationals and interlinking of the world
economy. Companies responded to this uncertainty by introducing
flexibility – by providing more diversified products for individual
customers (i.e. niche marketing) – and applying computer technology
not only to each stage of the production process but also to the integration of all stages into a single, coordinated process. In the car
industry, for instance, Henry Ford's famous boast that 'People can
have the Model T in any colour – so long as it's black', is replaced
by a multitude of choice in colour, style, price etc. for every customer.
Economies of scale can now be achieved on much smaller runs as
flexible, all-purpose machinery (which we discuss in the following
chapter) can produce a variety of products.

A good example of this approach is the Italian clothing firm, Benetton.
Their clothes are made by 11 500 workers in Northern Italy, but only
1500 work directly for the company. The rest are employed by subcontractors in small factories of 30–50 workers. The clothes are then sold
through 2000 tied retail outlets, all of them franchised. Benetton *coordi-
nates* operations in line with computerized daily sales returns which come
to their headquarters from all parts of Europe. Such returns also allow
companies to identify markets, which means they 'make what they can
sell' rather 'sell what they can make'.

As Thompson and McHugh (1989) point out, mass production
will not suddenly disappear, nor is it incapable of handling diversi-
fication within flow lines, but the trend towards more flexible approaches can clearly be seen as companies 'downsize', and this has
profound implications for the ways people work. Handy (1989) suggests we are seeing the emergence of 'shamrock organizations' (divided into three parts) where the labour force is segmented between
a *core* of permanent, skilled, well-represented, full-time employees;
a *peripheral* group of dispersed, unskilled, often female, poorly paid,
weakly organized, part-time workers; and external *subcontractors*
who are brought in when needed. Over the past two decades, we
have witnessed a move away from standard nine-to-five, five days
a week, eleven months a year, full-time work to a varied range of
different patterns.

- *Part-time work*

The number of part-time workers nearly doubled between 1970 and 1990. By 1994 there were five million women and 990 000 men in part-time work, and a survey by the Institute of Management and Manpower predicted that, by the turn of the century, major companies can expect more than half their workforce to be temporary or part-time.

- *Flexitime*

Many companies have introduced flexible working, whereby workers have to work certain core hours but retain some choice over their working time. Such arrangements have become more practical as technology controls production operations on a 24-hour basis.

- *Short-term contracts*

Temporary work – which grew by a third in the first half of the 1990s to 1.5 million – seems certain to become more common over the next decade. It has particularly affected female workers and the manufacturing sector.

- *Job sharing*

Job sharing, whereby two people share a full-time job on a part-time basis, has grown in popularity and is particularly attractive to workers who may not wish to work five days a week but would like to retain some job security.

- *Teleworking*

As a result of new technology, teleworking (which we discuss in Chapter 5) is becoming increasingly common. It is calculated that, by the year 2000, one in every hundred European workers will be connected to office computer systems from their homes and, by the year 2003, over eight million people in the UK are expected to spend the majority of their time teleworking.

- *Self-employment*

The government has continually encouraged people to start small businesses and over three million people (1 in 8) are now self-employed in Britain – 22% more than in 1984.

These new work patterns (and we do not suggest our list is exclusive) are profoundly affecting the way people work.

The optimistic view

Writers such as Hirst (1989) have labelled these developments 'flexible specialization', and largely welcome the move away from standardized factory work. Notwithstanding the wider range of goods and services made available to customers, optimists believe that the new work patterns also offer many advantages. They claim that both employer and employee can benefit: the employer can recruit an appropriate number of workers with the required skills, while the employee enjoys greater flexibility. DoE surveys in 1994 showed 75% of part-time workers (many of them women) claiming that they *preferred* part-time work: only 13% said they took such work because they could not obtain full-time employment. In addition, the worker's position may be enhanced because the skilled use of sophisticated machinery demands both greater autonomy for the worker and greater trust between worker and management. Indeed, if employers wish to hold on to key, core workers they will offer them attractive 'long-term part-time contracts', which could mean power passing, in certain respects, from employer to employee. Studies also show that flexible working can reduce overtime costs, improve morale, boost productivity and reduce absenteeism. Teleworking too offers many advantages: greater work flexibility, reduced traffic, less pollution, less stress and the renewal of the nuclear family. Finally, self-employment is seen as providing greater flexibility and high levels of job satisfaction.

The pessimistic view

Pessimists, on the other hand, maintain that such arrangements can increase fear, insecurity and stress. Writers like Murray (1985) see 'flexible specialization' as technologically determined and refer instead to 'neo-Fordism'. They focus on the new approaches to restructuring production, which, they insist, have come about not as the result of new technology but in response to changing market conditions which require capitalists to adopt new strategies if control is to be retained over the working population. Change is not directed by policy but by market forces. The increased flexibility results in 'numerical flexibility' (e.g. short-term contracts) as a management control strategy and the growth of a 'hire and fire' culture, despite the protection which European legislation provides to part-time workers. Pessimists claim that the move to part-time and contract work is not because workers desire it but simply because they cannot obtain full-time employment. People seek security, and permanent work, even of a part-time nature, still appears preferable to most people. Some working in job share schemes have also become disillusioned, finding their influence within the work organization greatly reduced. Teleworking too is seen by pessimists as having a downside: studies show that teleworkers can suffer social isolation and difficulties in managing their working day. Finally, many self-employed people have seen their businesses fail, and critics would maintain they received less government assistance than they needed.

Demographic changes

Another key factor in this discussion is the demographic change we can expect over the next decade. First, the birth rate – which reached a peak in the 1960s and caused an additional 2 million people of working age between 1976 and 1986 – dropped in the 1970s: consequently, the labour market grew slowly up to 1995 as 16–19-year-olds fell by 23% (i.e. 600 000). The number of 18-year-olds in Britain should pick up from 1997, but figures will remain low into the next century. Secondly, the elderly are increasing in numbers, both because of the rising birth rate in the early part of the century and because people are living longer. This will include an increase in the *very* old: those over 80 numbered 1.8 million in 1985 and this will grow to 2.4 million by 2001. But thirdly, and highly significantly, the birth rate in Britain rose again (for no clear reason) during the early 1990s and the number of children under 15 will rise to over 12 million by the turn of the century.

The effect of all this will mean a *smaller* working population providing for a *growing* number of old people and children. It is calculated that, by 2030, there will be less than three people at work for each senior citizen. This will have a profound effect upon employment patterns.

- With 30% fewer young people entering the labour market, employers will continue to recruit more women. While only 57% of women were at work in 1971, this had risen to 71% by 1994 and experts predict it will rise to nearer 75% by 2006. (The corresponding figures for men are 91, 84 and 82%.) Moreover, many of these women will wish to work part-time. This will require flexible working patterns, more nursery places, creche facilities, job sharing, statutory maternity leave etc.
- There will be greater demand for staff to look after the elderly, at a time when fewer people of school-leaving age will be entering the job market to take up these posts.

- A rising number of children will also mean an increased requirement for teachers when there are fewer school-leavers to take the jobs. At present, roughly 11% with two A levels enter teaching, but this needs to rise to 20% by the late 1990s – a figure thought by many to be unobtainable.

This suggests that many of the new jobs we shall need – nursery supervisors, nurses, teachers etc. – are not the sort that can be automated by information technology, and the terms under which they are undertaken will have to remain flexible. This rather supports Stonier's 'social policy response' and suggests a key role for government in developing and supporting the caring professions. Secondly, it could also mean more people working from home on an 'individual' basis rather than in factories or offices. Retired people, for instance, might also take on part-time work from home. IT makes this possible – and optimists welcome this – but it will require continuing investment in higher education (with 50% graduates by the end of the century), the development of a national electronic grid, distance learning, flexible working patterns etc.

The end result will be that – as a result of longer education, earlier retirement, flexible work patterns and increased life expectancy – more people will spend less time *at work*, in a formal sense, and certainly less time constrained within the rigid work patterns that have pertained hitherto. Indeed, for those who experience increasing affluence, work itself could become a matter of choice rather than a necessity. These and other issues – which raise questions over the very nature of work in industrial society – are discussed in greater depth in Chapter 11.

CHAPTER FOUR

Manufacturing

In the next two chapters we examine the changing nature of work, focusing more on the qualitative changes as opposed to the quantitative. There are broadly three things that can happen to people's jobs as a result of new technology: they can be eliminated, upgraded or deskilled; and having dealt with the first of these in the previous chapter, we now consider the other two.

Industries such as precision engineering, motor vehicle manufacture and printing, and service sectors such as banking and insurance, have already been substantially altered by information technology, and the range of applications and workplaces that could ultimately be affected seems unlimited. What will the effects be? In the final analysis, every application is unique and must be viewed as such, but given that social science requires some degree of generalization to say anything at all, we shall focus on manufacturing and office technologies in a broad sense and not discuss the intricacies of specific jobs in particular industries. At this level, we can observe what various writers think might occur, although we repeat that what *does* occur will depend very much on management choice.

We again find two main schools of thought – the optimists and pessimists – with regard to the likely effects of applications in the factory. The first group believes that new technology will in general enhance work – that it will 'reskill' in the sense of providing greater skill opportunities – while the latter foresees further 'deskilling' as technology downgrades factory work. In these two chapters, therefore, we often refer to the two camps as the reskilling and deskilling writers.

THE RESKILLING ARGUMENT

We saw in Chapter 2 that, for Bell and the convergence writers, one of the key features of industrial society is the growth in technical skills and professional competence among the workforce. This extends further in post-industrial society as work becomes ever more sophisticated and mechanization raises skill levels: workers require greater knowledge, particularly in science and technology, and the pace of change makes education a fundamental prerequisite. Work is therefore reskilled and upgraded as microelectronics removes drudgery and repetitiveness and releases people from boring, dirty and dangerous jobs to apply their skills to more meaningful tasks.

This view gained expression in the work of Robert Blauner (1967), who adapted Marx's concept of alienation to consider job satisfaction in various American workplaces, but saw alienation not as a consequence of private property but rather as the result of particular forms of technology. For Blauner, alienation is a 'feeling', an individual experience, while for Marx it results from structural forces and is an inevitable outcome. Of course, Blauner was writing before the advent of IT, but his model – and the subsequent discussion as to whether increasing automation ultimately removes worker alienation – is useful for our purposes. Blauner presents four dimensions of alienation which can be best understood if contrasted with their non-alienative states (Table 4.1).

Blauner tried to measure the levels of alienation in different workplaces and suggests that this is primarily dependent on the dominant form of technology. He studied four types of industry – printing, textiles, car assembly and chemicals – which he saw as representative of four distinct types of technology – craft, machine-tending, assembly line and process technology. It is in the last case where computers have been used most extensively for production control. Capital-intensive plants that refine or process raw materials – chemicals, electricity, gas, food, petroleum, cement, paper etc. – are increasingly structured so that information on

Table 4.1   Blauner's dimensions of alienation.

Dimensions of alienation	Non-alienative states
Powerlessness	Control
Meaninglessness	Purpose
Isolation	Social integration
Self-estrangement	Self-involvement

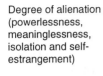

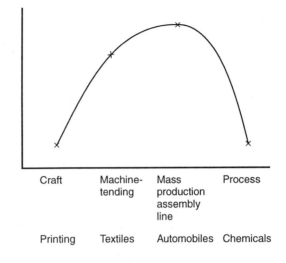

Figure 4.1   Blauner's 'inverted U curve' relating alienation and technology.

operations throughout the organization can be linked through computer-controlled networks. Sensors can measure and report details on flow rates of liquids, quality of materials, pressure on valves etc.

His findings led him to conclude that alienation was low on all four dimensions in the craft printing industry; high on three (with the exception of social isolation) in the case of machine-tending in textiles; and rose to its highest levels on the car assembly lines. However, he found in the process production of the chemical plants that alienation fell once more to the low levels of craft production, which produces his famous 'inverted U-curve' (Fig. 4.1). Workers were no longer tied for long hours to assembly lines where they carried out boring, repetitive tasks, but a small number of white-coated, trained technicians now used their expertise to check highly automated plant. This enlarged their jobs and permitted them to apply their skills and knowledge in work that provided far higher levels of satisfaction.

Blauner's work has been criticized on many counts, but it has proved influential, and provides us with a useful model for considering the impact of information technology. The main implication of his thesis, as the title of his book *Alienation and Freedom* suggests, is that as technology advances so the drudgery of work is removed, alienation is eliminated and workers are free to develop their skills. It suggests that mass-production assembly lines are best seen as a passing phase of history, and the model implies that information technology – which, thanks to micro-controlled robots, allows car factories to resemble chemical plants – affords the opportunity to return to high levels of job satisfaction found in earlier forms of craft work. This received support from John Collins, President of the British Robot Association in 1989, when he maintained that people and robots would increasingly work in teams, 'adding dignity to grotty jobs while removing the grot'.

Clearly we would not wish to overstate this, for there are subtle and important differences between continuous-process production and the way IT is applied, and there is perhaps now a need to add a fifth form of technology to Blauner's model. But, in broad terms, it represents the optimists' view that microelectronics will remove work alienation and provide a growing number of highly skilled jobs, mostly in the computer-related field. First, there will be a growing demand for engineering skills, particularly in the relating of microelectronics to control, production and mechanical systems. And secondly, there will be a continuing need for logic, systems and software skills, and general data-processing awareness.

APPLICATIONS OF INFORMATION TECHNOLOGY

It is not difficult to see why the optimists are excited by information technology: it can do amazing things. It can assist design, machining of parts, assembly, production control, quality control, stock control and maintenance. The range and variety of possible applications seems endless, and for convenience we shall adopt a series of headings and subheadings to consider the major changes that are occurring in the factory situation.

Computer-aided design (CAD)

At the design stage of manufactured production, computers are increasingly used in areas such as production planning, engineering, architecture and dress design. CAD can be used in two broad senses: first, to help design the production process within a manufacturing context and, second, to design the product itself. A factory production manager may use CAD to model the effect of a particular design on manufacturing schedules, while a skilled engineer might use it for creating a particular product. The computer's value as a design aid stems from its capacity to store, restructure and display vast amounts of information – on dimensions of components, raw materials, location of suppliers, unit costs of production, etc. – and it therefore doubles as both an electronic design board and a technical library. CAD offers big gains in accuracy of measurement, time and the testing of strength/stress factors.

Designers at computer-based workstations devise, plan and simulate the eventual design, size, cost, performance etc. of new products. This provides considerable advantages. In the first place it removes much of the drudgery from the designer's work and allows the validity of various alternatives to be tested before a commitment to manufacture is made. From a technical point of view, CAD allows the product, building, dress or whatever to be viewed from a number of different angles. Three-dimensional models of houses, aircraft, power stations etc. can be created, allowing the designer to identify (and thereby rectify) any problem areas – such as stress factors – before the product is assembled. The architect, for instance, can experiment with variations in heating systems, wiring rings and window sizes, and calculate the cumulative effect they have. Perspectives can be changed swiftly with a light pen and features added and deleted. Trillions of bits of information can thus be stored in the databank and recalled, possibly years later, for safety checks or design changes. In car plants, CAD 'vehicle impact simulation models' are used to 'crash' cars in safety tests. (CAD can do the simulation and cars no longer have to be crashed.) In 1981 there were only around 5000 CAD systems in the world, but they are now increasing at a rate of 50% a year.

As in other areas, CAD is increasingly affected by technological convergence. A good example is the link that has developed with laser technology. Designers' scale models can now be 'filmed', whereby the surface of the model is subjected to light from a laser, which creates an image in thin air. This technology, termed holography, allows three-dimensional models of prospective products to be used in sales presentations. Potential customers can walk round a building, bridge or car and view it from all sides, even though it only exists as an image. Medical scientists are also using the technique to visualize microscopic phenomena previously only conceivable as mathematical equations and computerized research data.

CAD thus offers many advantages. It can greatly increase the productivity of design staff, remove boring and repetitive tasks, reduce the lead time from design stage to final product, lessen errors, increase product quality, cut the costs of updating and modification, and allow orders to be swiftly repeated.

Computer numerically controlled (CNC) machines and tools

Once the product is designed it is then manufactured, and computer technology has played an important part in this stage of the production process ever since the emergence of computer numerically controlled (CNC) machines and tools in the early 1960s. In those days, numerically controlled machines were programmed by punched paper tape, but this progressed to the use of more sophisticated computer control and what is today termed computer-aided manufacture (CAM). Such equipment is extensively used in milling, drilling, and lathe work.

Machine tools were a prime target for automatic control because they work in a predetermined and repetitive fashion. A series of operations can be programmed into the machine, which then performs the task endlessly without tiring. Various aspects of the machining process – cutting angle, speed, tool selection etc. – have therefore come under preprogrammed control, and any decisions are now made by the machine rather than the worker. Most engineering machine shop work is done in small runs of components, and the coming of CNC machines and tools has provided far greater flexibility. Moreover, their cost, thanks to microelectronics, continues to fall, and their adoption becomes ever more widespread.

In some instances, CAM has been directly linked to the earlier CAD stage – to provide what engineers term computer-aided engineering (CAE) – as happens in electronics when integrated circuits are planned by CAD techniques and then sent direct by computers to the chip manufacturing stage. Under CAE, a single system can design components, display them graphically, produce design drawings, plan production schedules, prepare programs for machine tools, supervise production, maintain quality control and reorder parts.

Remarkable though CAM machines are, however, they are designed for particular functions, and though they can be reprogrammed (e.g. to cut at a different angle) they cannot be switched between totally different tasks. It is when machines can be reprogrammed for totally new operations that the factory obtains a flexibility it never had in the past. This moves us into the realm of robotics.

Robotics

The continuing convergence between microelectronics and mechanical engineering is having a substantial impact on manufacturing industry, and this most often takes the form of robotic applications. The essential difference between a machine and a robot is that the former is purpose-built to perform a specific task, while the robot's microprocessor brain allows it to carry out a series of tasks, and can be reprogrammed to amend or totally change those tasks. Once programmed, the robot can perform its tasks *ad infinitum*, and with far greater precision and regularity than any human. Degrees of precision are now astonishing – with robots able to thread needles etc. – and this will continue to increase.

The advantages of robots are fivefold:

- Because of their greater consistency, the quality of production is enhanced. Robots do not tire, need tea breaks, suffer boredom, sabotage machinery, fall ill or go on strike.
- In that robots can be reprogrammed to perform different tasks, they offer far greater flexibility in production processes than traditional machinery.
- Robots can work in atmospheres hostile to human health, e.g. paint spray shops, coal mines, ocean beds and battle zones. They have been introduced in many areas of dangerous, dirty work where absenteeism has traditionally been high.
- Output can be adjusted exactly to meet demand. At Fiat car factories, for example, robots are stopped if too many cars are being produced and, apparently, do not mind being 'laid off'!
- In the long term, robots offer considerable savings. Because their movements can be perfectly controlled, they do not waste materials (e.g. robot paint sprayers use 30% less paint than their human counterparts). With regard to labour costs, the Fiat robotic line, though it initially cost 30% more than a conventional line, now only needs 25 workers instead of 125 to run it. At Rover, energy costs were cut by over 50% when robots were introduced in 1985 as they do not need to work in heated or lighted factories.

The industries most affected by robotics include metal and plastic fabrication, instrument engineering, electrical engineering, shipbuilding and marine engineering, vehicles, electronic components, office machinery, chemicals, printing and aerospace. Comparisons between robotized and non-robotized factories can be frightening in production terms. In 1980, British Leyland were producing only 3.7 vehicles per employee per year compared with 69 at Toyota in Japan, and half as much overall as Volkswagen with a 20% bigger workforce. Robotization has now become imperative for car manufacturers if they wish to remain competitive, and Britain needs to invest extensively to keep up with competitors.

In 1996 Britain had 21 robots for every 10 000 workers (around 1000 in total) compared with 31 in France, 33 in the United States, 69 in Germany, 76 in Italy and 338 in Japan.

In medicine, robots are able to carefully move bedridden patients and allow surgeons to perform operations by remote control from thousands of miles away. In fighting crime, there is a robot that can make enquiries, temporarily blind a suspect with its spotlight, and call for help through its siren. In dealing with terrorism, robots can be used to detonate explosives. In agriculture they are used to shear sheep, pluck chickens and classify fish. Fire-fighting, nuclear power operations, deep sea diving, you name it – the list is endless. In 1989 a robot guitarist even played for the first time at the Singapore music festival.

The robot of science fiction has always resembled the human being (see, for example, the cyborgs in films such as *Robocop* and *Bladerunner*) and though the industrial robots of today are somewhat different, at a simple level the analogy still holds. Robots consist of three main elements – the mechanical structure, the power unit and the control system – which we can interpret as the body, muscles and brain. Staying with the human analogy, the three key parts of a robot are the brain, the arm and the hand (or as the technologists would term it, the 'grippers'). With rapid advancement in microelectronics, the first of these is now increasingly cheap, highly reliable, considerably sophisticated and capable of controlling a wide variety of tasks. The arm too, with advances in mechanical engineering, is increasingly versatile and dependable. It is the third area, the grippers, where robots are still weakest, though advances now provide multi-pick facilities to dramatically improve throughput. The various gripper heads available for the AR4 Argonaut palletising robot, for instance, can handle sacks, cartons, bins, drums and even perfume bottles (Fig. 4.2).

Not surprisingly robots have, to date, predominated in heavy engineering and been used in two main ways. First they have been used for various 'pick and place' transfer operations such as moving metal components from one position to another, sorting or packing parts, and loading or unloading equipment. Robots can do all this most effectively, particularly where the workpiece may be heavy, hot or sharp. Secondly, robots have been used to undertake repetitive tasks with tools, especially various forms of spraying, welding, cutting and grinding. This they also do effectively, for once the tool is fixed in the robot's hand it requires no particular dexterity on the part of its fingers. Because the grippers remain the weak part of the robots' anatomy, they have to date not been used extensively in assembly (at least not in Britain) and certainly not outside

Figure 4.2   The AR4 Argonaut Robot Palletiser, designed by Production Robots Ltd, manufactured and installed by Bankside Industrial Engineers.

the field of heavy engineering. But major changes are afoot: a second generation of 'intelligent' robots – mobile and multi-armed, able to 'see, hear, talk, and smell', and possessing a finer sense of touch – is being developed (particularly in Japan) that can perform most of the remaining tasks (e.g. quality control) on the factory floor. The grippers – like the rest of the anatomy – will continue to improve, and industries like food, cosmetics, and chemicals seem certain to be transformed.

Flexible manufacturing systems (FMS)
Convergence has been one of our recurring themes, and the next evolutionary stage from CNC machine tools, CAD, CAM and robotics is for all these various techniques to be linked, through computerized communication and control systems, to form what are termed flexible manufacturing systems (FMS) which integrate all stages of the production process into a single automated operation.

As the title suggests, the great gains from FMS are increased flexibility (allowing small batches to be run without great difficulty) and more consistent quality of output. Because an FMS can be instantly reprogrammed to make new parts or products, a single system can replace several different conventional machining lines, yielding huge savings in capital investment and plant size. Production machinery is interlinked by automatic handling devices (such as robots), automatic transfer systems (such as guided pallets) and communication lines. The whole operation is supervised by a computer (or group of computers) which knows at any particular time where a specific workpiece is and what is happening to it.

FMS is very much the key to 'flexible specialization', which we introduced in the previous chapter. Mass production gives way to batch production; 'economies of scale' are replaced by 'economies of scope'; and products are 'customized' to meet specific requirements. This can be seen in the car industry where, instead of standardized models, companies now use robots to build individual cars to customers' specifications with a variety of different accessories. With 'niche marketing' the production cycle is keyed to the customer's order rather than manufacturing first and trying to sell the products later, greatly reducing the risk element from a manufacturer's point of view. In the past, batch manufacturing required machines designed to perform single tasks; and for each product change they had to be rebuilt or replaced. FMS brings a level of diversity never before obtainable, for different products can be made on the same line at will. Aircraft, tractors, office desks, large computers – all are now made in batches rather than mass produced, which makes it easier for manufacturers to enter new markets and keep abreast of changes in fashion. Hirst, however, notes that such systems are not widespread in Britain. This is due to prohibitive costs, unsuitably trained operatives, poor relationships with subcontractors and old-style management practices.

Computerized stock control and warehousing
An important part of FMS is computerized stock control and warehousing, which has given rise to Just-in-Time (JIT) systems and allows parts to be delivered precisely when needed, thus saving costs on warehouse space. It is estimated that up to 40% of Britain's gross national product is spent on the storage and handling of goods produced in factories, and the economic gains from automation could be considerable. Automated fork-lift trucks, which can be programmed to go to particular parts of a warehouse, appeared in the late 1970s, and Japan now has thousands of fully automated warehouses, compared with around 500 in Germany and

nearer 100 in Britain. If stock could be turned over as quickly as in Germany, UK stock levels could be reduced by 40%, equivalent to releasing £20 billion of working capital. Japanese warehouses that once used 25 staff now operate with four, and the gains in speed, accuracy and access to information are considerable. At Volvo's plant in Köping, Sweden, stock inventories were cut by 20%, giving an annual saving in interest charges of over £100 000.

But investment in Britain seems likely to remain piecemeal. The reason for this is that the component parts of computerized warehousing – trucks, fork-lifts, cranes etc. – are made by different companies, and we do not think in terms of linking them together in systems as others appear to do. Rover, however, are one major company that have been adventurous in this field: the vast automated parts store at the Longbridge West works is run by seven minicomputers which record and check the quality and quantity of all parts. When needed, the items in stock are not retrieved by hand, but by robots. The parts store itself is linked up to every other section of the factory through four-and-a-half miles of video data cable. This provides a continuous flow of information on stock levels, quality control and production levels. Managers anywhere in the plant can tap into the system through visual display units (VDUs) to see how other sections are operating. Needless to say, the whole system was designed on a computer.

Towards the automated factory

The impetus towards technological convergence seems unstoppable, and just as electronics, telecommunications and computing converged to form information technology, so CNC tools, robots and automated materials handling are converging to form flexible manufacturing systems and, ultimately, the automated factory. Eventually, the whole system could work like this. In response to an order, computerized plans are produced from the factory's design office, instructions go to the warehouse for certain raw materials, and these are taken to the point of production by automated fork-lift trucks and robots. The parts are machined by CNC machine tools controlled by robots and, when machining is completed, robots carry out the tasks of assembling, welding, painting and quality control. Volvo have calculated that such a factory can be designed with existing technology to produce 1200 vehicles a day using a workforce of 12. So we move towards the factory that just has one person and a dog: the dog is there to make sure no one touches the machinery, and the human is there to feed the dog!

The most celebrated FMS example is the Fanuc plant just outside Tokyo, where robots controlled by computers make other robots. Fanuc (a subsidiary of the giant Fujitsu group) makes 100 robots a month with the minimum of human intervention, and during the night shift, one employee does the work that previously occupied 200. Fanuc estimate that it would have needed ten times the capital investment for the same output with conventional technology; it would also have needed about ten times the labour force of around 100. All in all, the plant is about five times as productive as a conventional factory. In terms of FMS, Japan is way ahead of any other nation. But automated factories are emerging in the USA, Russia and certain European countries, including Britain.

Britain's first automated factory opened in Colchester, Essex, in 1982 – not just as a government-sponsored showpiece, but as a fully operating factory – and illustrates how such a plant works. It consists of a £3 million small batch production line making a variety of shafts, gears and discs in steel, cast iron and aluminium. The raw component is loaded automatically on to a pallet and carried on a conveyor belt past various machine tools (drilling, cutting, chamfering etc.). The robot picks up the component and presents it to the appropriate machine tool for machining. After this, the robot releases the component and passes it along the conveyor for the next machining operation, while sensor devices monitor progress and a technician checks the VDUs. When one batch of components is finished, the technician resets the program for the next batch (Fig. 4.3).

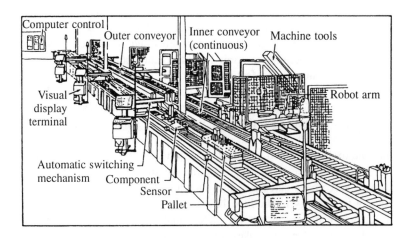

Figure 4.3   The automated factory (source: Zorkoczy and Heap, 1995).

The factory can produce finished components in a three-day cycle, whereas the former manual operations took 10–12 weeks' work and involved 50 separate handlings of the different small batches of orders. As we noted earlier, the advantages from such a factory lie not so much in labour-saving as in its adaptability – reducing stocks and manufacturing time-cycles, overcoming unsocial working hours, reacting quickly to market changes etc. The only people employed in the factory are a handful of white-collar operators to switch on and check operations.

Automated plants have become more common in Britain. Rolls-Royce turned a Derby tram shed into an automated plant to make turbine blades for the engines of the Boeing 757. Blades can now be made in 45 seconds instead of 6 minutes, and six workers are employed instead of 30. Inventory costs have been halved and productivity has increased by 28% per employee.

In Somerset, Normalair-Garrett have a £1 million automated plant for the production of bomb-release mechanisms. The manufacturing cycle time came down from four months to two weeks; stock is turned over six times faster; only two to three operators work on each shift; and output per employee increased from £67 000 per year to £210 000.

Cadbury's cocoa-processing plant in North Wales is totally automated. All operations, including the chocolate-making process, are undertaken on computers; presses are computer-controlled; and those workers that do remain are referred to as 'brainy' – as opposed to the 'brawny' operatives of previous years.

By the 1990s Britain had invested many millions in computerizing the shop floor, but the government was concerned that Britain should adopt the international standards MAP (Manufacturing Automation Protocol) and TOP (Technical and Office Protocol), for this allows different parts of the computerized business to talk to each other, greatly increase efficiency and cuts costs. For example, data design can be fed directly to machine tools and then into test procedures, and production planning can be coordinated with incoming orders, warehousing and transport. Many companies are now installing MAP/TOP (developed by General Motors in the USA) and major computer companies are designing their systems to fit in with it.

Computer-integrated manufacture (CIM)
MAP/TOP leads us to the ultimate convergence, where the automated factory is automatically linked with the electronic office and other information systems within the work organization to create what is termed

computer-integrated manufacture (CIM). CAM, CAD, monitoring and testing, automated materials handling – all are combined with management planning, production planning and control functions to form a total system. A computer – complete with database and data network – optimizes production flow and scheduling to meet the production plan, and all operations are interlinked so that production is tightly controlled at every stage. A British example is the JCB factory at Wrexham, which opened in 1985 and produces gearboxes for diggers at the rate of 40 a day. The factory operates with an array of interlocking computers, and the most important computer, programmed daily, is in overall charge of the factory. The £6.75 million investment paid for itself in three years thanks to increased production of 30%.

A similar venture is Pirelli's £20 million automated factory in Aberdare (Fig. 4.4) which makes household electric wires and is structured round multi-skilled employment, i.e. all staff are trained in 'computer literacy' and can switch between every job. Production and office computers are joined through a network of fibre-optic cables, so managers always know what is happening. FMS means that production can be quickly switched from one type of wire to another, so large stocks of expensive components need not be held. A central minicomputer handles office chores and passes customers' orders to the 100 production microcomputers, which then manage the microchip-run machinery. Overall, this involves around 120 million decisions per second.

Perhaps, as a postscript, we should mention that during the 1990s we can expect the ultimate in technological sophistication, high-tech factories in space, for some things can be done *better* in space (e.g. producing materials of great purity), while others can't happen at all (e.g. fluid flowing out of a container) because space has zero gravity, a near-perfect vacuum and extremely low temperatures. In microgravity, materials do not separate due to differences of density, which makes it possible to produce large, faultless crystals and to refine drugs to levels of purity impossible on Earth. Pharmaceuticals seems the industry most likely to initiate space manufacture.

THE DESKILLING ARGUMENT

The immediate impression is that there is much here to be welcomed. We would be quite happy to see robots go into paint spray shops and get their lungs filled with poisonous fumes rather than workers; we wouldn't

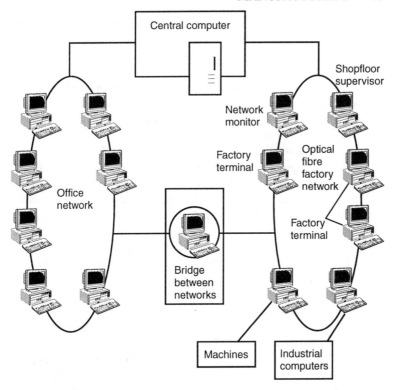

Figure 4.4   Computer-integrated manufacture at Pirelli, Aberdare, Wales.

mind if robots lost their fingers on machines rather than operatives; and we would welcome the release of humans from tedious assembly-line tasks. Robots can help us automate out of existence some of the most boring, repetitive, noisy, dirty, unhealthy and dangerous jobs in industrial society. If, in addition, the work that remains can be made more skilled and responsible, then this seems all to the good, and one can see why many welcome microtechnology as liberating and beneficial.

Why, then, are others sceptical? In the first place, as we saw in the last chapter, there is fear over job loss. Even if new jobs are created, they seem unlikely to be in manufacturing companies employing robots. The whole point of robots is that they are designed to replace humans, and while they did not arouse initial hostility – when used to undertake unpalatable work like paint spraying – resistance can be expected as they spread further in manufacturing industry. Moreover, as Gann and Senker (1993) point out, while Japanese companies tend to introduce robots by modifying existing equipment – and agreements are struck with in-house unions – UK companies seem to prefer a 'quantum leap' approach, whereby new technology suddenly replaces old. Workers' fears are understandable: numerous studies predict continuing labour displacement in Britain as a result of robotization.

As to more qualitative issues – the main concern of this chapter – the pessimists are equally despondent that the tasks people will be offered will become less skilled and rewarding. The argument has been most eloquently presented by Harry Braverman, who questions the suggestion that increased mechanization somehow raises skill levels, because the discussion is always couched in general terms and talk of 'averages' ignores specific work situations. While we might accept that 'on average' skills have risen as a result of technological advancement, Braverman maintains that this ignores the widening chasm between those with very high technical skills and those in increasingly unskilled work – the polarization that occurs with neo-Fordism. He graphically suggests that to talk in averages is like a man with one foot in ice and the other in fire saying that 'on average' he is perfectly comfortable!

He also questions the way optimists define 'skill' and interpret statistics on changing work patterns. As labourers declined and machine operatives increased, so the latter came to be labelled 'semi-skilled', but Braverman questions the case for doing this. Why is the labourer judged to be of lower skill than the operative? In that mechanization inevitably led to an increase in the operative ranks, this was bound to give support to the reskilling argument. Similarly, in the 1950s a further category of 'service' workers was added to the census statistics, and as 25% came from the 'semi-skilled' and 75% from the 'unskilled' this again provided another instant upgrading. However, it is questionable whether the growing ranks of white-collar workers – who are invariably placed higher than manual workers in terms of occupational grading – exhibit higher levels of skill.

As to the suggestion that an increase in skilled work is reflected in the growing importance of universal education, Braverman replies that literacy and numeracy are essential requirements for modern *society*, but not necessarily modern occupations. Some jobs may demand high levels of training, and the education system acts as a filtering device to identify this elite, but this does not mean that *all* the population need more education. For Braverman, the link between education and work is tenuous: he claims that most school-leavers are grossly over-educated for the work that is offered to them.

But the pessimists not only reject the reskilling argument. Continuing the Braverman tradition, Shaiken (1985), Noble (1985), Webster and Robbins (1986) and Thompson and McHugh (1989, 1990) believe there are clear signs that information technology (like its technological predecessors) will intensify the historical tendency for all work to be continually deskilled under capitalism. They maintain that future factory jobs will be every bit as tedious, high-paced and stressful; that employers will seek less skilled workers to 'mind' machines; and that managers will use technology to increase control. These fears can be considered with reference to the design and production process; health and safety factors; and work monitoring and pacing.

The design process

New technology can dramatically affect the factory in terms of its layout, organization and scheduling. A manifestation of this is business process re-engineering (BPR), adopted by many companies during the 1990s, whereby, through the use of sophisticated computing techniques, the central processes of the business are redesigned. Computer companies and senior management can then install systems which substantially alter and rearrange people's work – in terms of skills, supervision, work shifts etc. – and the deskilling writers insist that workers and trade unions should be fully involved in any installations. The Conference of Socialist Economists (CSE) writers (1980) stress that system design is first and foremost a political and organizational activity rather than merely a technical one, and therefore consultation should take place at all stages and be formalized in new technology agreements (NTAs).

Similar fears are expressed in connection with the design of the product and the adoption of CAD. While the computer can be used to carry out the routine or non-creative parts of the designer's job – drawing, listing parts, specification of techniques etc. – and provide new techniques and facilities which the worker decides how and when to use, it can also deskill highly trained architects and engineers by forcing them to operate within fixed constraints. The architect may no longer be free to draw on his or her imagination, but instead has to work with blocks of prescribed shape and length – rather like a child building with a Lego set – predetermined by the computer software. The outcome is that buildings grow depressingly alike – boring concrete blocks composed of standard parts – as the modern architect becomes incapable of ever conceiving a York

Minster or Brighton Pavilion. The same points can be made with regard to engineering and dress design: the creative abilities of the designer become restricted by the dictates of the software.

The production process

With regard to the production process, the CSE writers acknowledge that microelectronics offers the potential to re-humanize jobs but, like Webster and Robbins, they see little likelihood of this happening. In their view it will not be introduced to meet human needs but rather to boost private profit, and any benefits will be incidental.

The introduction of CNC tools is quoted as an early example of computer technology deskilling highly trained workers. Machinists in small batch production traditionally held high status as skilled workers who had gained considerable experience through a long period of training. Tasks included assisting with production planning, setting up the machine, and controlling its speed and operation. Workers had to confer with both the designer and management, and yet retained considerable independence in their own work. Now, pessimists claim, they have less opportunity for contact with others and experience a sense of isolation in the work situation.

With CNC machine tools, the skills of the machinist are broken down into their component parts and the computer programmed to control the operation of the machine tool. The machinist's job is now one of monitoring the computer-controlled equipment, a job that might be eliminated altogether once robots have been 'trained' to do it.

The pessimists maintain that while new technology may in theory make possible the fully automated workplace, it will not be introduced by employers unless it is judged economically viable. Britain is still a low-wage economy relative to many industrialized nations and, particularly in times of high unemployment, employers will use unskilled workers rather than invest in robotic equipment if it is cheaper to do so. This has the added advantage that they are seen as providing employment rather than automating people out of work with new technology. Britain's modest robotic development has therefore largely been as a *response* to the unemployment situation, not the *cause* of it. What seems more likely is that managers will introduce robots for highly skilled, intricate, heavy, delicate tasks (and save themselves the costs of skilled workers' wages) but retain unskilled workers (on low wages) in the more mundane, repetitive tasks. This could mean production lines composed of workers and robots in conjunction, in which the workers have to work at the pace of the impersonal, tireless robots. The CSE writers insist that companies should install telechrics (high-technology systems that are completely controlled by the workers) rather than robotics, and that where workers and robots work together, workers control the speed of work.

Health and safety

Health and safety have become major topics of concern, particularly in relation to the effects of VDUs. This will be discussed more in the next chapter on office technologies, but some factory workers may spend considerable time at terminals, and other forms of new technology may also involve hazards.

Cooley (1984) maintains there is a fundamental contradiction in the human/machine interface:

> The human being is the dialectical opposite of the machine in that he or she is slow, inconsistent, unreliable but highly creative. The machine on the other hand may be regarded as fast, consistent, reliable but totally non-creative.

Optimists may present these characteristics as complementary and supportive, but Cooley argues that as the computer dramatically increases the rate at which material is handled, so the stress on the workers trying to make qualitative judgements intensifies. He quotes American research which shows that those working with computers in the field of engineering design can experience creativity decreases of 30 to 40% in the first hour and 80% in the second.

While new technology may therefore reduce (or even remove) the strain of many tasks, their replacement with jobs that require the monitoring of dials and taking occasional action (in continuous flow production) can create strains of a new kind. The problems of physical fatigue may merely be replaced by those of mental fatigue. The machinery may require rapid responses from operating staff to avoid dangerous developments, and this can create considerable stress. Nor is concentration helped by the fact that the product they are working on could now be far less visible. Finally, the introduction of new technology may be accompanied by new patterns of shiftwork so that maximum use is obtained from expensive equipment. In 1954, only one in eight were shiftworkers, but this had risen to one in five by 1964 and is now around one in three. Studies in West Germany claim that ulcers are eight times more common among shiftworkers; the divorce rate is 80% higher; and juvenile delinquency among children of shiftworkers 50% greater.

The last two decades have witnessed substantial increases in absence from work, not just due to physical illness, but more especially psychological illnesses (e.g. neurosis, nervous breakdowns, ulcers, headaches, blood pressure). Seventy times as many working days are lost in Britain through sickness, and twice as many through accidents, as through strikes, and this could intensify further with new technology. Workers can experience stress if there are extremes (in either direction) of heat, noise, light, workload, responsibility, human contact etc. A satisfactory work situation requires a delicate balance between these factors, and certain types of work appear particularly prone to stress:

- repetitive, fast, strenuous production line work (e.g. manufacturing workers)
- tense, responsible, concentrated work (e.g. air traffic controllers, surgeons, miners)
- work which involves conflicting demands from those above and below (e.g. supervisors)

All these areas of work are being significantly affected by information technology; therefore increased stress can be expected.

Work monitoring and pacing

A lot of new technology applications have built in subsystems for worker monitoring and pacing which allow management to check the quality and speed of work at any time. Such devices enable management to (a) measure workers' performance, (b) determine the way a task is carried out, (c) collate information on employees, and (d) influence promotion prospects and career paths. Sewell and Wilkinson (1992) suggest that many management information systems provide minute control coupled with minimum supervision.

The autonomy of those who work with CNC machine tools, for instance, is reduced by monitoring systems which check daily output at a central control point and print out the exact output for each machine, and by systems that register at a control console if a worker is away from his or her position for more than the prescribed time. Advertisements for word processing staff often stress the fact that managers can easily determine the number of words inputted per minute and the number of mistakes made. The tachograph – the 'spy in the cab' which is now compulsory under EU regulations for long-distance lorry drivers – records a vehicle's speed at every stage of the journey, and any stops made. PBX telephone exchanges can print out all calls made, the extensions they come from, and their destination, duration and cost. Supermarket checkout machines have similar devices, and these can be expected to spread to other work situations. The CSE writers maintain that although the technology itself may be neutral, the functioning system is not and is usually designed in oppressive ways. Though such devices may be justified by employers in terms of greater efficiency and management effectiveness, the pessimists view them as mechanisms for extending management control and an unwarranted intrusion into individuals' work situations. To them it is the further spread of Taylorism into areas of intellectual work: it reduces independence, trust and responsibility, and is another stage in the deskilling process.

Alternative design

The CSE writers argue that, to counter these dangers, workers must insist on certain safeguards and companies think in terms of 'alternative design'. They make the following demands:

- New technology should involve higher pay and no loss of jobs.
- Workers should retain some control over the design process, and any changes to factory layout and working arrangements only be made in accordance with new technology agreements.
- Checks should constantly be made on health and safety factors in line with the 1974 Act.
- Companies should be encouraged to install telechrics rather than robotics. Where workers and robots work together, workers should control the speed of work.
- Built-in subsystems for worker monitoring and pacing should be designed out.

CRITIQUE OF THE DESKILLING ARGUMENT

Optimists level two main criticisms at those who advocate the deskilling argument. First they accuse them of adopting a short-term perspective (e.g. 20 years) and highlighting possible difficulties in the transitional period while ignoring long-term benefits. Though in the short run, microtechnology may create some job displacement, deskilling or work alongside robots, in the long term it should allow fully automated production and the Utopian society Marx always envisaged, without violent revolution. In the field of design, for instance, many maintain that, thanks to continuing advances in hardware and software, it is now possible to explore a *range* of alternatives before undertaking production. In short, this is similar to the long-term optimistic view of the previous chapter. The deskilling writers are accused of complaining about the nature of most modern work, but then moaning when new technology arrives to overcome so many of the problems they are concerned about. Capitalists have shown themselves adaptable in the past, allowing workers to improve their rights of citizenship and material conditions; why should this not happen again?

The second major criticism of the deskilling writers is that they tend to underplay the intrinsic characteristics of different technologies and their vast range of possible applications. Forester (1987), for instance, maintains that the pessimists' concerns are simply not borne out by the facts. Surveys show that many engineers prefer working with CAD systems, and in many factories the working environment has certainly been improved by robotization. Because new technology is rather viewed *as a whole* (i.e. as a tool of the ruling class), the fact that it can produce varying effects in different work sectors is somewhat ignored. Rosenbrock *et al.* (1981) take up this point, arguing that the *pace* of change can vary markedly from one sector to another, and present their arguments under three broad headings.

(a) Process production

In process industries (oil, chemicals, glass, paper, cement, iron and steel-making etc.) continuous production methods have been in operation for some time and microelectronics seems unlikely to have any marked effect, as levels of automation are already high. In such plants, microcomputers could well be used as an alternative to single, central, mainframe systems (i.e. new technology will be used to improve what is already done); there will probably be greater integration of operations through automatic data gathering; and in the long term some new processes might become feasible (e.g. through biotechnology). The labour force is already small, so further reductions are not a serious economic consideration and, for safety reasons, this may not be possible anyway. The nature of the work should not greatly change, though it is a matter of debate whether it is presently highly skilled.

(b) Engineering production

In this field, CNC tools and machines, and robots, are spreading, and CAD/CAM offers considerable scope for development. Certain workers in design sections and on assembly lines may well be replaced by technological advances, and those remaining may find aspects of their work deskilled.

(c) Office work

Office work – correspondence, ordering, invoicing etc. – has traditionally been labour-intensive, and this is dramatically changing, both in quantitative and qualitative terms, as a result of information technology. With word processing, desktop publishing, electronic mail (email) etc., considerable labour displacement can be expected, with the nature of the jobs for those remaining significantly changing.

The effects, therefore, could well be uneven, with change occurring more rapidly in, say, a car factory than a chemical plant. These arguments can be summarized as in Table 4.2.

Leaving aside the office – which is our concern in the next chapter – this has a similar ring to Blauner, and perhaps brings us full circle. The key point is that the optimists strongly emphasize the difference between manufacturing and process production, arguing that the latter produces more highly skilled work, and that as automation gathers pace and manufacturing plants turn to continuous flow production, so the deskilling aspects of factory work will evaporate. The pessimists, on the other hand, do not expect the production line to disappear overnight, and even when it does, they question whether process production in a capitalist society necessarily provides fulfilling, non-alienating work.

We find Rosenbrock's distinctions useful, and would actually take them a stage further. Further research (see Piercy, 1984) suggests we can expect considerable variation, not only between different areas of work, but even between different companies in the *same* sectors. Some companies, for instance, train their machinists to program CNC machine tools, which

Table 4.2   The likely effects of information technology on different industrial sectors.

	Industrial sector		
	Process	*Engineering*	*Office*
Labour displacement	Low	Moderate	High
Technological investment	Moderate	Increasing	High
Time-scale	Long-term	Intermediate	Immediate

can help provide a wider range of techniques for the skilled worker. Much also depends on national policies. In Sweden, for example, workers are automatically involved in all aspects of plant and system design, and at Volvo they have a say in determining the size of workgroups and whether robots are included. This reaffirms the point that it is dangerous to adopt a wholly optimistic or pessimistic view; it greatly comes down to choice.

CHAPTER FIVE

Office Technologies

If one regards most factory work as already severely deskilled, then the threat of new technology is to some extent muted. If work conditions are already pretty dreadful, is there that much to lose? If the pace of the line, levels of surveillance and the noise of the machinery are already so intense that one is unable to communicate with other workers, is working alongside robots that much worse? Could the removal of some tasks altogether, with the possibility of creating new skills, even outweigh the risk of deskilling? The impact of the technology, therefore, is relative to the existing situation. This, in part, explains why many commentators maintain that changes in the factory are less marked than those in office environments.

It is generally accepted that information technology has had tremendous impact on the office. Office workers are engaged in gathering, storing, processing and transmitting information – the very tasks that computers do so splendidly. We noted in Chapter 3 that there is widespread agreement that IT has led to considerable displacement, and similar fears are expressed over deskilling. But it goes further than this. Office work has traditionally been regarded as congenial, respectable, clean, flexible, quiet and non-authoritarian, and some fear that these characteristics are being destroyed. It is historically a form of work that carries higher status – partly because of the greater opportunity to mix with management – and this could also be lost. In particular it has long provided an attractive source of employment for women – 70% of clerical workers and 99% of secretaries are women – and information technology could adversely affect their job opportunities.

Why is it expected that change in the office will be even greater than in the factory? In the first place, while new technology for production processes is often purpose-made, most office equipment can be mass produced, which encourages ease of application and further cost reductions. But more important, the office has long been labour-intensive and under-capitalized in comparison with manufacturing industry: consequently, the increase in white-collar employment has not been matched in terms of increased productivity. Cheaper electronic systems now offer the opportunity to redress this balance. In 1980 there was one computer keyboard for every seven people working in the USA; by 1990 it was nearer one per person, with many having computers at home as well. The same sort of IT explosion has been seen in Britain and other parts of the world.

There are two phases to the so-called office revolution. In the first, technology has been used to assist with traditional tasks (the word processor replaced the typewriter, the microcomputer replaced the filing cabinet etc.) while in the second – brought about by the convergence of electronic data processing, telecommunications and office machines – many intermediary functions are eliminated altogether. This allows us to distinguish between 'information workers' (clerks, administrative assistants, receptionists, secretaries, word processor operators etc.) – involved in the routine entry, recording, storage and transmission of information – and 'knowledge workers', who analyse and utilize it. The first phase is the central concern of this chapter, while the second phase is considered in the next.

It is not just that the nature of office work could change for the worse, but the whole working environment. Consequently, the terms reskilling and deskilling are somewhat narrow for our purposes, and we usually revert to the wider optimistic and pessimistic labels. We shall draw in particular on the work of Vincent Guiliano (1982) and Hazel Downing, and – because 'information worker' is such a broad category – focus principally on secretarial work, which has been significantly affected by the most widespread form of office automation – word processing (WP). We also move to the centre of our continuum to consider the work of Webster (1993) who identifies the gendered aspects of office work and the need to be cautious when looking at the generalized predictions of the optimists and pessimists. Her research suggests that women's experiences of new technology are complex and contradictory, and influenced by *particular* social, economic and political circumstances.

OFFICE ORGANIZATION AND ASSOCIATED TECHNOLOGIES

Guiliano suggests that office organization has gone through three main stages of development, each involving major changes, particularly in the sphere of technological innovation. This is undoubtedly to oversimplify, for 'the office' can manifest itself in diverse forms, but the threefold model is conceptually useful.

The pre-industrial office

This emerged in the latter half of the 19th century and was characterized by low levels of mechanization and close personal relations. The 'counting house', which contained the three principal characters of boss, clerk and boy, was personal, small and involved little division of labour. In this Dickensian-style office, the clerk – who was almost certainly male, middle class and educated – would work for the boss very much as a personal assistant, and probably hoped one day to become a private businessman himself. Though sometimes called a 'secretary', his role was more the forerunner of such present day titles as company secretary, chief secretary or press secretary and stressed his managerial, as opposed to clerical, responsibilities. Even if his wages were humble, he was of a different status from the artisans because he possessed basic numeracy and literacy and was able to fraternize with the business class. Operations largely depended on the performance of individuals without much recourse to either systematic work organization or mechanization. Little conscious attention was paid to work flow efficiency or productivity of methods.

This form of office still exists today in many small businesses, professional practices, general management and executive offices; good human relations (loyalty, trust, respect etc.) are the key features and any information-handling devices (telephones, copiers, word processors etc.), while useful, are not utilized to maximum advantage. This structure is generally only effective as long as operations remain small-scale, and it becomes inefficient for handling large volumes of transactions or complex procedures requiring the coordination of different data sources.

Over time, the pre-industrial office faded in most organizations. We witnessed a growth in the number of clerks (from 0.8% of workers in 1851 to 10% by 1951); an increase in the number of female clerks (from 0.1% in 1851 to 59.6% by 1951); the growth of larger offices; the growth of an 'underclass' intake due to universal education; and the increasing use of mechanization. Thus we moved from the 'pre-industrial' to the 'industrial' office.

The industrial office

By the turn of the century, significant technological change had taken place. Steel nibs had replaced quill pens and typewriters were being manufactured. This was followed by adding machines, telephone switchboards, calculators, electric typewriters, photocopying machines, dictating machines, data-processing equipment etc., thus creating the industrial office we know today. But as with the factory, it was not the technology itself so much as the workplace restructuring it implied that was so significant. Just as the principles of Taylorism entered the factory, so they now entered the office, and workers became subjected to work study.

In the large, impersonal industrial office, workers were organized to serve the needs of a rigid production system. Work became simplified, specialized and regulated, with the result that jobs were often boring, repetitive and unsatisfying as the office became a 'production line' with paper moving horizontally between desks as each clerk performed a particular stage. To sustain this paper flow, workers had to work fixed hours, and the office became subject to the rigid work patterns of the factory. This approach proved particularly suitable for offices handling large volumes of customer transactions (e.g. insurance companies), and using batch systems for mainframe computers, for such work demanded standardization of jobs, transactions, technologies and even personal interactions. Thus in the industrial office much work became deskilled and akin to factory production.

Guiliano concedes that the industrial office has a number of shortcomings. From a human point of view, many find the work tedious, and this can become apparent to customers and managers with whom they often have to deal. If anything, clerical workers can become *more* alienated than their factory counterparts, as they constantly have to give the impression that they actually enjoy their jobs. (Witness the growth in customer care courses, where workers are trained to manage emotion, greet the customer, use appropriate language etc.) From a technical point of view, the industrial office is also criticized because many errors arise from the human-operated production process, and – because of the subdivision of tasks – these often become compounded rather than rectified. Finally, from the employer's point of view, office work is highly labour-intensive, and thereby costly.

The information office

Just as the pre-industrial office can still be found in certain instances, so we recognize that many aspects of industrial office organization remain as well, but we have now entered a further period of transition – as data processing and telecommunications converge – to form what has been variously described as the information, paperless or electronic office. The PC of the 1990s – complete with CD-ROM drive – can be used as a computer, telephone, fax machine, word processor and video aid. Terminal-based workstations can be linked with continuously updated databases to provide integrated systems capable of handling electronically almost every office function. This creates a world in which people, at the touch of a button, send messages to each other 10 000 miles apart; instantly obtain data for meetings from their company's electronic files; employ electronic calendars to schedule meetings at times when all colleagues are free; and chat simultaneously with people around the world in teleconferences. Paper ceases to be needed, as everything is done electronically, and we move from the industrial to the information office. These dramatic developments can be considered further under three main headings.

The written word
The machine most associated with document preparation, as we noted earlier, has been the typewriter, which evolved through its various stages – mechanical, electric, electronic – to the word processor and PC. The key change is that data is now processed according to a standard digital character code, making it compatible with computers, and allowing for the storage and manipulation of text and graphics before it is reconverted to hard copy. Digitization has created a convergence of voice, image and data and, in turn, between the telecommunications, electronics and computing industries. Graphics can now be incorporated directly into documents (i.e. desktop publishing); optical character recognition (OCR) equipment can 'read' people's handwriting; and pen technologies enable users to write with an electronic pen (which could make keyboards redundant).

This technological convergence assists companies with the considerable problem of organizational communication. Buildings are cabled to form local area networks (LANs) so that different sorts of equipment can be hooked together and data sent at high speed to various destinations. Just as one can plug different electrical appliances into various sockets on a wiring circuit in one's home, so data can be circulated to equipment at all points of the organization. A message originating on a word processor may travel to a central computer and on to a mini- or microcomputer in another part of the building. Once installed, the flow of computer-coded information can substitute for the flow of paper, and provide links with national and international data networks. With regard to distribution, the established methods of telex and fax are being supplanted by computerized teletex networks that provide far superior and swifter service. Satellites enable several hundred pages to be transmitted every minute compared with one A4 page every three minutes via traditional methods.

The spoken word

If the key technology for transmission of the written word has been the typewriter, for the spoken word it is the telephone. Advances in telephony have been equally remarkable – the 'yuppie' phone of the 1980s is just one of the more sophisticated aids that has now become commonplace. Early answerphones have been superseded by voicemail equipment, which enables messages to be sent, stored or transferred. The telephone network, the largest human artefact in the world, is complemented by radio technology (cellular network), infrared/microwave and satellite links.

Videophones have been developed, enabling callers to see each other and, although costs are prohibitive at present, many organizations are developing this facility to link regional offices. Video-conferencing, where several callers can link together simultaneously, is also increasing. Desktop video-conferencing is used by educational establishments to assist students in remote areas or who suffer from disabilities. Dictating machines are being superseded by voice recognition technologies which allow spoken words to appear on a screen instantaneously. Developments are currently taking place between voice recognition and language translation which will enable words to appear immediately in another language.

Numerical information

Developments in numerical aids such as spreadsheets and databases allow for superior data collection and analysis and greatly assist decision making. Their development can be considered at three hierarchical levels, with each stage emerging as technological sophistication has increased.

In the early days computers were introduced for 'number crunching' activities such as payroll. These systems are 'pre-specified', in that the processing functions are determined in advance and cannot usually be changed by the end user. They perform the role of collecting and processing the daily transactions of business. Office support systems (the second stage) are more 'personalized' and enable management and office personnel to process and obtain information swiftly and efficiently.

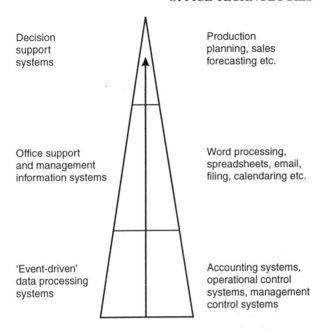

Decision support systems — Production planning, sales forecasting etc.

Office support and management information systems — Word processing, spreadsheets, email, filing, calendaring etc.

'Event-driven' data processing systems — Accounting systems, operational control systems, management control systems

Figure 5.1   The growth of computer applications.

The most sophisticated systems are decision support (or 'what if?') systems which allow one to simulate particular situations to assess the possible effects of particular strategies. Such systems are expensive and are, at the moment, mainly confined to top managers of large companies. All three systems overlap in the sense that one develops from another; all operate concurrently; and decision support systems rely on the data processing systems as a source for much of their data (Fig. 5.1).

THE OPTIMISTIC VIEWPOINT

Optimists, such as Guiliano, argue that the information office has the potential for combining systems and machines to the mutual benefit of both workers and clients. They see it as preserving the best aspects of earlier stages while avoiding their failings. Workers now experience a greater variety of work, for they control all information added to the central database, are responsible for making any corrections, and are able to handle a wider range of transactions. Much repetitive work (e.g. re-typing, manual filing and retrieving) is now eliminated. Productivity ceases to be measured in quantitative terms by the number of hours worked or items processed, but by the *quality* of the service the customer receives. Though Guiliano acknowledges that labour displacement could be as high as 50%, he optimistically concludes that those employees who remain benefit from a marked improvement in the quality of their working life.

With regard to secretarial work, Bevan *et al.* (1985) argue that 'large companies are experiencing a rapid convergence of role between manager and secretary, with secretaries carrying out increasingly complex admin-istrative tasks'. Secretaries assess the various technologies on the market; are in charge of recommending purchases; and need a high degree of computer literacy. Sylge (1995) suggests that, far from being deskilled, many information workers are IT-competent and poised to negotiate higher wages and receive more status from what has been traditionally regarded as low-status work.

Optimists see considerable gains in terms of administrative effective-ness. 'Information float' – where delay and confusion are often caused by the unavailability of material that is being typed, in the mail, missing etc. – is greatly reduced, and accessibility and retrieval vastly improved. Use of electronic mail, calendars and filing all make for swifter and more informed decisions. A further advantage is that cost reductions can prove considerable: email is only one-tenth the cost of conventional mail, and electronic filing is cheaper in that it saves a great deal of space. Such developments have led, in many organizations, to 'hot desking'. When workers arrive, they select a cordless phone, pull over a mobile workstation and drag a computer from a scissors lift. When they have completed their business, all is put away again. Nobody owns space: this provides greater efficiency and flexibility. Companies such as Digital Research and IBM have pioneered hot desking: at Digital's Basingstoke site, 700 people can now be accommodated in a space initially designed for 400, and many work at home three days a week. The company has saved £3.5 million through teleworking, and eventually expects to close half its UK offices.

As the power of the microchip has increased, operations have converged and refinement has followed. Computers have become 'part of the fur-niture': desktop computers have become laptops, and laptops are becoming palmtops. All this makes office environments more user-friendly – with greater attention being given to ergonomics (and the related issues of health and safety) – and flexible, as some offices increasingly resemble the traditional study at home while others become 'mobile'. As processing can be done at a distance, there is no longer any need to assemble all workers at the same time and place, for portable terminals and computers allow an 'office' to exist wherever the worker happens to be (e.g. for a worker with a laptop and mobile phone, a supermarket car park can act as an 'office'). With developments such as email and teleconferencing, home working has become commonplace and flexible new work patterns are being created, which the optimists see as beneficial to all. Toffler sees such developments providing solutions to social and transportation problems, greater personal freedom, reunited families, stronger communities and healthier societies.

Over a million people were working from home by 1996, and the Henley Centre for Forecasting maintained this could be nearer 12 million if we were prepared to build the necessary infrastructure. ('Telecommuters' work from home while 'teleworkers' are those who work anywhere outside the office, e.g. in cars or hotels, as well as at home.) It is thought that 50% of jobs could probably be done in this way, and surveys show that 70% of workers under 35 would be prepared to consider it. Optimists claim that this will mean savings in time, money and energy; a reduction in 'rush hours' and the stress involved in commuting; new employment opportunities for the handicapped; fewer road accidents; lower house prices; less need for companies to invest in expensive office space; and (as a result of greater work flexibility) more time for employee retraining, which would help ease the UK's skill shortage. Obvious savings are made on heating, lighting, rent and rates, safety and health requirements and security costs. There are also employment savings if telecommuters are made self-employed and lower-paid workers can be used: many companies now use home-workers in this way, particularly for small goods assembly work.

This is not to say that industrial-style offices are about to disappear, for people are used to a structured schedule and research (discussed later in this chapter) suggests that working from home and teleconferencing are not always popular. The office will also continue to house centralized forms of communications technology too expensive for the home, and we could therefore enter a transitional period in which workers still go to the office – but not as frequently as they used to – before it finally fades away as new patterns, possibilities and preferences emerge.

THE PESSIMISTIC VIEWPOINT

The contrasting pessimistic viewpoint is seen in the work of Downing, which, while concentrating on the secretary rather than clerical workers in general, argues that office work will become increasingly deskilled. The secretary emerged as a specialist office worker with the growth of record-keeping in industrial production and the increased utilization of typewriters, but the pessimists' fear is that with the arrival of information technology (and especially word processing) secretarial work has been hit detrimentally in four main respects: employment, health and safety, job satisfaction, and social relations.

Employment
With regard to employment, we saw in Chapter 3 that it is widely agreed that IT will reduce employment levels in the office sector – particularly in phase two of the office revolution – and Guiliano, of course, agrees with Downing on this point. However, the rate at which this will occur is largely unknown, for we do not know whether firms are using new technology to expand their quality and range of services or just to cut staff. Werneke (1983), in a wide-ranging international study, found that while new office technology was unquestionably labour-saving, it had not resulted in displacement because companies had been expanding their information services. But one wonders if this will apply in the long term: the various cases we mentioned earlier showed that the effects can be dramatic.

What is indisputable, however (as we noted in Chapter 3) is that tremendous changes are occurring in the *ways* people work and the skills required. The capacity to be flexible, creative, innovative and manage uncertainty are in high demand, and this places great stress on workers. Avner (1993) suggests that women, because of the dual responsibilities they have traditionally undertaken, are perhaps better placed to face the situation than men, but the signs suggest an uncertain future for all.

Health and safety
An area of equal concern – largely held over from the last chapter – is that of health and safety, particularly as it relates to possible ill-effects from working long periods at computer terminals. By 1995 there were over 16 million VDUs in the UK, and various studies have found evidence of people experiencing eye strain, painful necks or shoulders, back pain, hand cramps, irritation and general fatigue. In particular, questions have

been raised as to whether high levels of radiation emission provide a danger for pregnant women.

In 1985 a VDU Workers' Rights Campaign was launched (with the support of a number of MPs) which demanded the following:

- A one-hour limit on continuous work at VDUs, followed by a 15 minute break and a maximum of four hours work per day.
- Compulsory shielding of all terminals to eliminate electromagnetic radiation.
- The right of VDU users to transfer to other work when pregnant.
- Design requirements in offices to minimize 'visual, postural and ergonomic stress'.
- Regular eyesight and medical check-ups.

The campaign claimed that working at VDUs could cause miscarriages, eye strain, headaches etc., but, while in no way wishing to sound complacent, it has to be said that the evidence for this is far from conclusive. Causative links are often tenuous, and many studies have been anecdotal, poorly designed and unscientific. The Health and Safety Executive, as far back as 1983, concluded that VDUs do *not* give out dangerously high levels of radiation, and pregnant women should not be adversely affected, though there may be a slight risk for people susceptible to cataracts and photosensitive epilepsy. Any other soreness, headaches etc. they suggested were more likely due to lighting, workstation layout and other ergonomic factors. Other research supports this view – that it is probably not the technology itself that causes stress so much as the way it is installed, organized and operated. Studies from both sides of the Atlantic suggest that VDU operators appear vulnerable to stress-related disorders ranging from insomnia to depression, but this can be blamed more on job dissatisfaction and loss of job security than on such factors as radiation. Monotony and physical isolation seem to make the job less rewarding over time, and studies have found that absenteeism and sickness increase the longer VDU operators are in employment. Fatigue and frustration often result from tasks requiring sustained concentration, and this can only be reduced if operations are carefully planned and appropriate rest pauses introduced. Visual fatigue, and the consequent headaches and sore eyes, seem more likely to result from poor lighting, overcrowding, noise, unsuitable positioning of the terminal, poor supervision, unsuitable work arrangements etc. than from the screen itself. People with sight problems might intensify them by working on terminals, but this would be true with many other activities. Screen legibility is certainly better on some machines than others, but this is improving all the time and, hopefully, should cease to be a problem. Physical strain (e.g. backache) is similarly more likely to result from a poorly designed workstation with inappropriate furniture etc. We suspect ergonomics plays a more important part than technology, but we repeat that the evidence to date is inconclusive, and there is no cause for complacency.

Repetitive strain injury

During the 1990s a great deal of publicity has been given to repetitive strain injury (RSI) – a blanket term for a range of injuries to hands, wrists and arms brought on by repetitive movement, including tenosynovitis, the painful inflammation of tendon ducts caused by fast movements of the fingers. Many workers have been confirmed as having RSI, but to win compensation requires detailed medical evidence and, in a legal case in 1993 that achieved considerable notoriety, Judge Prosser denied its existence and ruled that RSI 'has no place in the medical books'. In the USA, IBM and Apple both successfully defeated compensation claims in 1995 (which makes it unlikely that employees will quickly obtain awards in that country) but, in Britain, Kathleen Tovey won a record £82 000 damages from the Inland Revenue in 1996. This led to fresh procedures at the Inland Revenue, whereby RSI sufferers no longer have to go to court to obtain compensation.

The fact is that *more* people are likely to be afflicted by RSI – or work-related upper limb disorders (WRULD), to use the broader label that is increasingly used – because more untrained keyboard users are now using terminals. Up to 15 years ago most keyboard users were formally trained, and professional typists let their upper arms and shoulders take the muscular strain. Legal cases have revealed workers using only the middle fingers of both hands to make over 11 000 key depressions an hour for 150 hours over a four-week period. This is highly likely to create the problems associated with RSI.

The Health and Safety (Display Screen Equipment) Regulations 1992

Legislation (following a European directive) was introduced in 1992 which now affects over seven million workers. It covers aspects such as lighting, noise, window covering, screen quality, keyboard, software, work surfaces and furniture (Fig. 5.2)

Any new workstations must adhere to the regulations and all unsuitable equipment be phased out by 1997. The law, however, requires employers

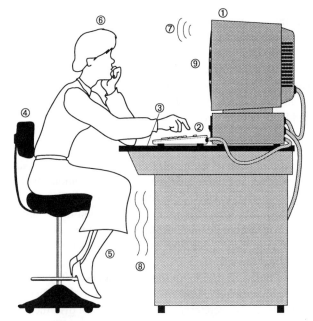

1. Screen: readable and stable image, adjustable, glare-free
2. Keyboard: useable, adjustable, keytops legible
3. Work surface: allow flexible arrangement, spacious, glare-free; document holder as appropriate
4. Chair: appropriate adjustability, footrest
5. Leg room and clearances: to facilitate postural change
6. Lighting: provision of adequate contrast, no direct or indirect glare or reflections
7. Distracting noise minimized
8. No excessive heat, adequate humidity
9. Software: appropriate to the task and adapted to user's capabilities; provide feedback on system status; no clandestine monitoring

Figure 5.2   Issues covered by the 1992 Regulations.

not only to assess workstations but also to determine 'regular' users – and this is far more difficult. Employers must provide eye tests (and even spectacles, where needed) for regular users, but critics claim that the legislation remains vague – words like 'significant', 'habitual' and 'normal' are not defined – and most organizations are taking little action.

The issues surrounding VDU safety seem certain to rumble on. Unfortunately, conflicting reports and minimal legislation often allow management to dismiss symptoms of fatigue and exhaustion, including RSI, as part of the general malaise of clerical workers and representative of their poor work attitude. Women in particular are viewed (by male managers) as 'peripheral workers', exhibiting little company loyalty and high turnover, and scant attention is often paid to health and safety factors in their work. Added to this, the fact that management often expect too much from the technology and are over-demanding of the operators, further adds to their anxiety and depression.

Job satisfaction

Job satisfaction therefore seems very much the key to health and safety, and it is with this, and the related issue of social relations, that Downing is most concerned. It is often more difficult to obtain firm data, because we are dealing with subjective considerations, and one cannot produce numbers as with labour displacement, or test findings as with health and safety, but it is in these qualitative aspects of work that she believes the effects will most be felt.

Pessimists maintain that when the perpetrators of Taylorism finished changing the factory, they turned their attention to the office and began to significantly divest secretarial workers of control over their work – by mechanizing it, automating it and generally making it more 'efficient'. This involved the introduction of ever more technology and the subdivision of tasks into separate departments – accounts, wages, sales, reprographics etc. Compared with the factory, however, the process remained less advanced. The typewriter, the primary form of office technology, essentially changed little from its invention in 1873, and control of the machine always remained in the hands of the typist. The office remained backward in Taylor's terms because technological application and investment were less, and labour was still largely unregulated, allowing 'costly' periods of 'non-productive' time.

Pessimists have suggested that information technology will alter this and result in the deskilling of secretarial and other forms of clerical work. In the first place, as we noted in the last chapter, computers can have supervisory and monitoring elements built into them – to check time spent at the machine, work speed, error rates etc. – and transfer control from the typist to the machine itself.

WP operators become wary that comparisons can easily be made between workers which allows the rates of the faster ones to be imposed on all. In the office, managers have traditionally relied on informal methods of control, and have perhaps even turned a blind eye to workers engaging in non-work activities during working hours. Many women workers are

controlled (by male management) through flattery, praise and encouragement rather than technological surveillance, but this is now destroyed.
With the storage of documents in the memory, the secretary no longer
even has to move to the filing cabinet, and work can be carried out
continuously in front of the machine. All this greatly increases the control
management has over the work process and allows for easier checking
on quality and output.

Moreover, the word processor can perform all the elementary functions
of typing – indenting, centring, tabulating, layout etc. – which can take
a person years to perfect. These may seem trivial points, but it has provided
the typist with some degree of control, and in a work environment based
on flattery and praise, it did provide for some degree of individuality and
the recognition of skilled work. (For instance, it has been known for
secretaries to develop filing systems which only they can understand so
as to create some element of personal indispensability.) Now a less experienced typist – a 'keyboard operator' – can produce the same quality
of work at much faster speed and considerably less cost. Deskilling is
further increased if the printing is done elsewhere and the operators are
prevented from seeing their place in the whole work process. Finally, in
that the decision over which type of word processing system to install
depends on the study of workflow, so office workers become subject to
detailed time and motion studies as the office is reorganized and jobs
further fragmented.

The introduction of expensive new office technology also means – as
in the factory – the likelihood of changed work schedules. Word processing
becomes cost-effective if machines are used virtually continuously, and
this invariably means the introduction of shift work and the creation of
WP centres akin to the former typing pools. The work may contain less
skill and mobility, but still requires high levels of concentration, and as
a result operators can feel socially isolated. Studies have found that some
workers feel intimidated by the machines; inadequate in understanding
what goes on inside them; and perceive such systems as 'unnecessary
alien intruders' in the office. Cooper and Cox (1985) found that job
satisfaction was significantly higher among traditional secretaries and
copy typists than among WP operators. Those who work long hours at
terminals are more prone to experience stress and illness than those who
use computers in a more interactive manner (e.g. coding, programming,
text modification). They maintain that this is due to (a) lack of role clarity
– over job descriptions, pay scales, job expectations etc. – and (b) a
feeling of limited career prospects. In short, those who say they work *at*

VDUs experience greater levels of stress than those who claim they work *with* VDUs. A survey by the Alfred Marks employment bureau in 1989 found VDU work was particularly disliked and topped the list of unfilled vacancies.

Similar points can be made with regard to telephone operators working with information and communication technologies (ICTs). Richardson (1994) examines this in relation to 'call centres', which provide customer services via the telephone, and argues that automatic call distribution, interactive voice response, automatic power dialling and computer-supported telephony are all systems which allow increased management control. Performance can be accurately monitored; workflows can be adjusted between individuals; and detailed information can be provided to plan staff resources. In the banking company First Direct, operators are monitored by what is described as a 'slave board'. Supervisors can identify exactly how many calls each operator takes over a given period and the nature of these calls. The screen also refers to 'idle' time, which means that the operator is not engaged with a call but could be doing other work. Terms like 'slave board' and 'idle' reflect some interesting assumptions regarding employees.

Social relations
The office is an area of work where relations between boss and secretary, and between work colleagues, have usually been more personal. It is the destruction of this 'social office' that Downing especially fears. She maintains that secretarial work, despite the claims of college prospectuses and secretarial manuals, does not have a conventional career structure, and in particular does not facilitate progression from a secretarial position to other branches of management. A secretary's position does not primarily depend on her speeds in shorthand and typing so much as the status of her boss, and becoming secretary to a top director invariably demands other 'feminine' features, such as looking the part, smart grooming and refined speech. The structure of secretarial work encourages women to be feminine and, consequently, it is often the companionship of other women rather than the content of the job itself that keeps them within the work organization. This reduces alienation and boredom in office work and enables women to develop an informal work culture, which cannot be penetrated by 'masculine' work standards.

Resistance in the form of industrial sabotage, absenteeism, lateness and high labour turnover is often regarded as the preserve of men, but Downing maintains that female office workers have also developed their own 'culture of resistance'. Because conventional typewriters relied on the control of the typist, the female worker could adopt any number of strategies to cease working and appear busy when she was not. If work was late, then 'the ribbon got stuck' or she had to call Mr X and couldn't get through. She could leave the typewriter because she had 'run out of paper' or needed something from a file in the other office, where she 'accidentally' met someone for a chat. She could even perform an act of sabotage by dropping a paper clip into the typewriter and waiting for the mechanic to arrive. In short, the female typist had a certain amount of control over her space and movements and, in addition, there were the various tasks that women are expected to perform simply because they are women, such as making coffee, organizing leaving presents and arranging parties. All this enhanced her role as 'office wife', but also created time and space away from the routine of typing.

The pessimists maintain that this is destroyed by new technology. No longer is the female secretary able to 'create space' and socialize with other workers, but is tied for hours on end to her workstation. The separation between the conception and execution of work (or the mental/manual division of labour) that Braverman identified is seen as having entered the office as well as the factory and will intensify due to micro-electronics. As a footnote, we might add that Pringle (1989) doubts whether women themselves will do anything to rectify the situation. She found that most of the 500 secretaries she interviewed were antagonistic to feminists like herself; preferred working for men; enjoyed the role of 'office wife'; and were cool about more women moving into management. A good secretary, like a good wife, appears to have no qualms about being defined by her relationship with a man; she is helpful and discreet, and does not think that she is being taken advantage of. Here is the paradox: the very qualities that make for a good secretary militate against any overall improvement in her status.

CONCLUSION: OVERSTATING THE EFFECTS

We therefore have two contrasting views on office work in the future. We have focused on the role of the secretary, but the same points could be made in relation to other areas of office employment (e.g. direct banking). Guiliano is close to the post-industrial writers in that he adopts a technologically deterministic approach and is optimistic that IT will not only radically, but beneficially, transform the office. He foresees considerable gains in efficiency and cost for employers, and in greater flexibility, variety and job satisfaction for workers. Downing, on the other hand, views these changes within the context of capitalist society and is pessimistic that the office will follow the path of the factory. For her, history shows that technology is not necessarily utilized for the benefit of workers, but only introduced where it costs less than employing human effort and/or enhances managerial control. For the pessimists, the coming of information technology changes little, for the structures of capitalism remain untouched and the deskilling process continues unabated.

Moving towards the centre of our continuum, other writers have stressed that IT is bound up with social and political factors, and workers engage with technology in complex and contradictory ways. Webster (1993), for example, is cautious of sweeping, generalized approaches, suggesting that such accounts fail to take account of secretaries *themselves*, many of whom are able to exercise choice in how they engage with new working practices. Many office workers, she concludes, continue to bring considerable expertise and competence to their work, and these have not been eradicated by the implementation of new office technologies.

Our own position is similar to the last chapter. Like Webster, we feel that both sides are over-deterministic and rather underplay the considerable disparities between different installations. Consequently, they are each apt to overstate the likely effects of IT. Guiliano, for instance, is subject to the criticism that he ignores the political, human context of technological innovation and rather supposes that what could theoretically happen will happen. Admittedly, he acknowledges that the information office will not occur overnight, but early signs are that his transitional period might last longer than he seems to think.

A reluctance to embrace the 'new'?
There is no doubt that IT is widespread in offices world-wide, but the rearrangement of work patterns that was expected to accompany its introduction has been far more uneven and uncertain than many predicted. Why is this? There are a number of reasons, which we can consider under two main headings.

Individual attitudes
Individuals are unpredictable in their response to new technology. The fact that workers can work from home, for instance, and hours of work become more flexible, does not mean it will instantly happen. Teleworking is a good example of a working arrangement that has met with considerable

resistance and been slow to take off. An experiment by Rank Xerox International, which involved six senior male executives becoming telecommuters, showed that their wives expected them to help more with household chores and that they experienced feelings of low status, especially from neighbours who no longer saw them as doing a 'proper job'.

Surveys show that homeworkers need considerable self-discipline, not just to get their work done, but to combat compulsive eating and smoking. Many need their time organized for them and experience time management problems with telecommuting. Whereas office work is usually clearly defined (i.e. from nine to five), with homeworking one has to organize one's own working day. The danger is that one can easily do too much and not know when to stop or, conversely, one can find the day taken up with domestic tasks – cleaning, shopping, repairs etc. – which causes guilt feelings and stress. Some find they cannot work at home because of constant family interruptions, while others simply miss the gossip and social life of the office. Some also believe (probably correctly) that they are less likely to be trained or promoted while working from home, as they are isolated from office politics.

Bibby (1995) found that the biggest growth in teleworking was in satellite offices on out-of-town industrial estates, away from corporate headquarters. Visiting a number of British 'telecottages' – drop-in centres where desk space can be rented by the hour – Bibby found women predominated, as their jobs involved routine secretarial and administrative work. Pessimistically, he describes these workers as part of 'a parallel informal labour force', with no career prospects. He sees them as belonging more 'to the world of domestic outworking of the early industrial revolution than to the glossy world of high tech, high skills and high pay with which telework is wrongly identified'. Teleworking encourages the flexible specialization that we discussed in Chapter 3; workers become 'peripheral', literally, and the core workforce is reduced.

The Trades Union Congress (TUC) expressed concern over teleworking in a 1995 resolution: employers were seen as introducing it to drive down costs, avoid responsibility for child care and to dilute union influence. Some homeworkers have to pay for the hire of equipment; are only paid for the time they work (not including breaks); and have no benefits, vacation time or sickness cover. As with other types of homeworking, there is plenty of room for exploitation and, as we noted earlier, it is often a ploy to obtain cheap labour. By 1995 Britain had the highest proportion of teleworkers in Europe, and in its report *Communicating*

Britain's Future the Labour Party (1995) called for a European code of practice to protect the growing number of teleworkers.

Likewise, teleconferencing systems (which have technically been available for some time through closed-circuit TV) have not sold as successfully as predicted because many apparently prefer to meet face-to-face. Though participation may be wider, the emergence of opinion leaders can be suppressed, thus making the reaching of decisions more difficult. Studies have shown that those who are *not* speaking in a meeting like to be able to pass notes, make faces etc., while those who are prefer to present their arguments in face-to-face situations. In addition, fears have been expressed over confidentiality, and managers appear hesitant to discuss delicate matters over electronic systems. However, teleconferencing may become more popular now that it is possible with desktop PCs.

Management attitudes
A second factor is the attitude of management, for they too may be disturbed by the organizational and economic implications of IT. They will not want to bring in flexible work schedules, work from home etc. unless they judge it to be advantageous in terms of control, as well as economically viable. With new arrangements they might find supervision and delegation more difficult and expensive. Traditionally, office workers are paid for attendance rather than performance: measuring the former is easy, but the latter is more difficult – even dangerous, if telecommuters won't accept it. In addition, the cost of much new equipment is still prohibitive, though it is continually falling. Guiliano himself admits that many companies have been slow to embrace the information office and introduce new work patterns and equipment, but never questions why this should be. A survey by BETA Exhibitions Ltd of 500 top UK companies found that 50% did not understand the full potential of office technology, 61% of senior managers still relied on secretaries with short-hand, and 74% admitted they were not using existing office space effectively. Of those who had introduced new technology, the majority were generally dissatisfied, and more than a quarter of installations were failing to carry out the function for which they had been purchased. The conclusion was (and other studies support this) that most companies were not rushing into IT – hot desking, teleworking, email etc., though increasing, are not the norm – and those that were did not seem too sure of what they were doing.

But equally importantly, most managers still prefer traditional work arrangements and are anxious to keep their personal secretaries as a status

Secretary/Personal Assistant to the Advertisement Director

Circumstances beyond my control mean that the third most important woman in my life (after Wife & Mother) is leaving me! But I am not too upset because I know that there is someone out there who can fill the void she will leave. IT COULD BE YOU!

The job

This is not a straightforward 'sit there and do a bit of typing' job. The requirements are to take dictation, prepare and type letters and documents, deal with figure work, and compile statistics and departmental records. Professional presentation and good interpersonal skills are required. You will also be an ambassador for me and the company.

The person

You will certainly need to be bright, articulate and reliable. A positive and enthusiastic personality and smart appearance are essential. You will also need to demonstrate your ability to...

Figure 5.3   Job vacancy in a regional newspaper, 30 September 1995.

symbol within their work organization: as Pringle puts it, managers like to 'have' a secretary, for 'having a secretary' signifies power. Despite the increase in new technology, therefore, the signs are that office work has not changed fundamentally, and this is mainly due to the attitudes of managers. The newspaper advert in Fig. 5.3 reflects the continuing image of the secretary as an 'office wife'.

Linda Thompson (1989) argued that while IT may be transforming office work, it was doing little to change the way bosses viewed their secretaries: they were still classified as 'dolly birds' or 'old dragons', and seen as 'appendages' to computer terminals, able to 'effortlessly process and retype mountains of documents, reports and papers for numerous executives, producing immaculate printouts complete with graphics and tables of figures'. Clearly, employers' attitudes have to alter, and the technology become more economic, before significant changes can be expected. Because of these various factors, we can expect a considerable 'technological time-lag'.

The key factor is not technology, but the way secretaries are employed by managers. The recession led employers to consider ways of economizing on office staff, and one strategy – no doubt resisted by many managers – was to organize secretaries so that they served more than one person. In 1970, 70% of secretaries worked for one person only, but this had dropped to 50% by 1981, and has continued to fall since. This move to secretarial 'teams' also affects a secretary's status (which is obtained from her boss) and makes the job less 'personal'. The declining use of shorthand (only 37% now use it as against 51% in 1981 and 83% in 1970) and its replacement by audio dictation has also reduced personal contact between boss and secretary. Shorthand dictation is restrictive and takes up two people's time, while audio dictation and typing are more flexible, if less interesting. WP centres work more effectively with audiotyping, which can mean the operator being plugged in from head to toe.

These developments seem more in line with Downing's predictions, but the point we would stress is that they were already taking place *before* the introduction of word processing (more as a response to economic recession) and not because of it. Mechanization of the office is nothing new and, if not on the same scale as the factory, has steadily increased over the past century. The early mainframe computers encouraged the development of industrial work patterns; clerical tasks have continuously been subject to fragmentation and subdivision; and deskilling has long been a characteristic feature of much office work. The industrial office is well established and, in describing the 'social office', Downing seems to rather idealize the secretary's role and understate the considerable deskilling that has already taken place. Secretarial work has long since been subdivided, with typists located in their 'pools'. It is *these* employees who are moving to the newly created WP centres, not the private secretary to the chief executive. Studies have already identified a large degree of dissatisfaction, disappointment and disillusionment with typing roles, and it is questionable to what extent word processing increases this. In short, it seems that the social office was being destroyed well before the advent of microelectronics, and that in many instances offices were already a great deal more like factories than the pessimists appreciate. In concluding this discussion, we must look at two particularly significant factors: organizational choice and polarization.

Organizational choice

There is no doubt that the effects from office technology can vary according to how firms choose to introduce and organize it. Webster (1986), in her studies of eight different organizations in Bradford, found a massive diversity, both in terms of the technology adopted and how workplaces were organized. Some WP operators complained of boredom, routine and lack of responsibility, while others preferred the new work situation and felt that the machines freed them from many of the previously repetitive and lengthy typing jobs. Some also preferred a work situation where secretaries play a less 'sexist' role and can be judged more by their work output.

Studies suggest that the deskilling effects can be considerably ameliorated by office organization, and this appears to take four main forms:

- The word processing centre, where all correspondence secretaries are located to undertake all typing within the organization.
- Satellite centres, in which both correspondence and administrative secretaries are housed to serve a sub-unit of the organization.
- Back-up centres, providing overload facilities for traditional secretaries.
- A decentralized system, in which word processing facilities are located in normal departments and less division occurs between administrative and correspondence secretaries.

The less centralized the system, it seems, the less the likelihood of deskilling and polarizing secretarial skills. This, of course, is a political decision, not a technical one. Pringle maintains that information technology *can* offer scope for responsibility if employers would only give more thought to delegating and organizing secretarial work effectively. WP installations can therefore result in either reskilling or deskilling, and this is largely dependent on organizational choice and operators' perceptions towards their work. Technology itself does not determine a particular job design; people's values and attitudes remain the overriding factors.

Polarization

Polarization in terms of skill has occurred in a number of areas and will be discussed more fully in the next chapter, but it is particularly relevant to secretarial work. Many companies have created WP centres, but managers often bypass them because they wish to retain their personal secretaries. This has reinforced a growing division between administrative secretaries, who specialize in non-typing secretarial functions, and correspondence secretaries (in the centre), who concentrate solely on typing. As Webster notes, there is an 'essential difference between the job content of secretaries and typists'. In the case of administrative secretaries, her studies found little evidence of fragmentation, deskilling and greater management control, but many typists complained that their jobs were as mundane as they had ever been. This gap could widen further as a result of word processing, and the administrative secretaries – who will still be needed for confidential, non-standard letters, references etc. – come to form an elite. Standard typing will now go to the word processing operators – the semi-skilled keyboard operators – in the WP or satellite centre who will rapidly lose any secretarial skills they once possessed, making the gap between the two groups unbridgeable, and further stunting the growth of any secretarial career ladder. (Pringle even fears that men could take over the best paid, most prestigious jobs, while women are left with the routine VDU work.)

We are suggesting that word processing could further deskill the work of correspondence secretaries (though they have been significantly deskilled already), while administrative secretaries may not be particularly affected. In other words, the pessimists' scenario could apply to the former group, and the optimists' to the latter. But in the main we agree with Webster and Pringle that generalizing about the effects of technological change on secretarial work can be dangerous and that we need to consider users' perceptions as well as the particular circumstances surrounding each installation. More than anything else, it seems to depend on how the equipment is introduced and organized, and early case studies suggest that sweeping generalizations are dangerous.

CHAPTER SIX

The Work Organization

In this chapter we ascend from the workplace level of the factory and office to the corporate level of the work organization as a whole. Information technology is spreading out to affect not just production and 'information' workers, but 'knowledge' workers and all levels of management. In this connection, we shall focus upon different functional areas of management, middle management in general, and computer management in particular, and extend the discussion of polarization introduced at the end of the last chapter.

Since the 1950s, forms of computer technology have altered dramatically, and a major debate has been whether such changes have resulted in greater centralization or decentralization with regard to company structure and management. Again we find that many regard computer technology – and microelectronics in particular – as beneficial to the work organization, not merely administratively and economically, but in human terms. The optimists maintain that it will not only remove a great deal of drudgery and repetitiveness from a manager's role, but will encourage greater participation in decision making at all levels of the organization. Information technology is presented as a democratizing influence in that it decentralizes and spreads power and decision making. Pessimists, on the other hand, question this and believe IT can equally result in more concentrated power at the higher echelons of the organization, the deskilling of middle management, and a greater polarization between high and low management grades. The debate raises many of the issues discussed in previous chapters, but particularly highlights the question of 'centralization' and 'decentralization'. To explore this we shall begin with a few words on the development of computer technology and its effect on organizational patterns.

MAINFRAMES AND MINIS

Technologists talk of 'generations' of computers, and we are presently moving into the fifth. The early mainframes of the 1950s were based on valves, which gave way in turn to transistors, integrated circuits and large-scale integrated circuits. The next (fifth) generation of computers is based on very large-scale integration (VLSI) techniques. These dramatic developments are creating new forms of computing power, allowing industrial companies to introduce wider applications, and resulting in major changes to the internal structures of large-scale work organizations.

In the 1950s, those companies big enough to be able to justify and afford the early, cumbersome mainframe computers purchased them (as we saw in the last chapter) primarily for data processing operations. Data would be batched on sheets at various points in the organization and sent to the mainframe to be processed. This created new specialist work tasks, intensified the bureaucratic structure, and undoubtedly had a centralizing effect within companies. As applications needed to be coordinated, the expertise of staff maximized and responsibility for the service located within a particular division, the function had to be centralized. Companies began to create computer services departments – usually consisting of systems analysts, programmers and operators under a computer manager – to take charge of all operations. In larger, multi-site companies, this was usually located at head office so that computer staff developed direct access to senior and top management, and the fact that it was spending considerable sums on the company's behalf also enhanced its prestige and power. Operations too had a centralizing effect, for batch processing did not particularly disrupt the work patterns of lower management and the general clerical staff. In practice, computers were used to solve the problems of the past rather than the future, and little consideration was given to the social and organizational effects that would follow. The computer services department worked in relative isolation at the apex of the organization, providing mainly financial information for senior and top management.

The computer manager was invariably answerable to the financial director. As most of the early applications involved financial procedures – 'event-driven' operations such as payroll, purchase and nominal ledger, and sales ledger – data processing was usually placed under the accountants. Little thought was given to this choice; it just seemed the natural thing to do. It seemed appropriate not only that the computer should be initially applied to accounting routines, but that it should be located within the finance department. This was the pattern for the majority of early users, and only rarely was the computer attached to other functions such as sales, production, or personnel.

This approach, however, had a number of drawbacks. In the first place, the concentration on accounting procedures, which meant that the computer was used for saving rather than making money, effectively blocked other applications for some time. It also led to computing becoming synonymous with accounting in the eyes of other managers, who distanced themselves from applications. Thirdly, it meant that the experience and expertise of computer staff were accumulated from converting well-structured, established procedures, which was to prove unsuitable for later more complex routines requiring a more creative approach. Finally, placing the computer within the accounting function often restricted its political role and meant that the scope of the computer manager to influence senior management remained limited. Many potential users became sceptical of the contribution that computers could make to their areas and, overall, the close association between computing and accounting was a barrier to progress. In some instances, the computer manager was promoted to board level, but this was rare.

Early computer services departments were usually subdivided according to the three main functions – systems analysis, programming and operations – but as this often caused problems in applications development, many companies moved to a project-based structure, with up to half a dozen staff forming a team, which allowed the systems analyst control over all aspects of an installation. Figure 6.1 shows the structure that became the standard form for computer services departments, particularly in medium-size and larger companies.

As computer technology advanced, cheaper minicomputers became available and batch processing for the mainframe was replaced by on-line terminals. Both developments had a decentralizing effect, in that machines could now be purchased at departmental/site level and general management and staff became directly involved for the first time in the processing of data. No longer was data batched on large sheets and returned to the anonymous central computer department; it was now input to terminals at site level. A wider range of staff participated in operations and a greater volume of data generated within the organization. This increase in installations made the structure over-complex in some instances – as a greater divide occurred between production activities and specialist support services – and some companies created separate administration sections or moved towards more elaborate management services departments. These

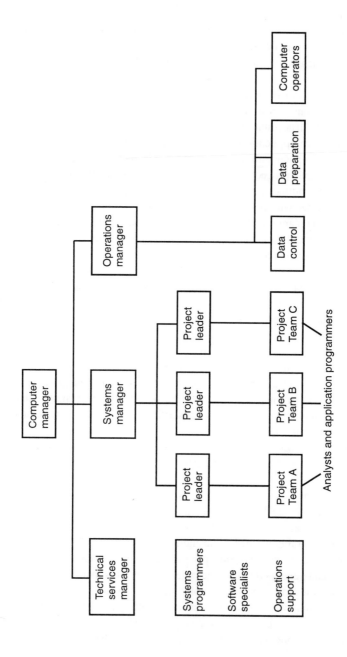

Figure 6.1   Project organization of computer services department (Rowan, 1986).

incorporated organization and method and operations research, as well as the computer, which now became seen as one of several tools available to management.

THE MICROCOMPUTER

The coming of the microcomputer (or personal computer) has had a further – and far more significant – decentralizing effect on the work organization, for it has placed the equivalent power of an early mainframe (at a modest price) on the desk of every manager. It can be used for a whole range of management applications and encourages the growth of client/server technology whereby workstations (clients) are linked to a 'server' (anything from a powerful PC to a supercomputer) which provides data and programs. As well as a computer, a multimedia PC can now be used as a telephone, a fax, an answering machine, a TV and a gateway to network services, all of which facilitate the distribution of information throughout the work organization. It also reduces management's dependency on a centrally based computer services department, and, during the 1980s, many large UK companies broke up their central divisions and established a trend towards 'distributive processing', whereby computer specialists were dispersed to various parts of the organization. Here they were (significantly) retitled business analysts rather than systems analysts, and performed an advisory role, assisting managerial colleagues with small-scale installations. This meant computer specialists taking on a more *consultative* role – advising on technology and applications.

Outsourcing
A stage on from this (during the 1990s) has been 'outsourcing'. Outsourcing takes place when an organization elects to have a function or specialized service provided by an outside source. This is more than 'facilities management' – as often occurs with transport, catering, property management etc. – for the provider becomes a 'strategic partner' and has a say in company policy. IT, up till the mid-1990s, was considered unsuitable for outsourcing (on the grounds that technology and data were assets that should be protected from outside exposure), but certain IT services (e.g. payroll processing) have long been outsourced by various organizations and some began to consider whether this could be extended.

Eastman Kodak rocked the business world when, in 1989, they announced a massive programme to have company data centres, networks and workstations provided by outside suppliers, and in 1994 British Aerospace (BAe) became the largest British company to follow this path when it outsourced its entire IT function to Computer Sciences Corporation (CSC) of the USA. Under a ten-year agreement, CSC bought out BAe's entire IT function, including most staff, and provided a full IT service. The benefits for BAe are that they receive first-class technical advice and optimum deals on the very best equipment and systems available, while managers can concentrate on their core skills and need not be directly concerned with IT. The downside with outsourcing, however, is that the provider may not know the organization's business in sufficient detail; it can cause disruptions and dissatisfaction among staff; the organization has reduced control over IT strategy; there is the added management responsibility of maintaining control over the outsourcing relationship itself; and an outside party obtains access to sensitive company information. This highlights the fact that outsourcing is no easy option. Early indications are that most contractual arrangements do not run their course and many companies are already cooling over the idea. A survey by PA Consulting in 1996 found one-third of organizations considered that the problems outweighed the benefits, though the report concluded that outsourcing will continue to grow for the strategic benefits it can provide. There are, of course, varying degrees of outsourcing, and many may settle for piecemeal solutions whereby certain areas are outsourced rather than adopting a full service. The various changes we have described, including those in computer technology and applications, are summarized in Table 6.1.

Table 6.1   Generations of computer development.

Changes in computer technology	Changes in computer applications	Changes in computer organization
1. Valves 1945–54	Batch processing on mainframe	Finance department
2. Transistors 1954–65	On-line processing to mainframe	Computer services – function-based
3. Integrated circuits 1965–	Minicomputer with terminals	Computer services – project-based
4. Large-scale integrated circuits 1972–	Microcomputer	Distributive processing
5. Very large-scale integration 1985–	Microcomputers in integrated information network	Outsourcing

Table 6.2   Possible computer applications in the organization.

Level of information	Field of vision	Amount of detail	Typical systems	Probable hardware
Corporate (e.g. company)	Long term	Little	Financial	Mainframe
Area (e.g. site)	Medium term	More	Manufacturing	Large mini
Department (e.g. production area)	Short term	Even more	Stock control	Small mini
Individual (e.g. production line)	Immediate	Much more	Personal data	Micro

It is not suggested that these 'generational stages' are distinct and precise, with clear-cut lines of demarcation between them: we are painting with a 'broad brush' and the stages should rather be seen as approximate and overlapping. In the USA, for instance, the time-scale would be some way in advance of Britain, while the length of the developmental time-span will vary between companies.

Nor should it be thought that the emergence of a new phase means the disappearance of another. The central computer department, for example, will not totally disappear, for it can still perform certain functions more effectively – namely project management skills, software selection, quality control and identifying needs within the organization. But it will certainly change and exist in a modified and narrower form.

Likewise, the company mainframe will not suddenly vanish – mainframes are improving all the time and remain highly effective for certain operations – but it will be supplemented by and linked with a growing arsenal of other machines. For instance, linking micros to mainframes gives them access to far greater sources of information. These different machines may well be used for different tasks at different levels (Table 6.2), from top managers operating 'what if?' decision support systems to shop floor managers requiring personal data for immediate tasks.

THE INFORMATION CENTRE

A further development, along with distributive processing and outsourcing, has been the emergence of the Information Centre (IC). Companies have increasingly been faced with two changes occurring simultaneously:

while computer experts have been providing their expertise to all parts of the organization, general managers have been independently (and often unsuccessfully) developing their own applications. This creates a particular problem with the linking of micros into LANs or the development of services such as email, where specialist advice is critical. The problem – largely caused by clashes and ill-feeling from the past – is that neither side trusts the other. The specialists are hesitant to impose their views through fear of being rebuffed, while managers are loath to approach computer services. Hence the need for an Information Centre.

The idea of such a centre is that it provides a neutral location in which end users can approach specialists for advice, and also allows the company to control the proliferation of hardware. During the 1980s, most major companies in the USA (and many in Britain) created ICs. It is rather like a technical library, providing information, equipment and expertise whenever and wherever the user perceives a need for it. The aim therefore is not that *data* should be held and maintained centrally (as occurred with traditional mainframe systems), but that end users should be provided with tools to process their *own* data. The main functions of an IC can be summarized as follows:

- to provide access to computing and software tools
- to listen to end users' problems, provide help swiftly and generally improve the user–specialist relationship
- to give guidance, training, support and hands-on experience
- to control the spread of microcomputers and provide some order in computer growth
- to help users create their own applications, especially with regard to decision support systems
- to help users with software applications that they might have produced themselves
- to provide facilities for access to external databases
- to help develop a new role for the computer services division

The current role of ICs, therefore, is to make available to users *tools* that allow them to do their own computing, including hardware, software, advice and training. Increasingly, however, as end users become more expert, this role will change. Sticking with the library analogy, the IC of the future will not teach people to read so much as let them know what books are available. It will supply as many computing alternatives as possible and assist in the selection of the most appropriate.

In theory, the IC should be an independent service section within management services, but in practice, because of the specialist staff required, centres are more likely to arise from within computer services departments or be provided by outsourcing suppliers. This ties in with the thorny issue of funding, for purists would argue that if an IC is to retain its independence it must be financed separately, with end users paying for any service – equipment, usage, staff time, data store or file management costs etc. – that they might receive. The danger with this, however, is that the costs could well discourage managers from approaching the centre, which is why many argue that it should be provided as a free corporate service. This seems the more likely alternative, but it runs the risk of over-expenditure and wastefulness. There is no ready-made answer, and while ICs seem certain to emerge in growing numbers, their form – especially with regard to the organizational aspects – will vary in each instance. The precise structure of each centre (and how it operates) remains a matter for management choice.

THE DECENTRALIZING ARGUMENT

The optimists welcome the arrival of PCs and the accompanying decentralizing move to distributive processing, on a number of counts. They see IT as a tool for *all* managers, and feel that computer specialists are best employed educating colleagues in the various opportunities available and assisting with individual applications. There are many advantages with this approach: operation and processing at the point of activity should assist system maintenance; there are considerable cost savings; and greater interest and support should be generated among staff who see it more as *their* system.

The technology is therefore viewed as a democratizing force within companies, for more information is available throughout the organization; more managers participate in decision making; and overall organizational effectiveness is enhanced. Individual managers can, through networks, be linked to others both within and without the organization. All this provides a totally new climate within work organizations. Whereas the mainframe approach required one to think in *vertical* (and hierarchical) terms – from head office machine down to on-line terminals – with PC networks one starts to think *horizontally*, in terms of a series of small-scale micro systems. All this makes organizational operations more open, fluid and flexible, and allows skilled managers – Bell's 'technocrats' – to operate with greater effectiveness in a more egalitarian atmosphere.

This move from vertical to horizontal operations has been described by Alvin Toffler (1973). He argues that because of new information technology, conventional organizational hierarchies are collapsing. Bureaucracies – which rank people hierarchically and separate decision makers from others – are being altered, side-stepped and broken down; organizations are forced to change their internal structures to accommodate temporary units as 'sideways' becomes as important as 'up and down'.

Bureaucratic decision making, says Toffler, invariably goes through a series of vertical stages, which accounts for why it is so notoriously slow, rigid, and inefficient. It may well be suitable for solving routine problems at a moderate pace, but it becomes manifestly inappropriate, he argues, when things are speeded up and less routine. The pace of technological change is now so fast that every minute of 'down time' costs more in lost output than ever before; information must flow through the organization swiftly to meet increasing competition; more information is needed to deal with non-routine problems; those lower in the hierarchy must take more decisions to avoid the delays of 'red tape'; and horizontal communication increases as workers make greater use of specialists (e.g. computer experts) and immediate colleagues.

Toffler maintains that it will be some time before bureaucracy is obliterated because it is well suited to routine tasks, and plenty of these remain. However, it is precisely these tasks that computers can increasingly do better. Automation therefore ultimately leads to the overthrow of bureaucracy. Bureaucracies also stifle the imaginative and creative qualities managers now need in solving non-routine problems. He points out that wherever organizations are concerned with technological change, where research and development is prominent, and where problems are non-routine, the decline of bureaucracy is most pronounced.

For such optimists, bureaucracy is the form of organization for an industrial age: it was not needed in pre-industrial times and is inappropriate for post-industrial society. In future, problems will be solved by task forces composed of 'relative strangers who represent a set of diverse professional skills'. Executives and senior managers will function as coordinators for these various teams, and people will be differentiated, not vertically according to rank and role, but horizontally, according to skill and professional training. There will be greater mobility between teams and less group cohesiveness, as managers take their expertise where needed and obtain greater job satisfaction from applying their particular skills to specific problems.

This leads Toffler to conclude that bureaucracy is being replaced by 'ad-hocracy' and 'organization man' by 'associate man'. He identifies three key features of bureaucracy:

- permanence (in which the organization endures through time)
- hierarchy (in which the individual knows his or her ranking)
- division of labour (in which the individual occupies a well-defined niche)

and argues that these are now being replaced by transience, mobility and flexibility, respectively. The bureaucratic manager, faced with routine problems, was encouraged to provide routine answers, and unorthodoxy, creativity and imagination were discouraged. In the ad-hocracy, people operate in a constant state of flux, moving round within organizations and even between them. In this meritocratic society, people become more loyal to their specialism than to an organization – cosmopolitans rather than locals, and task-orientated rather than job-orientated.

Toffler also perceives a rise in entrepreneurship, albeit in a new form. Because of the increasing affluence made available by information technology and the security provided by the welfare state, managers become more prepared to experiment and apply their skills and imagination. 'Associate man' represents a new kind of entrepreneur for the post-industrial age (Table 6.3).

In taking Toffler as representative of the optimistic, decentralizing view, it is interesting to note how similar his discussion is to that of Bell. While Bell focuses on society rather than the work organization, they both talk in similar terms of post-industrial change, and stress the role of technology in this development. They emphasize the growing importance of knowledge, the rise of technocrats and the greater use of computers in decision making. Most important, they see this leading to a more open, fluid, meritocratic and democratic society – both within the organization and without – in which old-style class divisions dissolve and people are allocated tasks according to their expertise. In such an atmosphere, exploitation and conflict give way to teamwork and harmony.

In a sense, any form of computerized system has an 'unveiling' and thereby democratizing effect, for the logic of computer-based systems is to encourage open and equal access to information, as managers are forced to express decision processes explicitly so that they can be handled by software programs. But as Crozier (1983) points out, this may not result

Table 6.3   Comparison of Toffler's 'Organization man' and 'Associate man'.

'Organization man'	'Associate man'
Subservient to the organization	Owes only temporary loyalty to the organization
Immobile – fears for security	Mobile – takes economic security for granted
Fearful of risk	Welcomes risk
Seeks prestige within the organization: conscious of hierarchy	Seeks prestige without the organization
Fills predetermined slot	Moves from slot to slot in a pattern that is largely self-motivated
Solves routine problems according to well-defined rules	Solves novel problems with ill-defined rules
Orthodox and conventional	Creative and innovative
Subordinates individuality	Only temporarily subordinates individuality to a particular team
Seeks permanent relations	Accepts temporary relations

in practice, for new technology has to be introduced into *existing* organizations. Managers have power bases they wish to protect, and technological change cuts right across the established hierarchical, bureaucratic structure of which they are a part. In short, computers come to disturb the very decision-making procedures they are supposed to assist. Again we need to consider the political and human context, for if managers feel they are being forced to change (and feel their power base threatened) they will cling to established procedures. This may include top management, who become reluctant to release information that has traditionally been their prerogative. In this scenario, the computer becomes superimposed on an existing framework, which reinforces the *status quo* and ossifies conservative forms of decision making. While managers might expect computers to deal 'magically' with complexity, in practice they add to it, and can act as an agent for consolidation rather than change. It is for these reasons that some commentators see new technology as a force for greater centralization.

THE CENTRALIZING ARGUMENT

Pessimists would maintain that while there has clearly been a growth in horizontal communication, this has not been at the *expense* of vertical communication: there has simply been growth in all forms of inter-organizational activity as work operations have become increasingly complex. It is not a zero-sum situation in which the former replaces the latter, and as Blau and Schoenherr (1973) point out, paradoxically we are freer today from coercion through the power of superiors, yet at the same time people in positions of power probably exercise greater power than any tyrant ever has.

This point should be kept in mind during the following discussion. But first, a few words on 'centralization' and 'decentralization'. The difference between the two involves a tension between efficiency and flexibility. All organizations want to prove themselves efficient while still remaining flexible, but these two concerns often stand opposed to each other. Efficiency can be greatly enhanced by centralization, for concentrating decision making in the hands of top executives improves coordination, maximizes expertise, economizes on managerial overheads, locates responsibility and involves fewer people. Its weakness, however, is that as a strategy of control it can easily appear authoritarian and inflexible, may not always be available or appropriate, and can easily prove counterproductive. Consequently, many companies have been attracted to the decentralized, 'flatter' approach, for this enhances flexibility, allows swifter decisions from those closer to the action, brings the profit motive to bear on a wider group, and (supposedly) provides greater motivation, wider democracy and more effective use of expertise.

An important point must be made. It should not be thought that a decentralized structure implies a weak centre; it is simply an *alternative* mechanism for retaining control that only operates on terms laid down by the centre and is still control. It is maintained not by centralizing decisions towards the top, but by setting clearly prescribed tasks, rules and procedures within which people can operate. This less visible form of power sets limits on what subordinates might do, and provides a kind of freedom of manoeuvre within bounds; but it is still bureaucratic control.

It may therefore be misleading to suggest that with technological decentralization we necessarily witness some kind of movement in power terms from the centre to the periphery, or from the top to bottom. Certainly with microcomputer networks more processing can be done at all points of the organization, and this may well involve increasing use of horizontal communication, but none of this need mean that centralized, bureaucratic control is reduced, let alone removed. On the contrary, far from information technology passing greater decision-making powers to lower levels, it can as easily be used to provide greater central control throughout the organization.

It is therefore dangerous to suggest that microcomputers and their accompanying networks must enhance organizational democracy. Technological change clearly has implications for organizational structure, but while networked PCs may allow – or even encourage – more participative procedures, there is no certainty they will ensure it. In the first place, there will always be some centralizing tendencies. For instance, in large companies it is doubtful whether a totally decentralized computer operation – in which managers indiscriminately purchase and use whatever equipment they wish – could ever be justified long term by top management. There are indications that many companies allow individual purchases for some time – to encourage familiarity with new technology – but then impose restrictions to ensure a coherent strategy in terms of compatibility, utilization and costs.

But, more importantly, top management may prefer to use information technology to enhance their own position rather than disperse organizational decision making. The fact that PCs are increasingly linked into networks and mainframes means that information is instantly available from all parts of the company and those at the organizational apex can now more tightly observe every aspect of operations. In this way centralization is enhanced. A chief executive can sit in an exclusive penthouse office and electronically check not only on whether a particular worker has spent too long on a coffee break or a typist is working up to speed, but whether individual middle managers are performing as they should be. In short, the flexibility offered by decentralization is also available to top executives and allows re-centralization to occur: central control and freedom of action for decentralized units can coexist. What pessimists suggest is that if the PC networks encourage any form of decentralization, it is only in a restricted, *technological* sense. Computer applications become increasingly feasible at ever lower levels of the organization, but this need not mean all control and decision making pass to these levels. We need to distinguish the quantity of decisions from the quality: the fact that people are using new technology to make *more* decisions does not mean that they are decisions of greater importance. While technology may move down in organizational terms, control can move up (Fig. 6.2).

In terms of management control, new technology can thus increase central control within a decentralized structure. But we return to our central theme. There is no technical reason why this *has* to happen; microcomputers do not *necessarily* result in either greater centralization

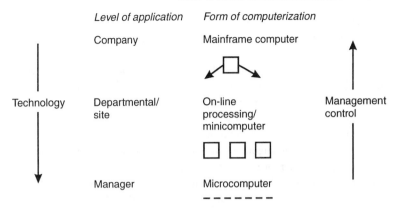

Figure 6.2   Computer technology and centralization/decentralization.

or decentralization. Computer technology does not determine the shape and nature of work organizations; it may suggest certain forms of structure, but it cannot impose. The outcome depends on the particular company and is a matter for managerial choice.

Information technology can certainly be used to facilitate more effective delegation and greater participation from both staff and management: this can be done by linking PCs with common file systems and other networks to provide access to all forms of information. Increased centralization also runs contrary to much research on motivation, participation, industrial democracy etc., but studies suggest most companies are unlikely to follow the decentralized path. Child (1988) refers to research into electronic point of sale (EPOS) systems in retailing, where the more precise information has been used not to provide wider information access for all staff, but to extend centralized control over ordering decisions, stock levels, size of labour establishment, in-store performance etc. Our own research at a biscuit factory, where large numbers of terminals were available to all ranks of personnel, also revealed that hardware was 'doctored' so that only certain data was retrievable at each level. The VDU operators were granted minimal discretion and felt less control over data than in their previous work situations. Staff found themselves working long hours at terminals; offices were rearranged, making communication with colleagues difficult; and working to a distant mainframe intensified feelings of isolation and detachment. In general, they preferred their previous work which they felt provided greater responsibility, variety, interest and satisfaction. Our experience is that it is difficult to view computer technology as some kind of 'emancipator' at the base of most work organizations.

The pessimists conclude that decentralization should not be viewed as in some way synonymous with democracy, though many top managers are apt to make this connection. To bring the profit motive and other responsibilities to bear on lower levels, and to provide them with new technology, may prove stimulating and motivating, but does not make fully participative management automatic. A particular form of computer technology is not more or less likely to result in decentralized management, nor is a decentralized structure necessarily conducive to wider democratic participation. Such factors depend on the strategy of management, for a decentralized structure can equally be used to maintain strong central control. Decentralization may *disperse* control, but it need not *dilute* it: and computer technology can prove a powerful tool in this process.

POLARIZATION

The conclusion we reach is similar to that of the previous two chapters. While the optimists suggest that new technology will rejuvenate the work situation, re-skill tasks, upgrade work and provide greater participation, the pessimists fear further deskilling through automation and an increasing polarization between those with high-grade technological skills and those with no real skills at all. Given that this process can be identified in certain instances in the factory and office, is it also applicable to management? Can the very people responsible for introducing and administering the new technology themselves become subject to its deskilling effects? In this final section, we wish to return and look more closely at the question of job polarization. A number of writers have, in their different ways, proposed a dual model of the work enterprise which suggests that the top part of the organizational pyramid is structurally different from the bottom part (Fig. 6.3).

While the top sector corresponds to a bureaucratic model, in which employees are provided with a vertical career structure though hierarchical grades, the bottom part is increasingly constructed according to Taylor's principles of scientific management, whereby people are arranged horizontally into simple, manual, specialized, repetitive jobs. The separation between the conception and execution of work is intensified as control

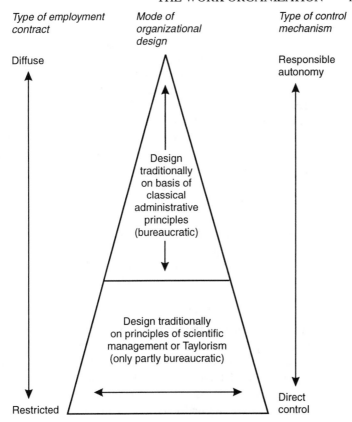

Type of employment contract	Mode of organizational design	Type of control mechanism

Figure 6.3   Two modes of organizational design (Watson, 1987).

of the work situation passes from the worker to those higher in the organization, and work in factory and office is increasingly deskilled.

Those above the organizational divide tend to have a more 'diffuse implicit contract', in which they are required to use discretion in their work, maintain high trust relations with their superiors and think in terms of careers. Those below the divide – in manual and, increasingly, routine clerical and service work – are characterized by a 'restricted implicit contract'. Here, work tasks are more closely prescribed and executed on the basis of a contractual commitment which is specific rather than diffuse; relationships with superiors are low trust; there is little potential career promotion; and workers are paid wages rather than salaries.

This model can also be applied to the changing position of management, and helps to synthesize the debate as to whether professional managers are becoming more important with the growth of the 'knowledge society' or are 'proletarianized' as their work becomes increasingly deskilled within work organizations. The model suggests that both processes can occur simultaneously depending on whether particular skills can be routinized, subdivided or taken over by a machine. This can be seen in the case of personnel, where a separation has occurred between the position of supervisor and personnel manager, or accountancy, where bookkeeping has been relegated in status while others exercise discretion and judgement as finance executives. This polarization is not dissimilar to the one we discussed in the previous chapter between administrative and correspondence secretaries.

Are other areas of management now likely to experience this process, especially as a result of information technology? Pessimists would claim that the model usefully shows how all branches of middle management could be affected.

- It will move the boundary line between the two sectors of the organization – between planning and performance – upwards. Just as planning was taken from the skilled worker, so it will now be removed from middle managers. Technology will take over supervision, record and process information and, finally, transmit that information. Their numbers could contract (as Jenkins and Sherman predict) while those who remain find themselves relegated to the lower parts of the organization.
- Large organizations will recentralize as top managers take on a greater planning role. The former planning tasks of middle managers are now transferred to the higher echelons of the company.
- The line separating the two parts of the organization will be drawn more clearly, making promotion more difficult from one sector to another. Fewer people will be needed, and managers will find it difficult to retrain and readjust.
- All managers will make greater use of computer technology, but for many this will result in repetitive, mundane tasks, and a fall in terms of skill, status and pay.

Some optimists would oppose this on the grounds that it underestimates the full role of management, which is still to negotiate, conciliate, inspire and lead. Managers often have to base decisions on information that is unsystematic, diverse and fragmented, and within increasingly complex modern work organizations, management – at all levels – remains an art that is not easily superseded by technology.

Pessimists, however, insist that a major part of middle management's role is the collection, interpretation and distribution of information, and because this can now be done so swiftly and efficiently by new technology, their position could become largely redundant. This will mean a reduction in the ranks of middle management, a contraction of hierarchical grades, and a slimming of staff and support roles below the strategic level.

We have not quite finished, for the pessimists would also claim that this process has, with the break-up of computer services departments, even hit the computer specialists themselves – the very people who brought in the technology that deskilled others. Ironically, they fall victim to their own devices. Braverman argues that computer work, which for a short period up to 1960 displayed the characteristics of a craft, with workers performing a number of different functions, has been subdivided into a hierarchy of separate tasks. The increasing availability of 'user-friendly' packaged software and high-level languages has lowered the status of programmers, and this has now extended to systems analysts and computer managers as hardware developments permit each manager a personal computer. Skills can be routinized, subdivided or taken over by the machine itself, which means that computer staff are relegated within the organization.

Without doubt, recent developments have adversely affected the career patterns of many computer specialists. From a period of sustained growth over two decades – during which they had the protection of head office and a strong central department around them – they have moved into an uncertain climate in which they are dispersed as 'consultants' to advise managerial colleagues or are transferred to other organizations under outsourcing agreements. Consequently, computer managers have not generally joined top management, but have in most cases remained answerable to the financial director. Not that other managers have shown much distress at these happenings: computer staff have generally been distrusted by their colleagues because they acquired (in a remarkably short space of time) a central position in the political framework of the organization and exercised considerable power over all aspects of operations. The computer department retained a monopolistic hold over its function (through the mainframe) and was not dependent on other departments or substitutable by them. While other branches of management (e.g. accountants, personnel) emerged to occupy central positions within organizations, they rarely created such levels of antagonism because they provided a service *to the organization* but did not require other managers to adjust. Computer services provided a service *to other managers* which demanded adjustments on their part, and it was this – especially when the service was thought to be of poor quality – that caused resentment.

The coming of the Information Centre, however, and the growth of outsourcing arrangements, suggests a continuing role for computer specialists, albeit in a new and modified form. The situation is perhaps akin to the Reformation, when the professional priesthood was dispensed with by many 'end users of religion', but then re-emerged to try to regain its former position. This is very much what computer specialists have done in trying to retain their professional status: as computer departments have broken up, so they have transferred their skills elsewhere.

The re-emergence of *powerful* computer services departments is therefore unlikely, for they would be resisted by other sections of management. Accountants, production managers, general managers and even top managers have clawed back ground lost to computer specialists and will not easily relinquish it. The power of the specialist department has been diluted in two main ways: first by deskilling the lower levels of computer work (e.g. programming) and secondly, by incorporating the upper echelons (e.g. the systems analysts) into general management or outsourcing them elsewhere.

CHAPTER SEVEN

The Internet – and Other Networks

We now turn our attention to networks. As noted in the previous chapter, these started to develop in various work organizations as local area networks (LANs), spread to local communities and, over recent years, have rapidly expanded world-wide to become wide area networks (WANs). Consequently, the distinctions between inter- and intra-networking have become blurred: computers are linked to networks and networks are linked to other networks to create 'network-centric computing'. This process also involves new technologies which, up to now, have only received passing mention, namely cable and satellite. It is these technologies that allow the chip to 'travel' and, as we stressed in the introduction, its full impact is only felt when linked with telecommunications. Digital technology – which makes possible the conversion of words, sounds, pictures and moving images into coded digital messages – is driving the computing and telecommunications worlds into ever closer contact, and networks allow this data to be distributed. In this chapter we therefore focus upon *communication*, the third strand, along with information and production, of the micro explosion.

CABLE

Coaxial cabling has been used throughout the world for some time to provide TV and other forms of communication, but it cannot carry a great deal of 'traffic' and has now been superseded by fibre-optic cabling –

hair-thin strands of ultra-pure glass – which is vastly superior in terms of service and provision. It is estimated that fibre-optic cable will be able to carry 2000 million bits of information per second by 2000, and optical power offers virtually limitless capacity to carry hundreds of video channels, thousands of phone calls, torrents of computer chatter and masses of information. Initial installation costs, however, are high and, because of this (and for various other reasons), adoption has remained uneven. Provision across Europe, for instance, is enormously varied – 92% of Belgian homes are cabled compared with less than 2% in Greece – but the prediction is that, by the turn of the century, 70% will be cabled in Britain. The problem with cable is that because of installation costs, outlying rural areas might be excluded, but its great appeal – particularly with fibre-optic cabling – is that:

- It offers expanded channel capacity.
- It offers two-way communication.
- It can easily be coupled with other communications technologies.

FLAG (Fibreoptic Link Around the Globe)

A good example of how cable systems can operate is the FLAG project (Fig. 7.1), accessible to three-quarters of the world's population, which was launched by Cable & Wireless Marine in 1996. When completed, the cable will stretch from Porthcurno in Cornwall to Miura in Japan with various landing points in Europe, Africa and the Far East. It will provide 120 000 high-speed circuits on a route chronically short of telecommunications capacity compared with the Atlantic and Pacific Oceans. Physically, FLAG consists of four glass-fibre strands, each about the thickness of a human hair, surrounded by armour to protect it against everything from fishing gear to sharks. It can carry 600 000 conversations simultaneously. Some 50 telecom carriers have agreed to purchase capacity on the cable, which will also provide medical imaging, video-conferencing, multimedia and high-definition TV. Many of the regions it will service have previously depended on satellite transmission, but FLAG will offer increased security, speed and accuracy of transmission, as well as the capacity for advanced, two-way transmissions.

With cable we can refer to a five-circle strategy. The first and innermost circle is the home, as home networks connect TVs, cookers, washing machines, alarm systems, personal computers, etc. The second circle is the workplace, which can be linked through local area networks (LANs). The third circle is the local/district loop, which connects homes, businesses

Figure 7.1   The FLAG cable system.

and services in a community network. The fourth circle is the national telephony network, and the fifth is the international circle created through satellite links, world-wide telecommunications and the likes of FLAG. This means that cable is about far more than extra channels of television – though this may act as the stimulus – for it allows the wired community to be created.

The British experience

Unlike many other countries, Britain did not have a tradition of developing cable systems, and the government's plan (as proposed in the 1982 Hunt report) was to rewire the country with fibre-optic cable to carry all electronic communications. The government had noted events in France where, with only six million telephone subscribers in 1974, a modern system of telecommunications was introduced. The TELETEL system now reaches nearly 30 million subscribers through six million terminals and carries around 15 000 different services. All subscribers are issued with a Minitel viewdata machine (a visionphone) which has many advantages over the traditional phone directory in that a printed directory is already a third out of date at the moment of issue – due to people moving, dying, installing a phone etc. – and, while initial costs are high, it does not need to be reissued and all information can be constantly updated. The computer base now holds millions of entries, and over 50 000 updates are made every day. The visionphone also incorporates a videotext service for local teleshopping, video films, TV channels, banking and mail-order shopping.

The British government was eager to move in a similar direction – the Hunt Committee was asked to consider *how*, not *if*, cable should be introduced – and believed that television would prove the main pull for cable development. Consequently, the resulting 1984 Cable and Broadcasting Act allowed the newly created Cable Authority to offer franchises of 15 years' duration to cable companies; permit pay-per-view TV; grant licences to operators to transmit 'suitable' programmes; control advertising quotas; allow programme sponsorship; and encourage two-way interactive services. The intention was that the Cable Authority should exercise a 'light touch' and intervene as little as possible, but should take action over unsuitable material. Cable providers and operators had to be companies under UK or EU control, and broadcasting companies and local newspapers were not permitted to control cable operations in their own area. Under the 1990 Broadcasting Act the Cable Authority became a division under the Independent Television Commission (ITC) and Radio Authority.

There are therefore three tiers of cable operators:

(a) the cable owners, who own the actual cable link
(b) the cable operators, who obtain the rights to sell and operate a package of TV channels along the cable
(c) The programme makers, who make and provide programmes to the operators.

In different parts of the country (or even in different parts of a city), these could be closely interwoven or totally separate entities.

In 1982, the Information Technology Advisory Panel (ITAP) – the advisory team to the Prime Minister – envisaged Britain beating the rest of Europe in a market-driven, private enterprise rewiring for multi-choice cable TV and interactive electronic services by 1985. It simply did not happen. Kenneth Baker, as Information Technology minister, had forecast 30 channels of cable TV for over half the homes of Britain, but in fact there were none. Cabling in Britain came to a grinding halt in 1984 with the government's decision to scrap tax relief on capital expenditure, and Britain did not rejoin the cable race until 1991 when the government (a) allowed cable companies to offer telephone services as well as TV, while (b) excluding British Telecom (BT) from providing TV and home entertainment services until 2002. (The aim was to generate competition for BT's near monopoly.) From this point cabling picked up: whereas in 1992 there were just 21 000 telephone exchange lines provided over cable systems, this increased, by the end of 1993, to over 250 000, and 20 000 new customers were subscribing every month. This resulted in an army of (mainly American) cable companies spending billions to establish monopolies in profitable areas where they could offer services, undercutting BT by up to 20%.

BT was, not surprisingly, frustrated by these arrangements: the company found itself with over two million miles of fibre-optic cabling carrying nothing more than telephone calls, though the potential was there to provide a host of other services. In 1995, Labour party leader Tony Blair announced a £15 billion 'understanding' with BT whereby a Labour government would allow BT access to the lucrative home entertainment and TV services market in return for connecting schools, colleges, hospitals and libraries (free of charge) to the 'Information Superhighway'. Under a 'rolling programme' BT would increasingly provide computer communication, so that by 2002 the company would be in a fully competitive position. BT claimed it would not have to dig up roads and pavements, as new equipment could be fed through existing lines and junction boxes. The cable companies reacted with alarm, pointing out that a third of UK homes already had cable running past them; that hundreds of schools were already connected; and that many hospitals, libraries and universities were also linked. The cable companies, understandably, feared that their investments could be jeopardized while BT welcomed a freer market.

By 1996 cable had reached around six million British homes, one in four of which had subscribed to cable telephony, but take-up for cable TV remained low. The feeling was that cable penetration would never equal that found in the USA. It is still early days – the cable industry is only five years old and more time has been spent 'digging streets' than gaining customers – but few predicted that the figures would be so poor. Whatever the outcome, the key point is that UK cable provision seems likely to remain within the private sector: neither major political party has seriously advocated that (as in France) an electronic network should be provided by the state.

Not that such a proposal hasn't been made. In a further 1985 report (which remained unpublished), ITAP insisted that local cable networks must still be built and that TV would be the drawing force, but that the money needed for cabling Britain would not just come from market forces, and the government had to become more involved, as in other European countries. Likewise, the NEDC's (National Economic Development Council) Long-Term Perspective group in 1987 called for work on a national electronic grid of fibre-optic cables (linking every home and business) to begin by 1990. They saw this as imperative if Britain was to compete in the 'information age', and argued that it could spur the whole economy, helping the growth of new firms, providing new services and creating new jobs.

Peter Large (1984) argues that, just as road, rail and canal networks were created during the first industrial revolution to provide a transport infrastructure, so now a fibre-optic national grid should be constructed by government to provide cable TV, interactive services, telephone systems, home technologies etc. to every home. This is what other countries are doing, and without such a grid we will end up with a plethora of systems and technologies and cable, satellite and interactive systems will fail to develop.

In Britain there has been uncertainty as to how cabling should be carried out. The most radical solution would be an integrated *European* grid of optical fibres – an option advocated by the Labour party until Tony Blair switched to his deal with BT – but while this has often been talked about it has made little headway. A second option is to allow BT to build a fibre-optic grid to serve the nation and provide all services – which Tony Blair advocated in 1995. The third option – and the one that the government adopted, because BT is a privatized company that should be subject to competition – is to allow cable companies to lay cable for all services but to restrict BT (in the short term) simply to telephones.

Critics claim that it is pointless digging up roads for cable when BT can provide what is needed and that, had an agreement been struck with BT a decade ago, Britain could now be well on the way to being the first country with 21st century infrastructure. This would have given British industry a head start in exporting all the peripheral equipment needed. In the end, however, both major parties have, in their different ways, advocated the grid being provided by the private sector.

The flaw in the government's strategy was the expectation that TV would provide the demand for cable. The fact is that many British viewers have been attracted to home video for feature films; others appear to retain a loyalty to the BBC and ITV; and most seem to have little desire for extra channels. Surveys suggest that the appeal of cable (and the two-way services it provides) lies first in home security (burglar alarms, front-door TV, electronic locks etc.); secondly, house management (e.g. checks on energy consumption, breakdowns etc.); thirdly, external services such as health care, education, home banking, shopping and other infor-mation services; and lastly, home entertainment. All this makes it difficult for cable TV to get established, and for the national electronic grid to come into existence, without government support. Cable illustrates well the point we have made throughout – that because a technology has a certain capability, it does not necessarily mean that it will be adopted. Evans may describe a world in which everyone uses interactive services, but political decisions will determine whether and how they are introduced into different countries.

Even if cable television does become established, there are still doubts as to whether this will lead to the development of interactive services for there are indications that those who are attracted to cable TV have little interest in two-way services. A 1985 study by JICCAR (the joint body representing both cable industry interests and the advertisers) suggested that the average cable TV viewer is likely to be a male, low-skilled, manual worker, with a larger than average family, living on an urban council estate, who expects all the family (from 18 months upwards) to be avid TV viewers at all times of the day. But he has little interest in two-way services. Hence the paradox: those with cable are least likely to use it for interactive services; those who might develop such services do not receive cable.

SATELLITE

The uncertainty over cable has led some to advocate satellite as a preferable alternative. Its great appeal is its universality: if you want it, you can get it. A satellite system can cover a third of the globe, cross national bounda-ries, provide up to 600 channels, and can be beamed down to anyone anywhere with the appropriate receiver. But the cost of a transmitter for interactive services would be considerable, and this is why they will not be developed by satellite alone.

Therefore, it is when satellite and cable are used *in conjunction* that their impact becomes fully apparent. This can be seen in the 'networked

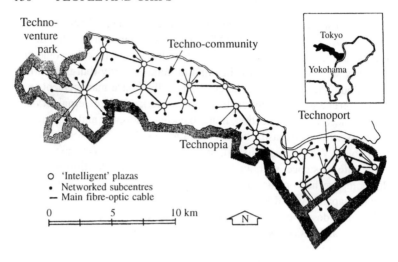

Figure 7.2   Kawasaki: the networked information city.

information city' of Kawasaki, Japan (Fig. 7.2), an industrial suburb, between Tokyo and Yokohama, of around one million residents. The plan links some 18 'intelligent plazas' (each being a constellation of 'smart' buildings) to form the beads of a broadband fibre-optic chain running about 30 kilometres through the city. More than 100 research and development centres exist and the plazas act as nodes with multiple gateways to the network. Four broad zones cover the city, and these are:

- Techno-venture park – concerned with the development of new technologies
- Techno-community – the industrial area, where new technologies are applied
- Technopia – the business sector of the town, where much new technology is installed
- Technoport – where port automation (e.g. robots) is extensively employed.

The intelligent plazas obtain information via satellite and distribute this through the various cable links, thus making available a vast array of information services and databases. Conversely, information can be sent via satellite from Kawasaki, and over 20 other Japanese cities have been designated for similar development, so that electronic links can be established between them.

Kawasaki illustrates the importance of networks – the linking of computing power through cable and satellite systems – and these developed extensively throughout the world during the 1990s. Most started as fairly small-scale LANs – across companies, communities or regions – but, in time, international networks became established. The impact of these has been immense, and one, above all others, has become particularly significant. It is now time to look at the Internet.

THE INTERNET

The Internet – commonly referred to as 'the Net' and founded in 1969 to shuttle data between two defence laboratories in the USA – is the largest computer network in the world. In 1990 the American government decided that it was far too important to be controlled by the military, and its administration passed to the National Science Foundation (which promotes science in the USA). The Internet has (reputedly) over 50 million users – around 1.5 million in Britain – and, with a new computer apparently connected every 30 seconds, we can expect 100 million users by the turn of the century. Anyone with a PC can obtain, through a modem and telephone line, information in words and pictures from any other computer in the world that speaks the same language. In addition to downloading software and information, email – the major commercial use of the Internet – offers enormous gains over telephone calls, faxes and letters, not just because it is substantially cheaper but also because it is not just text that can be sent: plans, pictures, sound and video can all be transmitted.

The Internet is therefore used by organizations to connect LANs – to create communities of computers – for this proves a lot simpler than sorting out leased lines and point-to-point setups, especially if only occasional inter-office links are needed. Companies create more structured electronic commerce mechanisms, with payments being made more swiftly and securely; products and services are advertised to customers; and all forms of communication are greatly improved. In short, the Internet alters the whole way in which we work and play.

The beauty of the Internet is that it can be whatever one chooses. For some it's the largest library on the planet in which to browse (or 'surf'), and through the World-Wide Web (WWW) users can visit museums, art galleries or libraries; access government information, sport databases and magazine archives; and obtain global weather reports, images of outer space and endless information on every possible subject. For others, it's the fastest, most reliable postal service in the world or, simply, a quick and easy way of meeting friends, discussing politics, sharing views and ideas or exchanging help and support. More serious users can use file transfer protocol (FTP) to download files to their own hard disks.

The following example illustrates the services that the Internet can provide. The Roman Catholic Church launched a 'site' on Christmas Day 1995, and millions of people have 'visited' it. People send email to the Pope, ask for personal prayers, request statements on Vatican policy, receive recent papal speeches (in six languages), download pictures of the Pope and seek general news and advice. More than 300 000 connections from 70 countries were made when the Pope was forced to miss Christmas Day mass due to sickness. For a world-wide community such as the Catholic church the Net clearly provides a swift and effective form of communication.

Some Internet activities, on the other hand, enter the realm of the bizarre. In 1996 a Californian couple (based in Venice Beach and Hollywood respectively) got married in cyberspace with friends and family 'attending' as virtual guests from all parts of the world, and the groom's father conducting the service from his church in Beverley Hills. In the same month another American filed for divorce after accusing his wife of electronic adultery on the Net: she was, apparently, conducting a 'virtual reality affair' with a man known as The Weasel. At the same time an anonymous subscriber in the village of Bruton, Somerset (population 2273), booked 1300 pages on the Internet to advertise the village! And so one could go on: the range of applications is endless. But, overall, is the rise of the Internet to be welcomed? Optimists welcome the new technology because of the *expansion* it provides, not just in terms of the vast amount of information cheaply and swiftly available but for the new opportunities that are stimulated for work, leisure and education. Pessimists, on the other hand, are primarily concerned to *protect* individuals' rights, liberties, privacy, security and traditional skills, and fear that the new technology could prove a threat to these. In this and the following two chapters we use this distinction between expansionists and protectionists.

The optimistic view
Optimists highlight the many gains provided by the Internet. Firstly, it can provide fresh opportunities for those living in less accessible regions.

In the Highlands and Islands of Scotland, for instance, it is providing fresh employment – former crofters now do editing work for publishing houses based in the USA – and training opportunities, which saves trainees having to make long, arduous journeys to colleges and training centres. Moreover, the Internet provides not only immediate delivery of learning materials but permits teacher and student to communicate instantaneously. This is a stage on from multimedia-based training (where communication is between student and machine) and provides a more rewarding, human interface.

Secondly, the Net can provide considerable benefits to the disabled and sick. Deafmail, for instance, an electronic deaf club created in 1993, allows deaf and hard of hearing people to 'meet' and exchange views and information, and similar groups exist for people with other handicaps. The Net can also be used by individuals suffering from rare complaints. A particularly heartening story occurred in 1995 when the parents of Matthew Fell, a nine-year-old suffering from the rare medical condition Trigeminal Neuralgia, put out a plea on the Net when British doctors said they could do no more to relieve his pain and, within hours, were put in touch with specialists in Pittsburgh, Pennsylvania, who were able to work on Matthew's condition. At the University of Humberside, where Matthew's mother worked, over £120 000 was raised to finance the treatment. In 1993 Cari Loder was diagnosed as suffering from the debilitating and incurable illness Multiple Sclerosis. As she gradually lost control of her body, Cari communicated with others on the Internet and, by sharing information on various medicines, pieced together a cocktail of drugs that produced dramatic improvements in her condition and offered hope to fellow sufferers.

There are also enormous gains in the distribution of information. On 1 January 1996, *The Times* became the first national newspaper to be published in identical form on the Internet. It immediately became a morning paper in London and an afternoon paper in Los Angeles, and arrived a day earlier than usual in Sydney. Readers are able to obtain it in a hotel room or office, 'call up' items of particular interest through search facilities, reply to and place advertisements, obtain news updates and browse through back issues. A scientist in Antarctica can receive the paper at the same time as a naval captain in the Pacific. Moreover, the paper can be received in parts of the world where censorship is practised, which optimists would claim offers a lifeline to free speech.

On this point it is worth noting that the Net has proved an invaluable forum for campaigns and worthy causes. Amnesty International, for instance, receives over 1500 'visitors' a day and provides an extensive library of updated reports on human rights abuses. Amnesty gets reports within hours and can respond critically and swiftly to abuses by authoritarian regimes. Optimists would claim that the English language, which dominates the services, software and content of the Internet, provides a linguistic unity which greatly assists swift, effective communication. This provides enormous advantages for Britain – what film producer David Puttnam has described as 'the cultural equivalent of North Sea oil' – and the opportunity to develop software services.

In response to those who claim that the Internet has become a hotbed for pornographic material, optimists reply that programs can effectively block the reception of 'inappropriate' material; are becoming increasingly available and sophisticated; and are used by many organizations. Most optimists favour such 'self-censor' programs over government controls – for this could restrict the Internet's development – but they would add that such controls have proved effective too. In 1995 a German court forced CompuServe in the USA – a major Internet access provider with over four million subscribers – to close global access to 200 sex discussion forums because of the nature of the material being transmitted, and in 1996 two Britons were brought to trial for distributing child pornography. Many national governments are investigating the issue, and rating systems, as used in the cinema, are being considered. Optimists would argue, however, that access providers should not ultimately be held responsible for the material others transmit and, while welcoming a legal framework, would want this to be as loose as possible so that the Internet is granted maximum freedom to develop. As far as Europe is concerned, a Directive on data protection was issued in 1995 and this must be enforced by UK legislation after July 1998.

In the business world the Internet is allowing companies to deal directly and swiftly with customers on a global basis. This will lead to dramatic changes in the nature of competition, and could squeeze out companies that 'link' suppliers and customers. Companies can advertise their wares to millions of potential customers for less than the cost of a single-page advert in most magazines. They can also gain access to vast amounts of information, can contact other organizations in the same field and generally find it an effective way to conduct business. Banks, for instance, are moving towards 'electronic money' and analysts predict a £400 billion Internet market by 2000. Internet security has been greatly improved and, ultimately, electronic money offers the perfect means of exchange, providing instant settlement, easy storage and savings on bank charges. The

Internet also assists the development of telecommuting (discussed in Chapter 5), which means reduced traffic, less pollution and less stress, and encourages the renewal of the nuclear family. And so one could go on. Equal educational opportunities for the world's population will become available: a child in a remote African village will be as close to the Library of Congress as a US senator. Super-optimists would even conclude that these shared experiences could lead to greater understanding and, ultimately, world peace.

The pessimistic view

Pessimists, however, present a different picture and are perturbed over *what* is transmitted on the Net: they are less concerned with the *expansion* of material and more with the need to *protect* certain persons from it. Pornographic material, for instance, is widely available – it has been calculated that around 50% of information searches are for pornography – and a particular worry is that children (with their IT skills) will obtain access to this while their less technologically minded parents are oblivious to what is happening. On-line 'chat' groups – where people type conversations with each other on screen – are a favourite recruiting ground for paedophiles. One in ten 'shops' on the Internet – outlets where goods can be bought by mail order – advertise erotica and sexual paraphernalia, while a similar proportion of computer bulletin boards are devoted to pornography. Pessimists question what protection is available from such influences. Paradoxically, while information is 'open' on the Net, subscribers' identities are hidden. Pornographers, child abusers and paedophiles hide with impunity behind an impenetrable electronic curtain and can use the Net to 'befriend' children directly, a danger that will escalate as schools, as well as homes, become connected.

Other forms of devious behaviour have been noted. Student newspapers in Britain carried adverts in 1996 for Gradnet (UK), a company prepared to buy and sell essays on the Net. Students were paid £10 for each essay accepted and could choose titles from various subject lists. Such practices create an academic world without standards in which anyone can obtain qualifications by submitting fraudulent material. Not that 'essay banks' are new; but the technology makes it easier.

Critics claim that the Internet is free parking for all manner of cheats, lunatics, terrorists and pornographers and that better on-line behaviour ('Netiquette') is badly needed. They are doubtful whether individual countries technically have the power to censor material, for censoring the

Internet is more akin to censoring a phone call than a book, and are wary that international agreements will become difficult to establish.

The lack of international agreement leads to a further problem – the retaining of intellectual property rights to information. Existing copyright laws deal inadequately with digital transmission, for information downloaded in one country may have originated anywhere in the world. The music industry, for instance, fears that digital copyright abuse will become a major problem.

The problem is that, although the Net emerged out of the US Department of Defense, it is not precisely clear who owns it or has responsibility for its upkeep, and this concern will increase as the Net expands world-wide. Pessimists fear that many will be denied access to the future infrastructure; i.e. the rich will get richer and the poor stay poor. They envisage a technological elite communicating across the globe, with an unplugged, disenfranchised underclass falling ever further behind. This worry is based on the fact that, unlike other great technological leaps, the Net is entirely in the hands of the private sector. 'Corporate America' may have little incentive to wire up poor and remote areas, a task which former telephone companies were legally obliged, and subsidized, to perform. Attempts have been made in the USA to introduce legislation to control the Internet's use, but many commercial interests are opposing this. The absence of any world-wide treaties could create considerable problems.

In the business sphere many see the Net being dominated by the powerful multinationals and providing an open door to anyone seeking to place money in tax havens, enabling floods of currency to circulate around the globe, far from the reach of nation states. With electronic money, anyone can send funds to some Internet bank offshore or set up a business anywhere on the globe without leaving home.

Pessimists also reject the notion that the English language provides some form of global unity. On the contrary, they fear that it will give English-speaking nations an unfair cultural advantage. In 1996, Accent Software (based in Jerusalem) introduced 'Internet with an Accent', a tool that made it possible to access, author, publish and distribute WWW pages and email in 35 languages. The company claimed that there was cultural richness from letting everyone express themselves in their own idiom and that this should be welcomed by multinational companies. Ironically, the once revolutionary Minitel phone system in France was, by 1996, being overtaken by the cheaper, faster, English-speaking Internet. France Telecom announced measures to harmonize with the Net, but people in France viewed the development with apprehension.

'Cyberwriters' (e.g. Castells, Jones, Featherstone and Burrows) insist that cyberspace is the new frontier, where new worlds meet and meanings and values are created. In a world where 'information is power' they question how our identities as human beings are constructed and how cyberspace influences the way we live and interact with others. Many fear that traditional languages and smaller national cultures will disappear as a world 'cyberculture' takes over; humans will physically deteriorate as they order everything from an armchair; children will become goggle-eyed couch potatoes, flicking across 500 TV channels, more used to a virtual world than a real one; subscribers will become 'hooked' on the technology in the way people are addicted to drugs; and on-line societies will forget the basics of community and neighbourliness. People will know how to 'log on', but forget how to 'drop in'; everyone will be lost in cyberspace.

Some insist that the Internet has been grossly oversold. Moore (1995) and Stoll (1995) both maintain that while the Net opens many doors, a lot of them lead to empty rooms: commercial opportunities are continually hampered by problems of security; exchanging information and software programs are threatened by copyright lawsuits; and end users can end up bewildered by a plethora of information. In the meantime, political extremists offer bomb-making recipes, while pornographers and child molesters prey on innocent users. That there is much to sort out with regard to the Internet is beyond question, but one cannot doubt its potential. How it develops will remain a matter for debate and, ultimately, choice.

The Internet and the IT industry

The growth of the Internet has had an enormous impact on the IT industry itself, and has been instrumental in many of the changes that have occurred. It is illuminating to study the changes that have taken place over the past decade and to consider how things might develop in the future.

It is staggering to think that, by 1984, with around two-thirds of world computer sales, IBM had a turnover greater than the gross national product of Greece. Its dominance was awesome, and seemed likely to continue when it entered the PC market and adopted Microsoft's MS-DOS as its operating system. MS-DOS became the industry standard, with 90% of the world market using the system, and Bill Gates (Microsoft's co-founder and later creator of the Windows operating system) became one of the wealthiest people in the world. By 1988, however, IBM was struggling, for it had responded too slowly to the rise of the PC and many successful 'clones' were being manufactured. In 1992 IBM lost £5 billion – its largest loss ever – and took only 12% of the world PC market. Within a decade Microsoft had become bigger than IBM in the personal computer market.

By the mid-1990s, however, the situation had changed again, for, just as IBM were accused of initially underestimating the PC's significance (and the fact that it would in many respects replace the mainframe), so experts now predicted that PCs would prove less important, in the long run, than the *networks* that linked them. It had long been acknowledged that 90% of PC owners used less than 10% of their machines' capabilities, and networking, it was argued, opened up more viable alternatives. The claim was that we were entering a network-centric world.

Larry Ellison – chief executive of Oracle, the world's third-largest software company (after IBM and Microsoft), and arch-rival to Bill Gates's Microsoft – stung his competitors in 1995 by branding the PC a 'ridiculous device' and predicting that it would prove a blind alley, for, instead of buying complex, expensive software suites (from the likes of Microsoft) computer-owners would simply download compatible mini-programs (to simpler, cheaper network terminals) from a network when needed. Oracle launched a network computer (NC) in 1996 – it had no hard disk, no floppy disk, and sold for £300 – and struck a deal with, among others, the British company Acorn to develop and produce the machines. To use an analogy: people would no longer purchase a car to drive on the motorway; they would hire one when needed. The dominance of Microsoft would be replaced by a new era of open competition.

Such a view also received support from IBM's chairman, Louis Gerstner, who acknowledged that distributive processing had proved a disappointment in many organizations where staff had become frustrated with the problems of incompatibility and surprised by the high costs of client/server computing. The PC had not provided all the answers. Gerstner's view was that 'client/server computing is, in fact, not a full-blown phase of computing. It is really the leading edge of what will be the next phase: network-centric computing.... Why not migrate a lot of the functions that currently reside inside the PC to the network – the applications, data, storage, and even some of the processing?'.

The exponential growth of the Internet had therefore, by 1996, created a network-centric frenzy and a new battlefield. Major IT companies were forced to fundamentally reconsider their business strategies. Many predicted, for instance, the demise of on-line services – commercially developed information sites such as CompuServe, Delphi, America Online (AOL) and Microsoft Network (MSN), available through Windows 95 –

for why should subscribers pay for such services when, through cheaper 'access providers' they can enter the whole of the Internet? Bill Gates had hitherto been largely steering Microsoft towards CD-ROM technology, but by the mid-90s this had started to look primitive. By underestimating the Internet he had missed the chance to create the dominating operating system as he had for PCs. (Sun Microsystems effectively did this with their programming language, Java, which was swiftly adopted by a significant slice of the industry.) Supporters of the on-line services, on the other hand, would claim that they provide ease of navigation. The Internet is a vast, unregulated ocean and belonging to an on-line community offers some coherence. Movement is easy and content is supervised by a team of regulators. Ellison's critics also express doubts about the costs and capabilities for the network computers and believe that he underestimates the desire of PC owners to retain local control. The rival companies were also being forced into alliances – previously unthinkable to Gates – to provide cross-licensing of technology. Microsoft agreed to take the Oracle Web browser and Sun Microsystems's Java and, having given up the attempt to dominate Net software, began to focus more on providing *content*. The company announced its own browser, Internet Explorer, and a set of programming tools for the Net; provided full access to the Net through Windows 95; and launched a 24-hour interactive news system (provided in conjunction with NBC). Gates admitted that the plan was to make the Internet an extension of the user's desktop, with Microsoft products providing the best gateway in and out of the Net. Such a switch in strategy was quite a turnaround for Gates – in his heart of hearts he probably still hoped that the Internet would not live up to expectations and that customers would continue using CD-ROM – but the rise of the Internet left him with little choice.

Whatever happens Gates will not suddenly disappear (just as IBM did not suddenly disappear), for there are still plenty of PCs needing software and he is clearly fighting for influence on the Net – but his dominance might well decline. By the mid-90s he was unquestionably facing severe competition from the likes of Sun Microsystems and Oracle. Ironically, in 1996 IBM turned in its best results for a decade, thanks largely to the policy of moving into networks, workstations and corporate mainframes.

The Internet is basically a network of networks and there are some (important) networks not, at present, included. In 20 years' time, however, with the development of multimedia and digital systems, we will receive all information in digital form on a single 'smart box' incorporating computer, telephone and TV screen. PCs will still remain important –

many predict that they will outsell TVs by 2000 – but 'communicating PCs' will provide a multitude of facilities – video-conferencing over telephone lines, digital modems for single-line voice and data, three-dimensional software support for modelling and virtual reality – and the interesting questions are how the Internet will develop and how PCs will be utilized. The Internet is the forerunner to the Information Superhighway – the M1 of a motorway network – which could ultimately draw all networks together and allow any person to access any information, at any time, in any place over cellular networks using pocket-sized devices. Precisely what form this will take is uncertain. BT's chief executive, Peter Bonfield, expressed the view in 1996 that 'there will not be a single national, information superhighway. There will be lots of highways knitted together. It is going to be a network of networks with increasing bandwidth across all of them. With DBS and digital TV the idea of a *single* fibre optic network is wrong'. Who knows?

It might be said that we have witnessed three ages of information technology. The first was dominated by mainframes and minicomputers, which processed vast quantities of data and helped automate many existing operations. The PC era brought the computer to the work desk, into the home and on to one's lap, and provided for individual applications. The third era is dominated by networks, such as the Internet, which allow computers to be linked across the globe and transmit all manner of data in digitized form. This highlights the extraordinary pace, not just of technological change, but also strategic change as the various IT companies are forced to reformulate policy.

CHAPTER EIGHT

The Response of Management and Unions

At this point we are including a chapter on industrial management and the trade unions. However, unlike earlier chapters, we shall not just be considering how information technology might affect various aspects of industrial relations – and if this could be for better or worse – but will also look at how managers and trade unionists *themselves* are responding to the technology. In other words, can they too be branded as either optimists or pessimists? Furthermore, we shall discuss 'industrial relations' in a broad sense, to include not simply collective bargaining procedures but also how IT is disturbing longstanding demarcations between the unions themselves and affecting different sectors of management. For reasons of space we are mainly focusing on the industrial sector – excluding such areas as finance, retailing and local government – though we acknowledge that IT applications are widespread in other fields.

How are industrial managers and trade unions responding to the new technology? Can they be classed as optimists or pessimists? Do we find different responses at the collective, sectional or local level? Which are the issues that cause particular concern? Will information technology change the very nature of industrial relations as we know it and usher in new forms of bargaining? And, most important of all, are the various changes to be welcomed or resisted? As with the Internet, which we discussed in the previous chapter, optimists welcome the new technology because of the *expansion* it provides, while pessimists are concerned to *protect* individual rights. Consequently, we again label these two groups the 'expansionists' and 'protectionists'.

It is important to note, however, that in this chapter we shall not just be working *across* our conceptual model (Fig. 2.2) (i.e. from optimist to pessimist), but equally *down*, from the macro to the micro level of analysis. In the case of industrial relations it is particularly important to identify the level at which analysis is taking place, and we shall consider the responses of the trade unions and industrial management at three separate levels – collective, sectional and local – which allows us to move down from the national collective organizations, through the various trade unions and industrial sectors, to individual workplaces. While passing reference is made to other countries, the discussion is essentially on Britain.

THE EFFECTS OF INFORMATION TECHNOLOGY

There is much speculation as to how information technology could affect industrial relations. One cannot be precise about this, but in previous chapters we have already touched on a number of issues that would seem highly pertinent, and significant change can be expected in the following areas:

- Labour displacement

Even if information technology stimulates new employment opportunities in the long run, there seems little doubt that some job dislocation will occur (e.g. in office work) and this is a major concern for trade unions.

- Opportunities for women

Many women work in areas such as office work, and their job opportunities may be hit at a time when more of them wish to enter the labour market.

- Smaller workplaces

Workplaces may well become smaller as a result of information technology, but trade unions have traditionally recruited and organized more successfully in larger plants, and union officials can service them more effectively.

- Diverse employment contracts

As more people telecommute and work from home, greater use could be made of subcontracting and consultancy. In some ways this is a return to earlier employment patterns, but the dispersed workforce makes trade union organization more difficult.

- Payment systems

With more people working part-time and from home, new forms of payment system will operate which will be more difficult for trade unions to control. Likewise in factories, if output is increasingly determined by machines, then flat-rate systems are likely to replace payment-by-results (for blue-collar workers) while, conversely, white-collar workers may move from salary scales to wages based on output. This could mean further growth in white-collar unions as more workers seek to obtain bargaining rights.

- Changes in skill composition

Whether information technology reskills or deskills particular jobs depends very much (as we saw in Chapter 4) on management strategies at shopfloor level, but either way, workers could now stand in a more *individual* relationship to the company (rather than a collective one), which will weaken the role of trade unions.

- Union organization

While there were over 1000 unions in 1900, this had fallen to 68 TUC-affiliated unions in 1995, and many predict that by the turn of the century over 80% of all trade unionists could be in just 10 unions. There were numerous mergers during the 1980s and early 1990s, and more seem likely. Information technology encourages this trend, and the conventional distinction between blue- and white-collar work will continue to fade. These developments should result in a more streamlined union structure and wider adoption of single-union agreements, which are particularly attractive to the growing number of overseas companies in Britain.

- Union membership

Over the past two decades employment growth has been fastest in *non-unionized* companies, while the biggest job losses were in unionized plants (i.e. high-tech workers are not likely to be in trade unions while shipbuilders are). Less than a third of private-sector workers are now in trade unions, and the growth areas seem certain to be in self-employed, part-time and female work – all groups that are less likely to be unionized.

- Work patterns

The trend to shiftwork (which we noted in Chapter 4) continues to grow and this makes it increasingly difficult for unions to recruit members. Moreover, the greater use of automated machinery undermines the unions' position and passes more power to management. Firms that sell robots are keen to point out that they don't join unions, go on strike etc.

- Information

Information technology makes available, both to management and unions, a wider range of information, more swiftly, efficiently and cheaply. This should greatly assist the effectiveness of all aspects of industrial relations, but some fear that it will equally encourage incursions into people's privacy.

- Management control

Many trade unionists fear that IT will be used to monitor working practices more tightly, to speed up operations and generally to enhance management control. This might well be done without due regard to health and safety factors.

All these points – and there are no doubt others – indicate the multitude of changes that can be expected in the field of industrial relations as a result of new technology. Whether they improve or jeopardize the quality of such relations is, of course, a matter for debate.

THE PRESENT CLIMATE

Before examining the impact of information technology in detail, we need to consider the changing shape of industrial relations over recent decades. What we might term 'the Thatcher years' were not, in most respects, an easy time, either for management or the trade unions. As we noted in Chapter 3, while 8.4 million people worked in manufacturing in 1966, this had fallen to 5.3 million 20 years later and, not surprisingly, this affected trade union membership. While there were 12.2 million TUC members in 1979, this had fallen to 7 million by 1995 – around a third of the workforce. This loss in membership meant a drop in subscription income of over £150 million at a time when trade unions were trying to do *more* – e.g. mortgages, legal advice, holidays – for their members. The areas of job growth that did occur tended to embrace self-employed, female and part-time workers, and, because these groups are less likely to join trade unions, this was not reflected in a growth of union membership.

The complexion of trade union membership also changed: by 1995, 38% of TUC members were managers or professionals; 28% were in white-collar jobs; 26% were in craft or semi-skilled work; and only 8% were unskilled. This is far removed from the TUC's traditional make-up and, as we saw in Chapter 3, the trend is likely to continue. It is against this background that we have to consider the impact of information technology. As we indicated earlier, we shall start at the collective level and work down to the local.

THE COLLECTIVE RESPONSE

1979 has been called 'the year of the microchip' – the year when Britain first woke up to the realities of information technology. Debates were held at all the major party conferences and the TUC produced its first official response in 'Employment and Technology'. From the management side, the CBI replied a year later with 'Jobs-facing the future', and these two documents still reflect the collective views of management and the trade unions.

The Trades Union Congress

In contrast to earlier technological innovations, when the trade unions were invariably forced to respond retrospectively, information technology permitted a considered, collective response. Because of the distinctive, confederal nature of British trade unionism – with its complex multi-union mix of craft, general, industrial and white-collar unions – this was not easy to provide, but 'Employment and Technology' offered a collective view and has remained the central position of the TUC. It contained an essential 'checklist for negotiators', which can be summarized as follows:

1. Basic principles. In anticipation of new developments, new technology agreements (NTAs) should be sought in advance: until agreement is reached the *status quo ante* should prevail. Union objectives (e.g. manning levels, working conditions) should be considered in full consultation.

2. Union organization. Joint union machinery should embrace all trade unions in the organization and be based on collective bargaining.
3. Information. Experts should be nominated to evaluate information, which should be provided regularly by employers. Training should be provided for trade union representatives (in work time and without loss of pay) in aspects of the new technology. In this way, expertise can be developed in areas such as health and safety.
4. Employment and output. The new technology should be used to increase output (products and services), *not* to cut manning. Job security should be guaranteed through retraining, and any necessary redundancy schemes should be negotiated.
5. Retraining. Mutually agreed training schemes should be set up.
6. Hours of work. Companies should aim for a 35-hour week, longer holidays, sabbaticals, earlier retirement, flexible working hours and the elimination of systematic overtime.
7. Distributing the benefits. Pay increases for any new skills should not create divisions between high- and low-skilled: benefits should be spread.
8. Control over work. Care should be taken over machines that permit employers greater control. Computer-gathered information should not be used for monitoring work performance. Trade unions should be involved from the design stage onwards.
9. Health and safety. Machines, such as VDUs, should be carefully monitored for any hazardous effects.
10. Reviewing progress. Joint trade union/management teams should be set up to monitor the effects of installing new technology.

Congress resolutions in 1994 and 1995 provided less specific recommendations – reflecting the TUC's growing view that IT applications had become increasingly diverse – but the broad areas of concern remain those first expressed in the 1979 statement. An unpublished internal report in 1996 called for trade unions to recognize the importance of IT in generating growth; to cooperate with employers in introducing it; and to be at the forefront of technological change and development. For their part, employers were called upon to consult workforces and trade unions, invest in training, ensure job security, address health and safety issues and not to use IT for monitoring purposes – all of which reinforces the earlier report.

While this viewpoint clearly reflects many of the pessimists' concerns discussed in earlier chapters, the TUC's response has been essentially neutral – at the mid-point on our continuum. In no sense has the trade union movement been antagonistic towards IT, for it recognizes that its adoption is essential to Britain's continuance as an advanced industrialized nation, but the TUC highlights the fact that union support is conditional upon certain safeguards being met. The statements are also sectional in outlook, focusing on how technology could affect the workplace, which is perhaps understandable given the trade union movement's more limited range of practical concerns – wages, job losses, work conditions etc. – but stand in contrast to the work of certain trade unionists (e.g. Jenkins and Sherman) who have discussed broader, societal aspects of information technology. However, like them, the TUC does not debate whether new technology is 'good' or 'bad', but rather concerns itself with the choices that must be made regarding its adoption. Consequently, the TUC is not providing policy statements so much as a set of *guidelines* for negotiators: the important choices have to be made in the workplace, the micro level of analysis, i.e. the bottom point of our model (Fig. 2.2). To summarize: the TUC's position is that Britain must remain in the vanguard of technological change, for (hopefully) this will result in greater wealth and less work, which should in turn allow for a shorter working week, more leisure time, earlier retirement and a higher quality of life. The concern is not with technological innovation *per se*, but how it is implemented and controlled.

The danger of adopting a 'middle of the road' position, however, is that it lays the movement open to accusations of being defensive, adaptive and cowardly, and critics (especially those of a pessimistic persuasion) have called for a more committed stance against possible dangers. To be fair to the TUC, a middle position needn't be a 'neutral' one, nor is to see technology as neutral necessarily the abandonment of a position, but unfortunately it is easily seen this way. The problem for the TUC is that it has to represent a disparate (and often feuding) membership; its influence over members (certainly in comparison with other countries) is generally weak; and it has limited research resources on which to draw when preparing reports. Most important of all, the movement finds itself increasingly faced with an acute dilemma: among its many concerns, two have traditionally remained paramount – the desire for improved standards of living and the need to preserve jobs – but these now seem to be in direct opposition to each other. The TUC needs to raise its sights and address more fundamental questions concerning the social role of technology, but this is not easy given its traditional concern with substantive matters. The outcome is that key issues become submerged beneath a tide of technological inevitability.

All the evidence suggests that shopfloor resistance is not an issue. Northcott *et al.* (1986), in a study of robotic applications in British industry, claimed that 17% of firms cited *better* industrial relations after introducing robots. A third expected shopfloor opposition, but only 2% experienced it: workers were favourable towards robots in 71% of factories and unfavourable in only 4%. Similarly Daniel (1987) (in a study of 2019 workplaces) found that workers generally supported the introduction of new technology and that trade unions were no obstacle to technological change. Management rarely had to use consultation or negotiation to win consent. Any resistance was likely to relate to 'organizational change' rather than to the technology itself, but even this was minimal. If anything, union shops were *more* likely to introduce technical change than places where unions were not recognized, and the higher the level of union membership, the greater the likelihood of change. Moreover, this picture is confirmed in comparison with other countries. In a major study of Britain, France and Germany, Northcott *et al.* (1985) found that union opposition proved a major difficulty for 16% of French firms, 14% in Germany, but only 7% in Britain. Such findings certainly dispel the myth of 'union resistance'. Robbins and Webster (1982) believe that the unions have largely accepted new technology on terms set by management: conceding to the 'imperatives' of technology, they have 'responsibly' accepted the pervading emphasis on profitability, efficiency and international competitiveness.

The Confederation of British Industry
In that business people and industrialists are essentially 'doers' rather than 'thinkers' it is perhaps not surprising that they have been largely absent from discussions over the benefits or otherwise of information technology. The central aim of employers has always been to optimize output, profits and control, and they have seen machinery and technology as important mechanisms for doing this. Microelectronics is no different; it is merely a further stage in technological progress and should not be treated as 'something special'. Consequently, as Lobban (1985) points out, managers have been keen to include new technology in normal collective bargaining procedures rather than negotiate NTAs, as separate agreements can cause damaging delays, cumbersome arrangements, problems over defining new technology and inflexibility in work patterns. Those managers who do express a view on the matter welcome the

removal of restrictive practices, the adoption of more flexible work patterns, the reduction in staffing levels and the greater opportunities for incentive payments and other productivity improvements. But, for the most part, the issue does not greatly concern them. The main requirement is 'keeping the show on the road' and remaining competitive: like their American counterparts they tend to hold to the dictum 'What's good for General Motors is good for America', and support new technology if it appears financially beneficial for their company and the UK. They would further argue that 'What's good for the company is good for the workforce', and consequently, like their trade union counterparts, tend to view new technology sectionally – from the standpoint of their company or industry – rather than from any global perspective. In that they find it advantageous to remain optimistic over most aspects of their work, so they tend to be optimistic with regard to new technology, though this is often by default rather than from any clear understanding of the issues involved.

This straightforward, if rather simplistic, viewpoint is reflected in the pronouncements of the CBI, which has generally welcomed information technology on the grounds that 'fuller employment will not stem from artificial protection of jobs but from the development of the economy: the primary need is for the British economy to be competitive and if this necessitates the adoption of new technology, then so be it'. As the title of the CBI report suggests, the focus is very much on jobs and competitiveness and is generally in line with the government's 'automate or liquidate' stance, which we discussed in Chapter 3.

But there are two separate senses in which we can consider managers as optimists or pessimists, and while many may be optimistic as to what IT might achieve and provide, they may be less so in terms of their ability to install it effectively. John Banham, then CBI Director General, made this point in 1989 when he maintained that British companies would be in deep trouble unless they prepared IT strategies, but feared that only a few were ready to do so. These two aspects – the technology itself and management's capacity to adopt it – will be discussed in more detail later.

What is interesting is that if one compares the collective responses from both sides of industry, and delves beneath the rhetoric and inevitable variations in terminology – the TUC talks of negotiation where the CBI talks of consultation – the differences are not as far apart as one might expect. While the CBI's overall stance might be considered more optimistic than the TUC's, it is similarly cautious over many issues and seems to give qualified support to many trade union views. There are certainly differences of emphasis – the TUC is less clear about union demarcation lines and the CBI less precise over job security – but both sides stress the importance of retraining, the fear of unemployment, the dangers of skill divisions, the case for sabbaticals and longer holidays and the key role of the state. Both sides acknowledge that information technology is an issue requiring close consultation and that trade unions have a central role to play.

THE TRADE UNIONS

It may seem ironic, but we have probably seen less division at the collective level, *between* the TUC and CBI, than *within* the ranks of the TUC itself. While the collective picture is one of unanimity and consensus, there has been considerable conflict between individual unions. The response of national leaders has been sectional – very much in terms of how their particular membership might be affected – and given that the primary duty of any trade union leader is to protect and project the interests of members, this is perfectly understandable, but it becomes a cause for concern if, as has happened, the stance of one union jeopardizes the interests of another.

Writing in the 1980s, Bamber (1980), McLoughlin and Clark (1988) and others made a useful distinction between

- those unions that saw new technology as providing benefits for members
- those unions who believed that new technology would lead to fewer jobs, but that resistance would not help the membership
- those unions who saw technology as a threat and only supported its adoption in accordance with strict conditions.

The central position, adopted by unions like the Banking, Insurance and Finance Union (BIFU) and in line with the TUC and most other unions, was largely led by white-collar unions which included workers that would be significantly affected by, but could also gain from, technological change. The former ASTMS and APEX unions were particularly prominent in this response, and the limited number of NTAs that emerged were overwhelmingly in the white-collar sector. Many of these unions held conferences, prepared booklets and policy statements, and even commissioned research, but their ability to influence decision making directly remained limited due to the rapid pace of innovation, the intricacy of the technology itself, unions' limited resources, the complexities of union structure, the power of the multinationals and the weakness of trade unions during economic recession. There tended, therefore, to be an air of inevitability about the trade union response: the technology would come, for better or worse, and little would be gained from trying to resist it.

Other unions, however, took a stance that was, in turn, either emphatically more optimistic or pessimistic. The likes of the Electrical, Electronic, Telecommunication and Plumbing Union (the former EETPU) saw much to gain from information technology because microelectronics would lead to some engineers being more accurately described as electricians, and indeed the EETPU were accused of 'poaching' members from the engineering union. The strategy of the electricians was strongly expansionist: they saw themselves in the vanguard of technological change and believed that their skills would grow in importance as IT became increasingly prevalent. The union recognized 'the need to foster the introduction of new technology enthusiastically in all sectors of the engineering industry'. Likewise, Post Office engineers in the National Communications Union (NCU) adopted an optimistic stance, helped no doubt by the fact that collective bargaining is centralized and only takes place with one central public sector employer.

The small group of unions who expressed resistance to new technology were mainly concentrated in broadcasting and the printing industry. They were strongly protectionist, concerned to defend the traditional skills of craft workers but, ironically (as Robbins and Webster show), their formal response in the early 1980s – in terms of policy statements, discussion documents, conferences etc. – was decidedly muted. Any thought that the new technology would simply go away, however, received a sharp rebuttal over the next few years. Matters came to a head with various disputes involving the Association of Cinematograph, Television and Allied Technicians (ACTT) and the ITV companies and between the National Graphical Association (NGA) and certain newspaper groups, including Eddie Shah's Stockport Messenger and Rupert Murdoch's News International. Even though neither union still exists in the same form, and to many these disputes are now a distant memory, they epitomized the problems that IT can create in the field of industrial relations.

The Wapping dispute
Though the events took place over a decade ago, the opening of Rupert Murdoch's newspaper plant at Wapping remains a watershed. It high-

lighted, remarkably clearly, the changes that can be wrought on an industry by new technology; the bitterness that can result from its introduction; and the divisions that can emerge within the trade union movement. Consequently, we discuss it in some detail.

The story really starts at the Stockport Messenger plant in 1983, when the owner, Eddie Shah, used the provisions of the new industrial relations legislation to prevent the NGA from maintaining a closed shop. Information technology had made it possible for newspapers to be produced more cheaply (with savings of up to 80%); swiftly (with stories written direct on to VDUs and transferred immediately to sub-editors for correction); efficiently (with stories beamed by satellite from anywhere in the world); and accurately (with typing errors being checked and rectified instantly). Shah's declared aim was to bypass the traditional print unions; negotiate a no-strike deal with the EETPU; and launch a new national newspaper, *Today*, by the spring of 1986. In doing this he would also circumvent Fleet Street, the traditional home of the newspaper industry, and break its long-established monopoly.

National newspaper proprietors quickly became aware of the implications of Shah's actions: a number renegotiated with the print unions, and Rupert Murdoch (News International) met them in October 1985 to negotiate a no-closed shop, no-strike deal for the production of the proposed *London Post* at his new factory at Wapping. He claimed that overstaffing and disruption had become serious problems at existing plants and were threatening the very existence of his company: consequently, he wanted a joint commitment from the unions and a new agreement. For their part, the print unions wanted guaranteed 'jobs for life' and inflation-linked pay agreements, but News International rejected this.

Murdoch clearly saw the situation as an opportunity to restructure industrial relations. Newspaper proprietors had talked for some time of introducing new technology and reforming Fleet Street practices, but it was Murdoch who 'bit the bullet' and made the first move. Though News International never confirmed the installation of 'direct input' technology at Wapping, computer systems had in fact been secretly assembled, tested at a warehouse in Woolwich, and smuggled into the Wapping plant. In January 1986 the company informed the unions that collective agreements with their members would be terminated; that the *Sunday Times* supplement would be produced at Wapping; and that the four national titles could follow. The Society of Graphical and Allied Trades (SOGAT 82) and the NGA, the print unions, announced a 5–1 ballot majority for industrial action, but News International considered that in taking such action the print workers were, in effect, dismissing themselves. Journalists were informed of the move to Wapping (which they accepted by a majority vote); EETPU and ex-NGA members were 'bussed in' to produce the papers; and arrangements were made for lorry drivers to distribute them.

On Sunday 26 January 1986, Rupert Murdoch proved that it was possible to produce two mass circulation Sunday newspapers without a single member of his existing print workforce; without using the railways; and with roughly one fifth of the numbers that he had previously employed. Fleet Street, as we had known it, had ceased to exist.

In an attempted compromise, the TUC proposed a seven-point plan for flexible working and a no-disruption agreement which would have allowed all the print unions to be represented at Wapping, but News International rejected the deal. The general council ordered sanctions against News International, while the company took out writs against SOGAT 82 to prevent unlawful picketing.

February saw the first mass picket – with 3000 taking part, 29 arrests and three police officers injured – but it failed to seal off the barbed wire-enmeshed plant. Furthermore, because the print unions had no members at Wapping it was deemed 'secondary picketing' and therefore illegal under the new industrial relations legislation (as it had been at the Stockport Messenger). SOGAT 82 were fined £25 000 and had £17 million assets seized under a High Court order. As compensation, Murdoch offered a £10 million printing plant to the unions (for them to print a new daily newspaper) and a series of settlement packages, but these were all rejected. The number of demonstrators rose to 7000, and in January 1987 News International announced that it would seek damages from SOGAT 82 and the NGA for continuing to picket following the granting of the injunction. In January 1987, the print union SOGAT 82 called off the dispute and were followed a month later, somewhat reluctantly, by the NGA. In 1991 the two unions merged to form the Graphical, Paper and Media Union (GPMU).

The 13-month dispute – which was not just between News International and the print unions, but within the ranks of all trade unionists – was especially bitter. Policing the dispute cost £4.7 million; 1058 people were convicted of public order offences; 400 policemen were injured; there were over a thousand attacks on drivers and vehicles; one worker was accidentally killed by a lorry; and another committed suicide. Over 5000 printworkers lost their jobs, of whom 1750 later accepted redundancy payments worth up to £60 million in total and 2000 found other jobs. The trade union movement found itself in a particularly difficult position:

papers were being written by NUJ members, printed by EETPU members and delivered by lorry drivers from the TGWU, while 5000 printers were out of work. Finally, it should be noted that there were even disputes *within* the ranks of the print unions themselves: many SOGAT 82 members in the provinces refused to support their London colleagues, and this was a key factor in the dispute eventually being called off.

Of crucial importance to the whole episode was the role of the EETPU. The union's general secretary, Eric Hammond, took the view that technological progress was inevitable and that just as blacksmiths were replaced by railwaymen at the start of the century, so printers were now being replaced by electricians: any temporary dislocation was unfortunate and uncomfortable for those involved, but it was the maintenance of a strong economy that would lead to new jobs and skills.

This compensatory view received little support from the print unions, who saw the EETPU as taking print workers' jobs at Wapping; colluding with News International in setting up the plant; and splitting trade union ranks. For their part, the EETPU denied any collusion with Murdoch, and were confident that if events resulted in the union being dismissed from the TUC, they could make it on their own. The events at Wapping put the TUC in a highly embarrassing position, with the print unions (and many supporters) demanding action against one of its largest members. After a series of debates the TUC Conference dismissed the EETPU in 1988, but it merged with the engineers to form the Amalgamated Engineering and Electrical Union (AEEU) in 1992 and was reaffiliated with the TUC a year later.

Information technology has transformed the newspaper industry. Protectionists find this depressing and lament the passing of traditional skills that craftsmen have taken years to perfect and the fact that thousands of print workers lost their jobs. They fear that a decreasing number of wealthy proprietors will continue to dominate the industry, making vast profits out of their newspapers, extending into other branches of the media, and maintaining a stranglehold on what people read and hear. In contrast, expansionists see information technology providing a more open and diversified newspaper industry. This has always been Eddie Shah's view: that IT allows for more, cheaper, well-produced newspapers; a better political balance between left and right; and the removal of Fleet Street's restrictive practices and outdated industrial relations. *Today*, for instance, – though it eventually folded in 1995 – was launched for the comparatively small sum of £20 million and kept going for seven years with relatively modest circulation figures. Likewise, the *Independent* –

launched with a similar amount and regarded by many as a certain failure from the outset – has managed, albeit with difficulty, to continue as a quality newspaper. (Others would add that we have also witnessed the *Sunday Sport!*) Having said this, we would not wish to overstate the case: new technology is still expensive to install and there have been spectacular failures (e.g. *News on Sunday*, *London Daily News*, *The Post*), but after Wapping things changed irreversibly. By 1989 all the major newspaper groups had moved out of Fleet Street – not just to new sites and new technology, but to new forms of industrial relations. By 1995 the Wapping plant had over 500 computer terminals – one of the largest concentrations anywhere in the world; the *Financial Times* was running its printing plant with 170 workers instead of the previous 600; and Associated Newspapers were adopting new advanced printing processes such as flexography.

As a footnote, we should also add that when Britain started producing national newspapers from computer keyboards, we were already, in comparison with many other countries, two decades behind the times: the 'new' technology of the mid-1980s was, in fact, old. Direct electronic publishing had already started and further advances could eventually mean the replacement of newspapers altogether (as we saw in the last chapter) and an end to thousands of tons of paper being carted around the country.

INDUSTRIAL MANAGEMENT

If we consider management in the way we have considered trade unions, i.e. in terms of different sectional areas, then it becomes more difficult to conclude that those in certain sectors appear noticeably more optimistic or pessimistic. While, as we saw earlier, the CBI may speak with a united voice, the fact is that across British industry and commerce the response to IT has been decidedly uneven. Sectors that have made increasing use of IT would include banking, finance and insurance, while areas of manufacturing industry – cars, aircraft, rubber, plastics, metal goods, mechanical and electrical engineering etc. – have invested significantly in CAD/CAM, FMS, and robots, but *within* particular sectors some companies (as we saw in Chapter 4) have adopted new technology far more extensively than others. The crucial factor seems to be the make-up of a particular company and much comes down to the commitment and expertise of particular managers.

As we noted earlier, some managers express optimism over possible uses of new technology, especially if they appear to assist day-to-day operations (e.g. gathering, processing and distributing information) and provide greater management control, and many IT applications certainly do this. Our experience has been, however, that many managers also acknowledge a debit side, especially with regard to deskilling and health and safety factors, which perhaps helps to explain why these issues have received greater attention in the UK than, say, the USA.

But, as we saw earlier, in the remarks of John Banham, the question of whether managers are optimistic or pessimistic about IT is not as important as whether British management are responding at all. In the early 1980s the government made extensive efforts to interest companies in IT (through the likes of their MAP programme), but, while around 100 companies a month were approaching the Department of Industry for assistance by 1983, over 50% of firms were still making no use of new technology. Surveys in the mid-1980s found that a quarter of British firms had made no significant change to their production methods since the 1970s; those companies who were investing wasted a fifth of their money as they were unclear what they were doing; few companies had a technical director at board level; many were using the shortage of skilled personnel and the high levels of unemployment as reasons for not innovating; and 40% had no corporate technology strategy. A survey by the Computer People agency in 1989 found little change: 40% of firms said they badly needed more IT skills but thought that things were unlikely to improve. Daniel similarly found that technological innovation was restricted by a shortage of qualified and skilled staff, low management confidence, inadequate investment and poor managerial awareness of IT. Our conclusion has to be that while UK management may be optimistic over the potential *use* of IT, they are highly *pessimistic* as to their own ability to apply it effectively. They know that IT can help them, but they also know that they lack the necessary skills to make use of it.

Richard Scase and Robert Goffee (1989) confirmed this depressing picture, finding two-thirds of young managers in large businesses ready to quit and almost all the older ones wanting to retire by 55. They often considered themselves inadequate, over-worked, tired, demotivated and under-trained. Around 75% of UK managers have never had any formal management training; 20% have no qualification at all; and only 12% have a degree. This means that many managers are poor at delegating, and indeed, if they do delegate, their subordinates invariably lack the necessary expertise as well.

There is a curious paradox regarding training in Britain. While it is irrefutable that Britain is under-educated and under-skilled, many managers claim that their output is not constrained by skill shortages. The problem is that, because so many managers are themselves poorly trained, they fail (in many instances) to recognize the new skills that are needed. They are locked into simple technology and simple techniques because they lack the expertise to get out of them (Thompson and McGivern, 1996).

In some respects Britain's adoption of IT seems, certainly at first glance, on a par with other countries. Northcott *et al.*'s European study of microelectronic applications in 1985 found Germany ahead of Britain – but only just – and France coming a poor third. The survey covered 3800 firms, and estimated that around 51% of German firms were applying microelectronics compared with 47% in Britain and 38% in France. Larger firms were more likely to use new technology, and factories employing microelectronics probably accounted for around 75% of manufacturing employment in Britain and Germany and 66% in France. However, *centrally organized* automation for several stages of production, while the norm in a third of German factories, was only found in a fifth in Britain and France. This highlights a British characteristic: while the use of chips in British factories trebled during the 1980s – by 1990 over 60% of factories were using chips to automate production to some extent, and 13% were using them to develop new products or update old ones – our automation has remained piecemeal. Less than 3% were using robots, and only 8% had integrated their overall production. The new technology was being used in *old* ways (i.e. to replace existing machines rather than to transform work patterns).

Northcott *et al.* also found that whereas a third of British firms expressed difficulty raising finance, this only appeared to be a problem for 19% in France and 18% in Germany. Furthermore, opposition came from 7% of top and middle managers in Britain, but was virtually unheard of in Germany or France. All this confirms the picture that we have been painting: the inability of many British firms to invest effectively in IT has stemmed far more from management resistance, a lack of coherent planning, poor awareness and an absence of financial backing than from any trade union opposition.

A survey by PA consultants for the CBI in 1989 found most British companies ill-prepared for competing in Europe. Two-thirds admitted that their IT strategy was inadequate; only 11% showed a strong executive commitment; 57% had computer systems incapable of dealing with different European languages; 44% had systems that could not handle European currencies; and 66% never expected computer projects to be delivered on time and within budget. Companies also noted the shortage of skilled personnel: 77% said that staff shortages were serious, but only 12% considered telecommuting as a possible answer. The report concluded that, although scepticism is gradually disappearing, most UK companies are 'unsophisticated in their use of IT and probably are not realizing the full potential of the systems they are using'.

A report from Pergamon Infotech (Griffiths, 1987) confirmed the fact that less than 10% of British companies (maybe 15% in banking) were using information technology to competitive advantage, and most managers were more concerned to get existing systems under control than to invest in new forms of technology. The report confirmed that many British managers are frightened of IT; lack the necessary education and expertise; and are suspicious of computer specialists. As a result, there is a lot of disappointment with IT: a third of all systems seem to be installed in the wrong place at the wrong time – probably by the wrong people. The report concluded that what is required is a new breed of manager: one who understands technology but is primarily business-oriented.

Awareness among functional managers

The conclusion we reach is that managers do not seem to divide into optimists and pessimists over how they view IT so much as over their ability to use it. Some certainly exhibit greater awareness, expertise and confidence than others, but one is hesitant to suggest that this is more prevalent in certain sectors. An alternative way of looking at the response of managers – and perhaps a more fruitful one – is to examine the responses from different *types* of manager, i.e. to adopt a *functional* approach. When we do this we find variation across different areas of management and discover that some seem more optimistic than others.

Figure 8.1 appeared in a report that a computer manager prepared for a major UK multinational on how he considered different departments were responding to information technology. The *x*-axis represents the amount of computing equipment and systems available to end users, while the *y*-axis indicates (in the computer manager's eyes) the degree to which departments understand how IT can help in meeting business targets. The range in computer sophistication is from 'ignorance' to 'omniscience', and his conclusion was that, while most departments had a fair amount of technology at their disposal, this was not matched with much awareness of its potential. No department appeared above the ignorance–omniscience

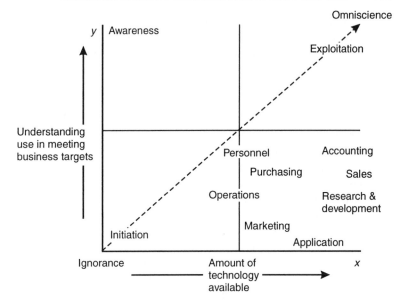

Figure 8.1   Responses of functional managers to information technology.

line – possessing more awareness than technology – though some did exhibit greater awareness than others.

This seems a useful model for analysing the varying levels of computer awareness and for assessing which functional areas seem most optimistic over using IT, and the computer manager's findings are, we suggest, representative of many other companies.

As we noted in Chapter 6, accountants have long been at the forefront of computer innovation – because most companies purchase their first machine for processing financial procedures – and, not surprisingly, score relatively high on both axes. Compared with their colleagues they seem optimistic towards the technology, both in terms of what it can do and as regards their capacity to handle it – they are expansionist and see many new forms of application that can be adopted – but this shouldn't be overstated. As we noted earlier, their dominance has, if anything, retarded applications in *other* areas, and accountants still tend to see IT as a cost rather than a tool; use it for yesterday's tasks rather than for developing competitive advantage; and fail to develop communications with other branches of management. Accountants may have computerized many routine functions, acquired personal computers and downloaded from large company systems, or even developed 'what if?' decision support systems, but their overall awareness is still limited. They may have moved from 'initiation' to 'application' but have not, as yet, moved to 'exploitation'.

Managers in areas like operations and purchasing are certainly not anti-technology, but their experience of computers is likely to be limited and they probably overestimate the power and flexibility of the micro. They may well have read glowing reports on information technology and expect it to answer all their problems, but they are quickly disillusioned if computers prove less effective than expected. Production and purchasing managers work in fast-changing environments, are stimulus-driven (problem-solving, fire-fighting, etc.) and do not tend to think strategically. They are not inclined towards detailed feasibility studies and planning meetings (which complex production and stock control systems invariably require); have a short attention span; dislike following specific procedures; and expect technology to work first time. Consequently, purchasing and operations managers have developed only limited awareness, and stock control and production systems are notorious for the problems they cause. Any optimism such managers may initially possess can soon become dissipated.

One might have expected that research and development (R&D) staff – in that they are likely to have a technological background, and are continually looking for and developing new ideas – would be an ideal group for IT applications, but this is not particularly the case. Take-up seems slow and numerous reports show that, although R&D staff have considerable access to the technology, they show little awareness. The main reason for this is probably that whereas systems relating to finance, operations or purchasing invariably interlink with others and draw from the same central database, those of R&D rather 'sit at the side'. Data used by R&D staff is usually 'self-contained' and, because of this, managers are often detached from developments elsewhere, which means they are less in touch with, and somewhat timid towards, IT applications in general.

Studies suggest that while sales is an area where managers show growing awareness and confidence – with the use of hand-held recording terminals etc. – marketing remains something of a backwater. This is perhaps puzzling given that, after accountants, marketing managers probably make most use of budgets, sales forecasts and planning data, but their low response perhaps reflects the considerable frustration felt towards computer departments; the fact that they are 'people-oriented' rather than technologically minded; and that they have rather been neglected by software companies. Overall they seem apprehensive towards the new technology.

The Pergamon Infotech report found that the response from personnel managers was low – 23% were still using completely manual personnel records – but, by the mid-1990s, things had altered with the coming of Computerized Personnel Information Systems (CPIS). No functional area should be more involved with computer innovation than personnel: central concerns such as labour displacement, deskilling, workplace reorganization, health and safety, training and data protection all require a proactive role from personnel specialists. In the 1970s and 1980s this was rarely forthcoming, due perhaps to the fact that, like R&D, personnel systems 'stand apart' from the rest of the organization, but we suggest it also reflected the non-technological background of many personnel managers. During the 1990s, however, personnel departments (often retitled Human Resources) came to play a greater strategic role and were transformed into a 'people accounting' function, providing employee data, reports, statistics and analysis. CPIS, especially in a period of recession, can assist in trying to utilize staff as effectively as possible and greater use has been made of IT over the past decade. Personnel, however, should not only use IT but should *facilitate* it – assisting others to make informed choices – in dealing with the many human issues.

Finally, it should be recorded that, even though they don't figure in the computer manager's model, computer staff themselves are not especially visible among the ranks of the optimists – in either sense. Ironically perhaps, they have not been the most widespread users of information technology. As we saw in Chapter 6, technological change has been staggering, and many computer managers, disturbed by such fast-moving developments, are apt to cling to old-style procedures. Many were brought up on mainframes, feel at home with them and, consequently, have shown little enthusiasm for IT – perhaps for the simple reason that they can get what they want, and more, from the mainframe. Because they are not IT-oriented they can remain unaware of new opportunities; are sceptical of micros; worry over demands from end users; and are suspicious of the departmental restructuring (e.g. outsourcing) to which they have become subject. Though they may have *initiated* change in the 1960s and 1970s, they have increasingly, like their managerial colleagues, become pessimistic over their place in the work organization and, as we saw in Chapter 6, protectionist towards their specialist skills.

RESPONSES IN THE WORKPLACE

This discussion of different trade unions, industrial sectors and branches of management provides us with a useful overview and allows us to draw broad comparisons between Britain and other countries. But our main conclusion has to be that there is great *unevenness* in the British response. Broad generalizations must not be allowed to mask the fact that while some unions and managers may be extremely well informed over IT, and confident as to their ability to handle it, others are not. Similarly, while some have strong views on the possible benefits (or otherwise), many express no view at all. Much clearly depends on the particular company, or even a particular manager or union official: in short, we descend to the level of the individual workplace, and while it is beyond the scope of a general book such as this to get embroiled in detailed discussions of specific applications, it should be noted that it is at this level, through the adoption of a case study approach, that some of the most illuminating discoveries can be made. The Wapping dispute, for instance, while highlighting many of the key issues that arise in industrial relations as a result of information technology, also reminds us that it is in the workplace that the issue is most critically addressed, for other newspaper companies went through very different experiences. Indeed, apparent consensus at national level – between, say, the CBI and TUC – might even heighten conflict between managers and workforce if the latter think that national union leaders are in some way 'collaborating' with employers.

We therefore need to consider the strategies adopted at the workplace level, and in this connection Willcocks and Mason (1987) discuss five main stances which they suggest managers might adopt towards new technology:

- 'Traditionalist' managers tend to be hostile to trade unions and believe that they, and they alone, should control the introduction of new technology. This approach may secure employee compliance, but rarely commitment.
- 'Sophisticated paternalism' exists where companies foster a strong corporate culture and attempt to render unions unnecessary. (This is typical of foreign-owned, high-tech companies, such as IBM.) Employees are encouraged to feel that the company has their best interests at heart and, therefore, they need have no fear of new technology.

- 'Constitutionalist' managers see collective bargaining agreements as the bedrock of industrial relations and believe discussions on new technology should only operate within these (i.e. NTAs).
- 'Pragmatists' are managers who tend to deal with issues as and when they arise, adopt a variety of tactics and rarely consider a strategic approach. Many managers respond to new technology in this way.
- 'Consultative' managers involve employees at all stages of technological innovation. This approach is not common, but when used it is often successful, and there are signs that it might be increasing in popularity.

All these approaches – which represent a progression from authoritarian to participative styles of management – can be observed in different workplaces, but we should note that none offers a view that is explicitly optimistic or pessimistic. Traditionalist managers (who believe management should take all key decisions) may, for instance, feel confident about IT and eager to expand its application, or may equally be protectionist – anxious that IT could threaten their present position, professional identity, access to information etc. Conversely, consultative managers might involve subordinates because of their expansionist philosophy and eagerness to involve everyone in applications, or simply as a result of insecurity.

There is, however, evidence to suggest that the consultative approach is more likely to *develop* optimism. The DEP Manpower Study Group (Sleigh, 1979) – while stressing that there was no 'one best way' – found from case studies that companies who experienced successful computer installations did seem to possess certain features: they seemed to inculcate a sense of company loyalty (and often moved to single status employment); were likely to have a technical director on the board; provided extensive training programmes backed by a firm personnel input; exhibited strong executive support at board level; and were likely to contain 'champions'.

This last point is very important. Scores of studies show that successful applications (in every sense) often depend on a 'champion' – a manager at any point in the organization with the understanding and vision to see how IT might be used to the company's benefit, the energy and political clout to champion its cause, and the ability and confidence to take others along with the idea. This does not depend on a manager's specialist area, hierarchical position, or even managerial style, so much as the ability to understand the workplace and see how IT might be utilized – very much the 'new breed of manager' called for in the Pergamon Infotech report.

In our company example (Fig. 8.1) the personnel director was a champion, but it could as easily be any other manager.

With regard to the unions, Francis and Willman (1980) suggest four main stances that might be adopted at workplace level – total opposition, concerted opposition, bargained acceptance and total acceptance. Again, though total opposition and total acceptance may appear to reflect the pessimistic and optimistic positions respectively, this need not be so: a union might be optimistic about new technology, but totally opposed to the way it is being introduced, while another might be pessimistic but prepared to accept it. In practice, the first two are rare (certainly in Britain, if not in France and Germany) and while some have adopted the third approach by negotiating NTAs, the fourth is by far the most common. Coherent union policies and bargained agreements seem more likely in single-industry and single-employer unions, or where the union represents a single occupation, but most unions have still not developed a strategic approach to new technology. Indeed, Williams and Steward (1985) found that even where NTAs had been negotiated they largely failed, in practice, to meet trade union demands. If trade unions are involved it still tends to be with *traditional* issues – such as pay, grading, redundancy, and health and safety – rather than with key decisions over investment, type of technology, job design, training or employee recruitment. As with management, the main conclusion has to be, not that the trade unions are particularly optimistic or pessimistic, but that they have failed, in many instances, to develop appropriate strategies.

Dodgson and Martin (1987) give five main reasons why trade union policies have generally proved inadequate:

- The structure of trade unions and collective bargaining

Trade unions are essentially reactive; managers propose technological changes which unions either accept or attempt to reject. They respond to new technology *after* it has been introduced, when many key decisions have already been made. Because of multi-unionism at plant level it often proves difficult to present a coordinated strategy, particularly if the new technology creates conflicting interests between different memberships.

- Economic circumstances

The TUC's essentially tripartite-based policy, devised in the 1970s, has failed to reflect changing economic and political circumstances.

- The policies themselves

Trade unions tend to regard technology as 'given' and to remove crucial areas for negotiation (design, organization etc.) from the bargaining arena. Union demands are often statements of what would be desirable in an ideal world rather than realistic objectives.

- Resources for research

The unions are severely hampered by their lack of research resources; few have a researcher responsible for new technology. This makes it difficult for unions to negotiate effectively with management and to keep up-to-date with technological change.

- Employer strategies

Managers are reluctant to make new technology a special issue and to separate it from normal collective bargaining. They wish to keep trade unions confined to traditional areas; to make this consultation rather than bargaining *per se*; and for such consultation to be as informal as possible. This 'softly, softly' approach has meant that, during recession, employers have been able to introduce new techniques much as they liked.

A great deal, therefore, depends on 'champions' in the trade union movement too, for information technology requires fresh approaches. With *traditional* technology, negotiation centred around the technology itself (e.g. machinery, materials, layout), but with IT discussion focuses on *systems design* (working conditions, skills, work organization etc.) rather than technology *per se*, and strategies that were appropriate in the past almost certainly no longer apply. Unions are used to bargaining on *substantive* issues (wages, working conditions, hours of work, discipline etc.), but now they are forced to become more involved with *procedural* issues (i.e. the rules of the game). All the signs are that the unions, like management, will be faced with a turbulent time ahead, as a result of IT.

We are conscious that we have devoted merely a chapter to a topic that has spawned complete books (some of which are listed in the Bibliography) but we hope this cursory view provides an insight into how IT is affecting the world of industrial relations and how management and the trade unions are responding. We are aware that the discussion has, of necessity, been brief and that many areas have been excluded, but we hope, nevertheless, to have provided a useful overview of the situation.

Curiously, in a chapter supposedly about the *two sides* of industry, we found that much of what we said about the trade unions applied equally to management. The pronouncements of the TUC and CBI overlap in many instances; most unions and managers have said little on the subject; and much depends on the roles of individuals – champions in particular workplaces. The picture that emerges, certainly in Britain, is one in which management, unions and employees appear, for the most part, remarkably placid (some would say complacent) about, and certainly not resistant to, information technology. A dispute like Wapping, which rightly captured the national headlines, remains the exception rather than the rule. In most workplaces little has fundamentally changed; few have expressed strong views on IT. While information technology may eventually prove a catalyst for new forms of industrial relations, the 'old' attitudes of management and unions still seem to underlie the introduction of most new technology. Though some may appear optimistic towards IT, and others pessimistic, the vast majority exhibit little understanding, curiosity or concern. Perhaps in this instance it is not so much a case of dividing between optimists and pessimists as between the interested and the indifferent.

CHAPTER NINE

Citizenship

If the optimists and pessimists, in their different ways, both predict such dramatic changes in the work situation as a result of information technology, it is hardly surprising that they expect the effects to spill over into the non-work situation. In this and the following chapter, we shall therefore broaden the debate, and for that matter the technology, to embrace the issues of citizenship and life in the home. How are our lives being affected by the fact that more information is available, not only to our employers, but to politicians, the police, the medical profession – even ourselves?

The new technology makes vast amounts of information available, at staggering speed, to all sorts of people. Much of this will be straightforward factual material, such as information on theatre tickets or train times, but it will also include more personal information, such as medical or work records. A hundred years ago, few records were kept – apart from births, marriages and deaths – but now data is held on social security, taxation, education, employment and a host of other subjects. Clearly, such a transformation has enormous implications for life in democratic society, and for individual citizenship.

The key question is: do such changes enhance the liberties of the individual, or are they more appropriately seen as mechanisms restricting personal freedom? We can again divide between optimists and pessimists, and between expansionists and protectionists: between those who welcome the *expansion* of new technology and information for the administrative benefits it provides, and those anxious to *protect* the democratic rights, liberties and privacy of individuals. We shall consider these contrasting viewpoints on citizenship with reference to the central issues of representative democracy and personal privacy. The first addresses the wider concerns of the political system as a whole, while the second focuses on the rights of the individual citizen.

REPRESENTATIVE DEMOCRACY

In Western industrialized society, we set great store by 'democratic values' and the view that democracy is a 'good thing'. It is the fact that our political system is 'democratic' that distinguishes it from totalitarian regimes, and this ideal is shared by most political figures in Britain, whatever their particular shade. The right-wing conservative will voice the 'democratic virtues' of individual freedom just as the left-wing socialist will call for the 'democratic rights' of equality, opportunity and justice. But what does 'democracy' mean? It could be argued that the system with which we are familiar in fact takes a very imperfect form and that, despite the extension of 'one person, one vote', we have in many respects moved further away from true democracy. The notion of a 'city state', in which all citizens join together in true democratic fashion to pursue their political deliberations, becomes quite impossible in an industrialized society of nearly 60 million people. Consequently we have adopted a 'representative', or 'parliamentary', form of democracy whereby citizens form into constituencies; elect individuals to represent them in various assemblies; and only indirectly influence political decision making.

This ceases to be true democracy in a number of respects. In the first place, the member, once elected, is more a representative than a delegate, bound by the views of a party rather than constituents. There are also many instances where members, even governments, do not pursue the policies and views they advocated at the time of election. Thirdly (and this particularly applies to Britain), there is often little relationship between the allocation of parliamentary seats to particular political parties and the total votes cast. The 1983 election best illustrates this: although the SDP/Liberal Alliance received 26% of the vote to Labour's 28%, they secured 186 fewer seats and, more importantly, the victorious Conservative Party received the support of less than half those who voted, and less than a third of the total electorate, but was returned with an overall majority of 144. The alternative of proportional representation (PR) could create equivalent problems, for it is mathematically more complex; might well involve a series of elections; is slow to produce a result; removes the single-member constituency; and invariably results in coalition governments being secretly formed in smoke-filled rooms. Does the coming of information technology therefore have any implications for representative democracy?

Cable systems

Post-war politics has already been dramatically affected by a new technology – television. Television has made politics more immediate, more visual and more personal; it has changed the kinds of faces, voices and personalities that win elections. This is now being re-shaped by the coming of cable systems and the provision of a vast number of channels to people's homes. The effect of this will be for broadcasting to be largely replaced by 'narrowcasting', which has considerable implications for the presentation of politics. Up to now, politicians have used television to send short, general messages to large audiences, but this could be replaced by longer messages to smaller audiences. Britain has come comparatively late to televising its national parliament, and in the USA many cable systems already broadcast city council meetings. Longer, more detailed, presentations could be broadcast for minority groups such as Roman Catholics, Devonians, the unemployed, or whoever. As technology becomes cheaper yet more widespread, so it will have a special impact upon local elections, and viewers can become as familiar with their councillor or member of parliament as they are with national political figures. In addition, local interest groups should be able to broadcast in the free time usually available on cable systems.

Optimists argue that this is encouraging. New technology should provide greater access to the electorate, particularly for poorer candidates and minority groups; live television coverage should make politicians more responsive to the electorate than to powerful lobbies; and it should generally increase public participation in politics.

There is, however, another side. While such developments may appear as a stimulant to democracy, it must be remembered that the potential television audience now becomes dissected across numerous channels, and pessimists fear we may end up with smaller and smaller groups knowing more and more about less and less. There is also the fear that those interest groups with largest resources will be able to buy greater influence through the cable networks. Moreover, as politics becomes more interwoven with entertainment and commercialism, the worry is that it will become increasingly trivialized and polluted. Narrowcasting may fragment our perception of events, encouraging us to pursue news items that interest us in detail to the neglect of others. But this would be no different from the situation that appertains to newspapers, where we already choose to read those stories that interest us (or those newspapers that interest us), and the small number of cable viewers watching a city council meeting would almost certainly be in excess of those attending in person.

Electronic polling

An even more dramatic change could occur with regard to electronic polling, and the development of 'wired cities' through the likes of the QUBE system, which first began in Columbus, Ohio, and has now been developed in other American cities. Such systems can offer hundreds of channels of cable television and various two-way communication services such as electronic shopping, information services, home security services and voter participation (see Chapter 10). The latter operates by subscribers attaching a small black box containing several buttons to their television set, and tapping in their particular preferences.

The television announcer poses the question, the viewer selects from four choices, and the result appears on the screen within seconds. Initially this was largely restricted to fairly flippant decisions over quiz shows and soap opera endings (in which viewers could vote for a sad, happy or 'come back next week' ending), but it is also used for local political issues. The city's mayor, a local school board chairman, or whoever, can present a case for a particular policy and a referendum of the whole electorate be instantly taken.

In the USA, a growing number now receive these facilities, which clearly removes many of the shortcomings to representative democracy that we mentioned earlier. The case against PR, for instance, is significantly weakened because mathematical complexity is now no obstacle (second preferences etc. can be handled instantaneously) and the time-consuming element of conventional vote-counting is removed. But the technology does more than this, for it raises a question mark over the whole system of representative democracy – in whatever form – as we know it. Optimists welcome the new technology as a truly democratizing force which allows the city state (or even nation state) to reappear. Masuda (1982) terms this 'participatory democracy' and believes that people will demand more involvement as political decisions have an increasing influence on their lives. He envisages a society in which all citizens are equipped with home terminals (which have become increasingly cheap) and are given the opportunity to vote on particular issues. For instance, it might be decided that, at seven o'clock on a Friday evening, the entire nation could vote as to whether or not it wished to restore capital punishment. The vote could be preceded by a full-scale debate, and the result known in seconds. Such a system would dramatically affect the role of elected representatives as we know them, and logically encourage wider electoral participation.

The pessimists, however, are less enthusiastic. Returns from Columbus were certainly biased in that poorer people were less likely to be subscribers and were therefore deprived of a vote. In addition, one could not know precisely who had voted: do we want a four-year-old or a dog deciding over comprehensive education? It could further be argued that such systems tend to measure people's immediate response to a problem and do not encourage deliberation and analysis. Swift decisions on the Irish question, for instance, would almost certainly prove non-beneficial. It might also be asked why voters are offered four (in the case of QUBE), and only four, choices when there may be various other alternatives. Four options may be convenient for the technology, but it could well result in political over-simplification. Even with four alternatives, the way the question is posed might also determine the outcome (as many say happened with the only referendum Britain has ever undertaken, on whether to leave the Common Market). Most important of all, who decides on the four alternatives and how they are worded? Active political participation in instant referenda could well benefit existing power structures more than citizens.

While electronic polling may strengthen the *vertical* links – between citizen and decision maker – it could simultaneously weaken *horizontal* links between sub-groups – local parties, pressure groups, workgroups, families etc. – which, it might be argued, represent the true heart of democracy. The picture becomes one of individuals confronting and deciding issues in isolation, and as they become *less* organized, so power increasingly passes to existing bureaucratic hierarchies. The information is now used by power holders to *predict* public reaction – which enables them to circumvent it more easily – and if citizens fear that their opinions are not just being listened to, but also recorded and analysed electronically, this could lead to higher rather than lower levels of political apathy. With conventional elections, although voting is secret, it is done *in public*, and it is this that enables us to ensure secrecy. We might replace free voting in public with coerced voting in private (e.g. with key family members imposing their views on others). And finally, some see dangers for a society over-dependent on computerized systems: a breakdown of such systems (or their sabotage by powerful groups) makes a democratic society highly vulnerable.

ore it is argued that technology can be both beneficial and
he gains of access, immediacy, participation and visibility –
d by the optimists – are counterbalanced by the pessimists'
rficiality, simplification, indoctrination and triviality. While
information technology may expand opportunities for political participation, it could equally threaten democratic rights that need to be protected.

PRIVACY

Of equal concern is the delicate issue of privacy. As the power of computers
has increased, so the electromagnetic storing of data has gained in popularity. With cheap microcomputers and improvements in telecommunications, systems can now hold and process huge amounts of data and
make it available on VDUs based vast distances away. Optimists maintain
that this offers many advantages in our daily lives: they value the new
technology for the administrative benefits it provides and believe that the
gains will far outweigh any drawbacks. The claim is that the expansion
of new technology and information will generally inform, improve and
invigorate our democratic society.

Large data-processing computers are already integrated into national
and international networks, and central government departments, local
authorities, the police, social services, financial institutions and employers
all make use of computerized systems for holding data on individuals. It
is not always realized just how extensive these now are. In Britain today,
three government departments alone – the Home Office and the Departments of Health and Social Security – hold over 113 million personal
records stored on more than 30 separate computer systems, covering
vehicle owners, blood groups, prison records, unemployment benefit etc.:
there are over 50 million names on the Health and Social Security computers and 25 million (including every car owner) on the Police National
Computer (PNC). In addition, every taxpayer's details are held on the
Inland Revenue database, and at local level databases exist for local
authority housing, the council tax, electricity, gas, water, telephone calls
etc. The government's £1.7 billion Health and Social Security computer
project, 'Operational Strategy', is one of the largest computer systems in
Western Europe, providing benefits for over 24 million people; incorporating 30 000 computer terminals in 1300 offices; and containing all
National Insurance records and social security benefits in one massive
database.

In 1996 the government announced plans to create a Whitehall computer network linking all the departments covering benefits, tax, passports, driving licences, student loans, and numerous state grants from housing to community care. The aim is to create an 'electronic shop window' which will allow people to order passports, fill in income tax and VAT forms, apply for driving licences and claim benefits over the computer network. (The government would be able to reduce staff costs dramatically and sell surplus office buildings.)

Most data held is in no way sinister, and helps meet the needs of both data user and data subject. For instance, data held on one's bank account is of use both to you and your bank manager, and it is in both your interests that it is accurate, accessible and not obtainable by others. Indeed, in the field of banking it is questionable whether modern financial institutions could now cope without computers, for they have greatly eased the arranging of credit and processing of cheques as financial transactions have increased in complexity.

Similarly, the better the records of social security or the vehicle registration centre, the more this benefits both these departments and the individual citizen. Social benefits can be distributed more equitably and efficiently and checks can be made on fraudulent claims. In 1995 the Countermatch system – which can 'recognize' signatures and could save the taxpayer, it is estimated, £600 million a year – was introduced in certain areas. Such systems can provide the public with a much improved service as the important (but often repetitive) demands of the unemployed, sick and elderly are handled by technology. Optimists claim that the gains from such developments are considerable.

Pessimists, however, take a contrasting view and maintain that, far from enhancing democracy, IT poses a direct challenge to it. They insist that the overriding importance is to *protect* the privacy and personal liberties of the individual citizen. This addresses two main issues. In the first place, they are concerned over the ability of the state (and others) to 'spy' on an individual through new technological devices. British Telecom's System X telephone exchange system, for instance, is designed to allow 'official' telephone tapping, and specific calls can be routed to special centres run by the Home Office or BT. Similarly, the interactive cable systems discussed earlier not only allow citizens to voice their various preferences, but could equally serve governmental and private agencies with data on people's political opinions, buying habits, financial status, leisure activities, and family and friends. Other data banks could supply sensitive information on religious beliefs, medical records, employment history or criminal activity. This view approximates to George Orwell's vision of 1984, in which, it will be recalled, Big Brother and the party were able, through two-way telescreens, to 'switch in' and invade all aspects of Winston Smith's personal life. Such a situation is not unrealistic, for laser systems can now pick up conversations through processing the vibrations of a window pane, and electronic bugging devices have become increasingly sophisticated.

The second concern relates to the accessibility that individuals have to data held on them. Protectionists would argue that access to such data is a fundamental right in a democratic society. Data kept on individuals may be purely factual, seem fairly innocuous, lie dormant for years and offer no particular threat to the individual's liberty, but this does not answer the point that the individual has the right to know of such data. The main danger, of course, is that data users may prove incompetent, may misconstrue their own interests, or may simply be devious and criminal. In such circumstances, computerized systems do not work for but rather against the interests of the private citizen. Data held may be inaccurate, available to unauthorized persons or used for improper purposes, such fears being particularly prevalent in the case of police and medical records. The fear is that those in power, far from becoming more answerable to the general populace, may use technology to maintain and enhance their control. The machine takes on an 'objectivity' which never existed in the case of the official, and citizens feel that they have little recourse against decisions it imposes. Rather like the lie-detector, the computer acquires a mantle of scientific infallibility that is by no means always justified.

It is this scenario, with its accompanying violation of civil liberties that causes concern, especially as more information of an increasingly delicate and personal nature becomes available. This view is therefore more concerned with privacy than efficiency, to protect individual liberties rather than boost the effectiveness of state administration.

Cross-referencing

Expansionists are more optimistic and question why there is so much concern about computerized data. After all, the retention of personal records is nothing new: the sheer complexity of modern industrialized society has meant that for years governmental and other institutions have collected information on members of the public, and this has been generally accepted. Record systems have long existed in manual form and, in principle, computerized systems are no different. There is simply *more* data on *more* people, and this added complexity, it is argued, if anything assists anonymity and privacy.

Tapper (1983) optimistically maintains that the dangers from computerized systems are no greater than those that exist already, and that computers get a 'bad press' simply because any shortcomings are far more visible. It is in fact easier, he argues, to ensure that data in computer systems is complete and accurate, as automatic checks and warnings can be incorporated. He rejects the notion that the computer has somehow converted good uses of personal information into evil uses; if this is so, the fault lies with the operators, not the machine.

But why have the protectionists expressed such fear and suspicion? Campbell and Connor (1986) point out that, with computers, data can be processed at virtually any distance, vast amounts can be stored and (most important) different indexes can be cross-referenced. This last point allows separate sets of data, probably collected for totally different purposes, to be correlated, and in effect allows data to be turned into new information. With a computer, the data previously held on various sheets of paper in different filing cabinets throughout a range of different departments can be correlated into a comprehensive dossier in a matter of seconds. This is why many (including the Data Protection Registrar) are concerned about the proposed Whitehall computer network which would allow different departments to use each others' systems, exchange information and, in effect, create profiles on individual citizens. The government insists that such exchanges will not take place, and that electronic safeguards will be installed, but many fear that cross-referencing will occur.

It was the natural constraints of the manual system that provided the protection for our privacy: manual systems can only take so much data before they become unworkable, and consequently only the most important data is selected for storage. With a computer, the amount of data that can be stored is virtually unlimited and the tendency is to retain information that is irrelevant, outdated or even inaccurate. The concern is a simple one: it is perfectly acceptable that our doctor should have access to our medical records, but not necessarily an employer or a tax official. Similarly, while the tax official may know of our financial circumstances, we may not wish these to be available to family and friends. So long as information is dispersed between different agencies, our privacy is preserved: cross-referencing on a computer can destroy this.

Of particular concern is the possible establishment of a Universal Personal Identifier (UPI) for each individual – a single identifying number that can be used to access computer information from all the national databases. When the Lindop committee (1978) considered the issue of individual privacy in an electronic age they warned against this idea, but pessimists claim that we have now, in effect, developed this by creating a cross-reference facility between National Insurance Number and date of birth which provides access to major state systems. Countries such as France have already officially adopted UPIs and many predict that (despite an announcement from the Home Office in 1996 that any plans for compulsory identity cards were shelved) Britain will eventually follow the European pattern. The overriding concerns are that it makes information in one area easily accessible in another; permits swift and comprehensive cross-referencing; and, consequently, poses a threat to individual liberty. This becomes a particularly sensitive issue in the case of police and medical records.

Police files

It is the computerized records of the police that have caused most concern in Britain. In this connection, it is important to draw a distinction between factual data, such as car registration numbers, and intelligence, which includes hearsay, speculation or the personal observations of police officers. The first Police National Computer (introduced at Hendon in 1974) became the centre for a network of around 300 computer terminals, serving police stations throughout the country. It held data on millions of people: there were around 5 million names on the criminal names index, more than 3.5 million sets on the fingerprint file, 1.23 million Special Branch files, 29 000 files from the National Immigration Intelligence Unit, 160 000 from the National Drugs Intelligence Unit and 67 400 from the Fraud Squad, as well as over 34 million entries on car owners from the vehicle registration computer at Swansea. The system could deal with over 250 000 enquiries a day and, through radio networks, officers anywhere could be given information from national records in a matter of seconds.

The original computer has now been replaced by PNC2 – a more elaborate, extensive and sophisticated system – which contains all criminal records, criminal intelligence, details of stolen property, direct access to records held at the DVLC, a major incident/casualty recognition service, updating of records and improved automatic fingerprint recognition. Pessimists fear, however, that as police systems become increasingly elaborate they can easily be linked to other government networks, allowing cross-referencing to take place. Police systems already interface with CEDRIC (the Customs system), NDIU (National Drugs Intelligence Unit) and the NFIU (National Football Intelligence Unit).

It is acknowledged that PNC2 contains a considerable amount of suppositional data. According to the Home Office, the Police National Computer is not linked to any other central or local government systems, but Large (1984) claims that there is evidence of information being passed between tax authorities, the vehicle registration centre and social security offices. There have also been indications in recent years that associations such as the Anti-Blood Sports League are noted on licence records, and it is such developments that protectionists see as infringements of personal liberty.

Expansionists would counter that if a citizen has nothing to hide, then that person has nothing to fear. If sophisticated computer systems can assist in more swiftly apprehending criminals, then they are to be welcomed, and without doubt the facilities for storage, swift access and cross-referencing enable the police to provide a far more effective service. This can be clearly seen in the infamous Yorkshire Ripper case of 1981, where it is now conceded that more effective use of computers would have almost certainly led to an earlier arrest of Peter Sutcliffe. His sixth victim, Jean Jordan, a Manchester prostitute, was paid a freshly minted £5 note by Sutcliffe, which was later found in her handbag. Manchester CID contacted their West Riding counterparts and, through the Bank of England, the note was traced to a bank in Shipley and identified as one issued to a number of local employers, including the company where Sutcliffe worked. But though he was interviewed a number of times, the police were satisfied with his story. Much data was being collated on the Ripper, but by different police forces, on different themes, and with manual systems. West Yorkshire police were pursuing other leads, such as the tape-recorded voice, and the various data remained disseminated. A quarter of a million names were held on the manual inquiry system; over 115 000 written actions were passed to inquiry teams; almost 31 000 witness statements were taken, and over 33 000 house-to-house inquiries were made. This resulted in 24 tons of 'paper-held' information. It is easy to be wise after the event, but had other information on the Ripper been correlated with the banknote, it would certainly have pointed strongly to Sutcliffe, and a further seven lives could have been saved.

The police enquiry system, appropriately named HOLMES (Home Office Large Major Enquiry System), is now available to all forces and can store information that pours into an incident room and give detectives rapid access to it by scanning statements at up to a million words a minute. The system equips all 51 forces with compatible software so that joint investigations can be made more effective. For instance, if a witness recalls seeing a red car, the computer system can provide every other reference to red cars in previous statements; it can combine information from separate investigations; and an officer making inquiries about, say, a blue jumper can also be given references to jerseys, sweaters and pullovers. At present, however, the system is provided by different companies to various regional forces, which means that they are not directly compatible with each other. To facilitate compatibility, when needed, there is a central facility at Hendon that can be used to interface between any two HOLMES systems.

The police have also introduced a supplementary system for analysing information which can be used in conjunction with HOLMES – not surprisingly, this has been nicknamed WATSON! – and many forces use this for crime pattern analysis. PHOENIX (Police and Home Office Extended Names Index) carries full details of every person with a criminal record and has now replaced the National Identification Bureau (NIB); NAFIS (National Automatic Fingerprint Identification System) will be totally operational by 2000 and available to all forces; and NCIS (National Criminal Intelligence System), based in regions, holds intelligence data that is shared with customs, immigration and military intelligence. Police IT systems are, therefore, a myriad of complementary systems that are networked nationally and come under the umbrella of the National Strategy, Police Information Systems (NSPIS).

Most would welcome such facilities, and in many respects we already accept various forms of 'technological policing' in our daily lives without particularly taking exception to it. Most of us do not greatly object to speed checks on motorways or TV surveillance in supermarkets. Rooftop cameras are increasingly used for major state occasions and have been introduced at football matches to help combat hooliganism. A Home Office report in 1995 claimed that closed circuit television (CCTV) was playing a significant part in cutting vandalism and burglaries. Digital editing techniques make it possible to bring a face into instant close-up and greatly help in apprehending troublemakers. At the international level, the development of increasingly swift computer systems assists police forces of different nations in tackling the problems of drug traffic and terrorism.

Nevertheless, pessimists express misgivings. The fear is that different information, much of it possibly impressionistic, can be linked together to provide a totally spurious picture. This can be seen in the celebrated case of Jan Martin in the 1980s. Jan worked for a company producing industrial films, but her company was told by one of its major clients that 'she would not be welcome on their premises' because they alleged she had connections 'with terrorists in Europe'. Because Jan's father happened to be a former Detective Chief Superintendent, she was able to establish that the accusation had been leaked from the Special Branch. It appears that while on holiday in Holland she and her husband were in a cafe where the proprietor thought her husband looked like a Baader–Meinhoff terrorist, and rang the police. The Dutch police didn't pursue the matter, but the accusation stayed on the file and was relayed to the Metropolitan Police Special Branch. Campbell and Connor, in their detailed work on the subject, record similar cases.

There is substantial evidence that many employers regard any kind of police record, no matter how innocuous, as a mark against an individual. One American study tested a number of employers with files of job applications containing varying police records, and found that employers were far more likely to employ those with no record at all, even if the record indicated that the individual was later acquitted. Many fear police harassment over perfectly legal activities (e.g. protesting over animal rights) and suspect that unchecked data can build up to create an 'information mountain' beyond the control of the individual. It is for these reasons that the protectionists are wary of the police use of computers.

Another controversial high-tech device being used by the police, which we should mention at this point, is 'electronic tagging'. Under this procedure prisoners are confined to their homes rather than prison and have tags fitted, either to their wrist or ankle, which (under 'active' systems) emit an electronic signal that is transmitted down a telephone line when a probation officer contacts the 'prisoner'. The alternative 'passive' systems monitor prisoners' movements and set an alarm off in a control centre if the prisoner strays more than a prescribed distance. Tagging is now used in a number of American states, and supporters claim that, overall, it is proving a success. Prisoners certainly prefer it: when offered a choice between tagging or jail the tag acceptance rate is virtually 100%, and it is estimated that, in Britain, at least 25% of the prison population could be dealt with in this way. It can also be used in non-criminal situations: in 1995 Safeway supermarkets introduced tagging for young children who might otherwise get lost in their stores, and Prince William has used a tag while at Eton! Optimists see tagging as a further example of information technology providing us with new, effective and 'humane' systems.

But pessimists (such as the Labour Party, the Prison Reform Trust and the probation service) have given the idea a cool reception on the grounds that – notwithstanding the fact that many offenders will not be on the telephone – it harms the important relationship between probation officer and prisoner, represents an intrusion into private life that can lead to family stress and social stigma, and may be subject to technical malfunctioning. Indications are that the technology works well: in 1995 the Home Office experimented with the idea and were pleased with the technical results. But further problems arose when some criminals simply broke the curfew. One convicted shoplifter defied the ban over 40 times in a matter of days, continued shoplifting and boasted to the national press of the computer printouts he had received!

Medical records

A second main area of concern is medical records. These do not usually involve as direct a threat to individual liberty, but they clearly contain information of a highly personal and sensitive nature. The situation is similar to the police: the state may wish to create large-scale centralized computer systems for administrative purposes, while the medical profession is wary that these intrude on individual privacy. One might say that the Department of Health has shown itself to be expansionist while the British Medical Association (BMA) has appeared strongly protectionist. Anderson (1996a), in a report specially commissioned by the BMA, speaks of 'the undoubted benefits that information technology can offer', but reminds doctors of their duty to apply 'rigorous ethical standards to its use'. The BMA remains deeply concerned over the Department of Health's project to computerize health and family details of children from birth, on the grounds that the system fails to comply with the BMA's nine principles over privacy and data security. The BMA is not against computerizing medical records, but insist that safeguards should apply and that different forms of information be kept separate. They are not prepared to accept that personal medical records should be interwoven with data held for administrative purposes.

Anderson (1996b), in a separate article, presents a set of security guidelines, calling on doctors to address such issues as careless disclosure (e.g. providing information through telephone calls and faxed messages), computer theft and data destruction, access control (in many hospitals *all* users can access *all* information), communications access (e.g. dial-up modems from branch surgeries), information security on wide area networks (e.g. Internet communication), and information disclosure to third parties (e.g. social workers, police, lawyers). Because of these concerns Anderson is unhappy over the NHS-wide network on three main counts.

There is no agreed security policy in force and the BMA lacks confidence in those technical security measures that do exist. But, most importantly, 'many of the applications that the NHS-wide network has been designed to support are ethically objectionable in that they will make personal health information available to an ever growing number of administrators and others outside the control of both patient and clinician'.

It should not be thought that the requirements of the Department of Health and the BMA are necessarily incompatible. With care and imagination, different systems might well be possible with appropriate safeguards, particularly in view of the various forms of hardware now available. In that the Department of Health requires detailed, centralized records, these can probably be most effectively held on large mainframe systems, while doctors' practices appear more suited to small-scale integrated micro networks, where each doctor could operate a terminal holding patients' records. Such a system is far more effective and secure than the manual system it replaces, and releases the doctor from a great deal of administrative work. Those entering data to the system could have personal code numbers, and machines could be barred so that different information is available to doctors, nurses and receptionists respectively. If desired, such a system could even be linked to the Department of Health system on terms agreeable to all parties. Once again, it is a matter of choice.

IT also makes possible the use of medical 'smart cards'. Imagine that an elderly woman, visiting her daughter in Scotland, has a fall while miles away from her home in Kent and, in pain, tries to explain to a strange doctor about her recent hip operation and the painkillers that can make her sick. Her problems would be greatly eased if she was carrying a smart card, containing her complete medical history. Within minutes, the woman's X-rays could be downloaded and the doctor could arrange for a hospital specialist to examine her via a video link. This became a reality in parts of Britain in the mid-1990s. As one doctor put it, 'It abolishes geography. It brings the service to the patient'.

Some commentators (who I would term expansionist) believe that during the next half century the very nature of the problem itself will change, particularly as a result of advances in artificial intelligence. Sir Clive Sinclair, the British microelectronics pioneer, has predicted the emergence of artificial 'super brains' by around 2020, which will take over from the family doctor and other professionals. He forecasts the arrival of meta-computers costing no more than a family car and able to supply all professional knowledge. The machine would know each individual, his or her medical history and personality characteristics and, like the doctor, would supply prescriptions, comfort or advice. Likewise, there would be no need to leave home for education or to consult a lawyer. Sinclair believes that in many ways such a system will prove more acceptable, as it will free us from any embarrassment, reduce travelling and provide far greater control over personal records.

Computer crime

Christopher Evans (1979) optimistically predicts that crime will decline as more financial transactions take place electronically, security is improved, and people have less need to travel by car. Credit cards become increasingly foolproof as people are issued with PINs and, in future, owners might even be identified through fingerprint patterns. Cable systems will provide improved security systems – direct links to police, fire and ambulance – and we can expect fewer motoring offences as people (thanks to electronic communications) have less need to travel; dwindling oil supplies make motoring an extravagance; and the cars that do remain have considerably improved safety and security devices. In short, new technology reduces traditional criminal activity, though Evans acknowledges a possible rise in civil disturbance as society readjusts to new circumstances.

Pessimists would respond that Evans underplays the potential the computer itself provides for fresh forms of antisocial activity. He maintains that systems will become increasingly secure, but evidence suggests that one person's ability to devise new security checks is matched by another's ability to get round them. 'Computer crime' is now big business, and though continual attempts are made to check the abuse, leakage and dissemination of information, the signs are that it will remain a never-ending battle.

It is estimated that computer crime costs British business in excess of £1 billion a year; and this is certainly an underestimation, as companies are reluctant to admit to it. It is thought that around 70% of computer crime is never even acknowledged. First, there is the theft of hardware itself, as computers are increasingly constructed from separate, extractable components. In 1995 computer chips worth £400 000 were stolen from a truck at Heathrow airport; an armed gang stole £150 000 of computer equipment from a factory in south London; a national newspaper had computer equipment worth £200 000 stolen from its offices; and a factory in Scotland lost chips worth over £2 million. Thieves are becoming more sophisticated, and British Airways, British Rail, the Automobile Association, ferry companies, travel agents and even the Department of Transport have all suffered at their hands. Moreover, other computer-related crimes – improper use of personal information, unauthorized access to confidential data, tampering with computer networks etc. – are all on the increase. It is curious, but many firms still seem reluctant to spend the necessary funds to make their computers secure, and Tapper insists that if they did the problem would be largely resolved. The truth is that many computer criminals do not break in but fall in. Banks and other financial institutions seem particularly prone to criminal activity, which can include taking advantage of 'bugs' in systems, stealing and altering software, erecting home-made cash-point machines and fraudulent use of credit cards.

The paradoxical situation, however, is that while governments may urge companies to improve their IT security, they don't want the security to be *too* good. Advances in modern computing and mathematics have made encryption systems virtually unbreakable – it would take a Cray supercomputer a billion years to crack some of the codes now available – but this reduces governmental control over digital communications. (British Telecom's A5 system for digital mobile phones has been criticized for being too effective.) The US government in 1995 devised the 'Clipper chip' – which allows the government to intercept and decode encrypted information, which they claim is essential for keeping tabs on drug traffickers and terrorists – and want it adopted as a standard international system. But many individual computer users see this as invading personal privacy and have developed powerful encryption systems which are now widely available on the Internet.

Hacking

A particular problem is 'hacking' – where someone illegally enters and experiments with another person's computer systems. In the 1980s, two American teenagers, using domestic computers, broke into the Pentagon's secret ARPA computer network; seven other teenagers tapped into computers across the USA to make free international telephone calls and move telecommunications satellites across space; and police in Pittsburgh unearthed a nationwide network of hackers who were illegally obtaining bank, telephone and credit card numbers to spend thousands of dollars on designer clothes, skateboards, stereo systems and TV sets. In 1988, Edward Singh, a British computer hacker, was found to have penetrated defence networks on both sides of the Atlantic and, in 1989, eight Germans were charged with infiltrating military systems and passing highly sensitive information to the Russian KGB. Criminals or whizz-kids?

The problem has intensified with the growth of the Internet. In 1994 the Internet hacking group Internet Liberation Front (ILF) broke into Pipeline, an American on-line Internet provider and software company, causing access to be shut down for six hours. On another occasion, hackers installed 'packet sniffers' – programs that scan the first few dozen bytes of every data packet and note contents – and obtained passwords and users' names. It is estimated there are over a thousand networks that form the Internet, and that, on average, there are four break-ins every day. However, as we noted earlier, poor security is often down to the users themselves rather than the network: around 75% of companies attached to the Net have little, if any, security.

Curiously, computers seem to be throwing up a new kind of criminal. He or she is likely to be young, well educated, in a position of trust, and relatively honest in most other respects. (Campbell and Connor even cite instances where police staff have improperly obtained information from the PNC.) They may have political motives – some hackers wish to challenge the power that controllers of large-scale systems appear to possess – but generally they enjoy the intellectual discovery and seem attracted to computers in the way that others are attracted to crossword puzzles. Hacking is largely a lone pursuit, but, like trainspotting, it has its own subculture. Hackers communicate with each other, form clubs, share information and compete to crack specific problems.

Computer fraud (which is often a form of hacking) invariably involves money. The perpetrators are usually personnel within the organization who find ways into 'secure' systems to divert money, create spurious accounts and manipulate data. The celebrated case of Nick Leeson's activities in the £860 million collapse of Barings bank in 1995 is a good example of this. It is estimated that over a billion pounds a year is lost in this way by banks, building societies and other financial institutions. Meanwhile others, instead of cracking codes or fiddling data, are copying software. Such people are called 'crackers', and they usually copy and sell the software to make money. The issue here, of course, is not new: technology has long since made it possible to violate copyright on records, tapes, videos and books.

A final threat that should be mentioned is computer viruses: These have emerged during the 1990s, and over 8000 now exist world-wide. These are programs that upset or harm the computer on which they run and, as with real viruses, they are self-replicating; they will copy themselves on to every disk they come into contact with. When a virus runs it may do no more than hide itself in the computer's memory, so the user remains unaware of anything happening. A particularly sad case occurred on Friday 13 October 1988 when a virus, triggered by the date, entered various computer systems across Europe, including that of the Royal National Institute for the Blind in London, where £4000 worth of valuable data was wiped out.

The Computer Misuse Act 1990
The 1990 Act made hacking a criminal offence in Britain and created three new offences:

- unauthorized access to computer material (i.e. hacking)
- unauthorized access with intent to commit or facilitate commission of further offences (e.g. use of electronic data for blackmail)
- unauthorized modification of computer material (e.g. viruses).

The law also tries to deal with the international nature of hacking: someone can be prosecuted so long as there is a 'significant link' with Britain.

But the act has come under attack from various quarters. Definitions of 'computer' are considered unclear; many feel that the 'terminology' relates to the 1960s world of mainframes (i.e. batch rather than distributive processing); and critics maintain much will depend on how magistrates choose to interpret the law.

The first prosecution came in 1995, when Christopher Pile (dubbed the Black Baron) – working from his bedroom in Plymouth – was convicted of planting viruses on the Internet, causing millions of pounds worth of damage. Pile even wrote a virus-making guide which he left on computer bulletin boards in America and Europe. It took police nearly a year to catch him. Attitudes to hackers vary. As Williams (1990) points out, some regard them as a social conscience in an increasingly 1984-ish world: they show that computers cannot dominate us; they provide a reassurance of human ingenuity, intelligence, resilience and creativity; and they provide a test area for the actual security of real systems.

Computer manufacturers, government agencies and data holders, on the other hand, invariably consider them criminals, and many would not share Evans's optimism that as technology progresses so criminal behaviour will decline. Computer 'virus-writing' kits – which provide blueprints for programs to penetrate and attack systems – are manufactured for hacking enthusiasts, and all the signs are that computer crime is flourishing. The dangers, in terms of loss of data, money and even life, are considerable. In one instance a hacker altered the alarm thresholds on a computerized health system and two patients died. The situation seems analogous to that of earlier technologies such as the motor car: cars today greatly assist the police to solve crimes, but they also permit a whole range of criminal activities previously unknown.

Data havens

Another important issue is that of trans-border data flow and data havens. Satellite technology has made it possible for data from one country to be processed in another and, in the 1970s, many European organizations discovered that the cheapest way to update their systems was to do this in the USA, at night, when computers were not being used. In the Swedish town of Malmö, for instance, the local fire brigade had an excellent computerized system containing details on all properties, and if a fire broke out they knew in seconds how many men to send, how to equip them, how long the ladders should be, whether elderly people were involved etc. The data for this system was updated during 'quiet time' on a system in Ohio, USA, and such services proved highly lucrative, particularly for America.

But this also provided an attractive sanctuary for those organizations wishing to hold data (perhaps of a dubious kind) that was illegal at home. Some countries became 'data havens' – refuges for data that was illegal elsewhere – and a good example is Singapore, which became a data haven for certain Australian companies. In the 1970s, Britain too gained an unsavoury reputation as one of the last remaining data havens in the developed world, and many countries wished to divorce themselves from such activities, partly because of the implications for their own data-processing employment. Just as pornography, drugs and great train robbers seem to gravitate to those countries with the most lax legislation, the same appeared to be the case with 'dirty data'.

Nations began to protect themselves by introducing data protection legislation. Sweden was first in 1973, followed by other European states such as Denmark, Norway, Luxembourg, Germany, France, Holland, Austria, Belgium, Portugal and Spain. These laws vary considerably, but most cover data held on individuals by both public and private bodies, and are legally enforceable. Sweden suspended the Malmö operation, as the USA lacked legislation, and the Americans became concerned they might be cut off from European operations. Along with Canada, they too introduced legislation, but it was weaker in that it only applied to the public sector and compliance was voluntary.

Other countries, such as Australia and New Zealand, also passed appropriate legislation.

Britain's response to the data protection issue remained somewhat dilatory, and protectionists became critical of this. As countries began protecting themselves, and made trans-border flow illegal with those not covered by appropriate legislation, so Britain became increasingly isolated. For instance, an English firm won the contract to produce national health cards for Sweden, but the Swedes withdrew because they were not prepared for their health records to be sent to a 'data haven'. Much of our existing law was simply obsolete for an electronic age. For example, under English law, orders by email, sent by satellite, were not proper orders as they were not 'in writing'. Most importantly, the situation meant that Britain had no effective means of dealing with the growing problem of international computer crime.

In 1981 a Council of Europe Data Protection Convention came into operation which in effect created an exclusive club of member states who, having accepted certain principles, would then transfer electronic data only between themselves. As Britain became a signatory, this in effect obligated us to introduce legislation. Had we been left out and member states denied data to us, this would have run serious risks for multinational companies, major banking and financial institutions, and scientific research. Overwhelming support for data protection legislation came from the business community, the trade unions, the computer industry and the professions.

The drafting of a Data Protection Bill in Britain was therefore very much in response to pressure from the international business community. With new technology, the multinational companies are particularly important, for they play a major role in stimulating trans-national data exchange and have become adept at transferring data much as they wish. A single multinational may now operate its own communication network serving over 500 computers in, say, 100 cities in 20 different countries. National laws have become increasingly difficult to operate, and if problems arise over the holding of data, companies can store it in one country and process it in another, while manufacturing and selling in others. Such tactics might also be adopted to weaken the power of particular trade unions or workgroups, or even to obtain cheaper clerical staff. Information can now be transmitted so swiftly and cheaply that its location is increasingly irrelevant to the function it performs, and Kerr and Bell would no doubt see this as representative of the convergence they identified.

The Data Protection Act, 1984

Parliament passed a Data Protection Act in 1984, although as we have seen (and government ministers admitted this) it resulted more from political and commercial pressures than any burning concern over individual privacy. The British act is more about data protection than freedom of information – more concerned with the control of those who hold data rather than the rights of those on whom data might be stored – although recent decisions of the Data Protection Tribunal have emphasized the importance of the data subject. The act also incorporated the important principle of an individual's 'right to know' and in this respect deviated from the earlier Lindop report. Individuals may see data held on them and correct it where necessary, as it should be accurate, kept up to date and only retained as long as needed. Personal information may be obtained, held, processed and distributed, but only for specific purposes, and it should be adequate but not excessive for those purposes. The storage of data for speculative reasons is illegal.

Any users of computer systems containing personal information (including police computers) had to register with the Data Protection Registrar by March 1986, and tell the registrar what information was being held, where it came from and what its purpose was. The Data Protection Register, which is held at the Registrar's office and sets out the names and addresses of all registered data users and classifies the data they are using, is open to the public. Any data user (apart from those who are exempt under the Act) can be made to supply the data subject with a printout of all computer data held on them. If dissatisfied, a citizen can go to the county court or to the Data Protection Registrar. Any unregistered person storing computerized personal information is committing a criminal offence, and anyone found using inaccurate information is liable to pay compensation.

The Act thus provides individuals with five rights:

- to check whether any organization keeps information about them on computer
- to see a copy of the information, subject to certain exceptions
- to complain to the Data Protection Registrar, or the courts, if they do not like the way organizations are collecting or using the personal information on their computer
- to have inaccurate computer records corrected or deleted
- to seek compensation for damage by the misuse of computer records.

By 1996 around 190 000 data users were registered, but thousands of organizations (mostly small businesses) had still failed to comply, and the Registrar complained of insufficient resources to track down culprits. The signs are that many find the Act confusing, and there are disagreements over interpretation. For instance, a BBC publication on the Act said that mailing lists were exempt, but the Registrar only accepts this under certain conditions. Or again, the Act leaves the question of medical and social records to be decided by order, but in 1987 the Home Secretary agreed that individuals be given the right to check medical records as long as medical opinion was that the knowledge would not harm the patient. The indications are that the Act will evolve over time: it has already been modified in the light of subsequent legislation, and the Registrar's office continually revises its Guidelines. Moreover, the EU's General Data Protection Directive 1995 has to be implemented into British law by 1998, and this may require a new Act.

To summarize the 1984 Act, it is based on eight principles which require organizations to ensure that all personal information is:

- obtained and processed fairly and lawfully
- held only for specified and lawful purposes
- used only for the purposes, and only disclosed to the people, described in the register entry
- adequate, relevant and not excessive for those purposes
- accurate and, where necessary, kept up to date
- not held longer than is necessary
- made available to data subjects in accordance with the Act
- protected by proper security.

However, there are still important exemptions, including national security systems, home computer systems, club records, and information held for payroll and accountancy purposes. Lawyers may also be exempt in cases where professional confidentiality could be breached, while examination results are granted limited protection. Nor can individuals check information relating to tax matters or the prevention or detection of crime (which in practice covers the most sensitive police files), and there are also various discretionary powers vested in the Home Secretary with regard to medical records. Finally, we should remember that the Act does not cover 'expressions of intention' as opposed to 'facts and opinions', data held on computer systems for less than 40 days and, of course, information held on manual records (i.e. clerical files).

Criticisms

The Act has attracted considerable criticism from protectionists. In the first instance, the BMA and National Council for Civil Liberties (NCCL) have complained that, unlike most other countries, the Act only covers computer records, when 90% of medical records, for example, are probably still manual. This allows people to simply choose not to computerize in order to stay outside the law. Hewitt (1984), for the NCCL, acknowledges that computers increase the *scale* of the problem, but insists that the principle of the citizen's right to know relates every bit as much to manual systems. The BMA, meantime, is uneasy at the considerable discretion granted to the Home Secretary to withhold data appertaining to individuals' medical records. Even the supposedly independent Registrar is appointed by the Home Office (and therefore by the political party in power), and under the Police Act doctors are still required to supply data for police purposes. The BMA is concerned over all these issues.

The NCCL is critical of the definition of 'national security' which allows a matter to be so certified if a cabinet minister deems it so. They also criticized the Act for including the registration of computer users, but not computer *systems*. This means that the Home Office, for instance, can register as one user even though it may operate 15 major national systems of personal data. The form of registration therefore makes it difficult to ascertain precisely what data is being kept. In the case of national security, the NCCL feels that the public should know what files are held, if not their content. Hewitt also criticizes the omission of Lindop's 'codes of conduct', and questions whether the proposed voluntary codes will ever materialize into anything meaningful. Linked to this is the fact that the Data Protection Registrar has fewer powers, a smaller staff and fewer opportunities for monitoring than the Data Protection Authority envisaged by Lindop. The Conservative government rather saw the DPA as a 'quango' (for which it had a marked distaste) and preferred a simplified scheme that involved the bare minimum necessary to protect personal data. Computer users will only have to abide by the general principles, not any detailed codes of conduct, and there is a Data Protection Tribunal to hear appeals against the Registrar's decisions.

Many pessimists question whether the government is seriously committed to data protection legislation, and feel that the Act is 'too little too late'. Campbell and Connor insist that the Act is over-regulatory on many small, private computer users, but simply ignores the major national databanks, which have been the main concern of this chapter. Moreover, they maintain that the pace of technological change will soon make the Act obsolete. After the Younger report of 1972 and the even more radical Lindop report of 1978, the Act is seen by many as a pale shadow of what it should have been. In general, critics argue that the limited powers of the Registrar, the exclusion of manual records, the system of registration, the lack of detailed codes of conduct and the considerable number of exemptions mean that the Act is minimal, weak, insufficient and barely meeting the requirements of the European convention. It was primarily introduced to ease trans-border data flow, is designed to answer the demands of business interests, national governments and multinational corporations, and far more meets the wishes of the expansionists than the protectionists.

CONCLUSION

This chapter has considered the possible impact of new technology on citizenship, with regard to both representative democracy and the question of personal privacy. In each case the technology poses both opportunities and dangers. With regard to democracy, the technology could result in wider and more regular participation, but could equally dissect the electorate and provide tighter surveillance of political expression and personal activities. Similarly, in the case of privacy, more accessible data can greatly assist the provision of police, medical and other governmental services, but at the same time lead to data (possibly false) being held and manipulated without the citizen's awareness.

The optimistic view tends to have a *quantitative* emphasis in that it stresses the expansion of data (and new technology) and suggests that this will prove to be to the overall benefit of society. Pessimists, on the other hand, are less concerned with the amount of data and more with its *quality*: their fear is not that we will experience more data so much as that it may be distorted and inaccurate.

There seems no doubt that in future we shall experience more information – the issue is whether this can be both *open* and *protected*. In the 'good society', public life should be open and private life should be private, but the fear with new technology is that we could end up with greater public secrecy and less personal privacy. As we have seen, the focus in Britain has been far more on the issue of data protection than on the question of freedom of information, but the two are intertwined. How do we make more information available to citizens, yet at the same time protect personal information from becoming available to others? In a democratic society, citizens demand access to decision making, but wish to express that right in private. They also demand access to information that is held on them, but equally insist this is denied to others. It is this fundamental clash between freedom of access and confidentiality that is so difficult to maintain in a society where information technology is increasingly prevalent. The central dilemma is this. If society involves more people in decision making, then their views are more likely to become known to all. Similarly, if it produces more data and makes it accessible to those it concerns, so it invariably makes it more accessible to others as well.

The issues of access and privacy provide us with a 'see-saw' situation, for it would appear difficult to improve one without jeopardizing the other. This is not a new problem for democracy, but information technology intensifies it and makes the whole issue of citizenship extremely complex. Pessimists, such as the NCCL, are eager for personal data to be made more available to citizens, and Cohen (1984), in a study of different kinds of record-keeping systems, argues that opening systems and respecting the rights of individuals actually leads to *better* systems and improved democracy. But clearly, greater openness increases the problems of protection. Interestingly Masuda, an arch-optimist, argues on similar lines and believes that more open access will come about as a result of participatory democracy. This brings together the two themes of this chapter. He argues that by giving citizens participatory rights, we at the same time give them greater access to, and control over, data that is held on them. In his 'citizens' society', information technology is autonomously controlled by citizens and privacy ceases to be an issue. The problem with this scenario – in which presumably everyone has total access to all information at all times – is that the fundamental democratic right of individual privacy no longer exists at all. Each society must seek a balance between these concerns and introduce appropriate legislative safeguards. New technology does not impose certain measures: this is a matter of choice.

CHAPTER TEN

Technology in the Home: the Special Case of Television

Just as new technology is invading the factory and office, so it is invading the home. Work and home are not of course separate spheres of activity, for we noted earlier that many may work from home in the future, but here we wish to discuss mainly non-work aspects of life – leisure, hobbies, domestic chores, family activities etc. – and how they are affected by technological change. Again, because of the vast range of applications, we focus the debate by concentrating on particular forms of technology and, in particular, television.

Technology in the home is of course nothing new. Television, the telephone and the washing machine are obvious examples, but established products are being transformed while other new domestic appliances and facilities are becoming available. Take the case of television. Not only is the set now infested with chips – for tuning, colour correction, channel selection etc. – but the various graphics one sees on the screen are created by computer, and the major news items that appear 'instantly' from all parts of the world are provided by 'electronic news gathering'. Chips similarly appear in washing machines, microwave ovens, dishwashers, CD players, sewing machines etc. Particularly important, in the 'smart' electronic, networked home (which we mentioned in Chapter 2) is the way the chip can be used to regulate services. In the USA, the Breslin computer system will wake you up; give you the time, weather forecast and your day's appointments; switch on the radio and make you a coffee; act as a burglar alarm; open the garage doors; control all heating, lighting and cooling; address Christmas cards; play *Happy Birthday* once a year;

and maintain all financial accounts. Most remarkable of all are the domestic robots that can dust, vacuum, serve drinks, water plants, wash dishes and even operate fire extinguishers.

Technology can be of particular benefit to the elderly and handicapped at home. Many local authorities have introduced sensor-operated systems in people's homes, whereby an alarm is raised if movement is not registered over an eight-hour period. Alternatively, residents can wear emergency buttons that they press if they have an accident or become ill. Such systems are also proactive, allowing social workers to contact individuals for reassurance if they desire it, and in this way the elderly and handicapped can retain the independence of their homes while also receiving a 24-hour caring service. In addition, many authorities have introduced hand-held terminals for social workers to ascertain welfare benefits to which clients are entitled.

Generally speaking, there is much to be optimistic about regarding new technology in the home. It will remove many domestic chores, which even the most dedicated cleaner would find difficulty enthusing over; it can increase safety and security; and it should provide extra time and opportunity for more fulfilling family activities. Toffler talks of the 'electronic cottage', where work will be reintegrated with domestic life, as it was before the industrial revolution. Electronic networks, such as the Internet, will offer the chance to revitalize the home as a centre for work and play, education and democracy. Just as the road infrastructures engendered social innovations, ranging from the supermarket to the suburb, so now fibre-optic electronic networks will provide a new infrastructure for communication.

Pessimists, however, argue that the danger of a Breslin system is that the technology becomes one's controller rather than one's servant. Just as working skills are transferred to machines, so the human activities of waking up, ascertaining the weather, remembering commitments, making decisions etc. are taken from us and we cease to think for ourselves. As a result, the routinized work practices of factory and office spill over into the home. Reinecke expresses concern over isolation and loneliness as more people use digitally controlled washing machines rather than go to the local launderette, and play computer games on their own rather than bridge with the neighbours. All the electronic leisure activities are concentrated inside the domestic fortress; they do not encourage its occupants to look outside it. Moreover, computer games are often criticized for being violent, greedy and materialistic, and even for fostering sinister values. In Germany, for instance, anti-Semitic, neo-Nazi video games have been illegally manufactured, which pessimists regard as a very unsavoury development.

In similar vein, Simons (1985) talks of 'computer phobia' and suggests that the imposition of new technology on people's lives can create states of psychological and emotional anxiety. We become fearful of being outdone by technology in those areas in which we most pride ourselves. Why bother to play chess when a computer can beat you? Why bother to learn maths when an expert system can perform all the calculations you require? Why bother to play the violin when a micro-controlled synthesizer can do it better?

Personally, we find all this a bit strong. In the factory situation, the worker may experience feelings of alienation – be prevented from applying skills, or compelled because of noise and line speed to work in a state of isolation – but in the home, these effects seem far less apparent, if only for the obvious reason that one is largely one's own boss. There is clearly an element of choice: one does not *have* to use an electronic diary to record all one's engagements; and if you prefer playing bridge with the neighbours to computer games, you are free to do so. And surely many enjoy playing chess or the violin even though they know they will never be a Karpov or Menuhin. The debate is similar to the one surrounding television, often branded the 'goggle box' and 'conversation killer'. While it can isolate people in their homes and feed them mindless pap or even promulgate questionable values, it can equally stimulate, educate and inform, and as easily serve as a 'conversation maker' when people enquire of each other whether they saw a particular play or news item. In some instances conscious attempts have been made to locate new technology *outside* the home, as a way of fostering social life. In Scandinavia, for instance, communal electronic centres have been set up in remote villages to help bring communities together.

THE BRITISH RESPONSE

The extent to which British households will adopt new technology is constantly underestimated. Despite our reputation, certainly in the industrial field, for being less technologically advanced, the British home seems fascinated by new forms of equipment and gadgetry. A classic example was colour television: in 1965 the BBC predicted 750 000 sets by 1975, and ITV 2 million; in fact there were 8 million. The same can be said of video recorders (an American invention largely manufactured in Japan), where Britain has become the world's best market. More recorders are rented or bought in Britain than the USA (with four times our population), and nearly as many as Japan (with twice our population), and over 80% of homes now have one. Most important of all, Britain has been particularly prominent in the use (and manufacture) of personal computers: nearly one in three homes now has one (over seven million machines) – the highest rate in Europe and twice that of the USA.

A point to stress, however, is that most of this personal computing boom has involved *one-way* communication; or 'standalone' technology. The real gains obtained from home computers are when they are linked with external services in *two-way* communication – what are called interactive home systems (IHS) (Fig. 10.1).

One might imagine a situation where you have to stay late at the office: you telephone home to reset the timer on the cooker, draw the curtains and set the video to record a programme you would otherwise miss. While driving home you receive an 'intruder alert' and are told that it has already informed the police. When you arrive home the doorknob recognizes your touch and allows you to enter. Later, when watching satellite TV while the robot cleans the house, the doorbell rings, and by using the front-door TV you see who it is before letting them in. And so the possibilities go on: smart houses are expected to be commonplace in the next century.

Such developments, however, require the chip to be linked to the technologies we discussed in Chapter 7 (telecommunications, cable, satellite etc.) and, in this respect, Britain has been far less successful. Prestel, for instance – a British videotex invention linking subscribers to computerized databanks through telephone lines – was expected to replace publishing as the primary means for distributing information, and millions of 'linked homes' were predicted by the mid-1980s; but its use never became widespread. By 1990 Prestel had only 80 000 customers, and was being overwhelmingly used by businesses (for such services as TOPIC, the stock exchange reports), travel agents, road haulage companies and banks. In 1996, Prestel Online was launched as an Internet service.

Multimedia

It is interesting that while one in three British homes now has a computer, most owners see it as detached from other forms of domestic technology, such as TV and hi-fi. Most PCs, for instance, are kept in bedrooms, studies or attics rather than sitting rooms, but this is likely to change as consumer electronics and computing converge with the coming of digital

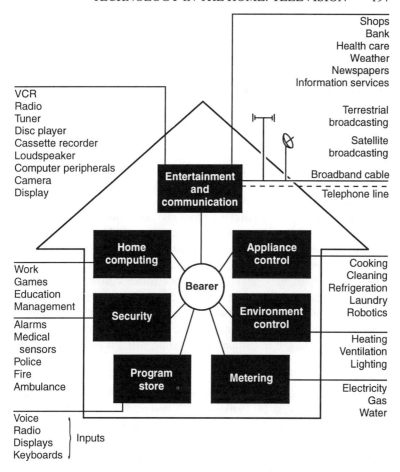

Figure 10.1   Application areas of interactive home systems.

transmission. The 'multimedia PC' will merge the various technologies, draw data from a range of sources – video, still photography, illustrations and speech – and mingle it with text and graphics created directly on the computer. Everything – computer, TV, telephone, CD-ROM, fax, on-line services – will become contained in the one 'smart box' which, in turn, will encourage the development of networking and interactive services. Banks and retail companies are aware of this. Barclays Bank, for instance, has launched a credit card division, Barclays Merchant Services, which allows subscribers access to the UK's first interactive virtual shopping mall.

In this chapter we therefore explore various new technologies in the home and focus on what is probably the most important, and contentious, piece of domestic technology – television. We use this as a vehicle to illustrate, once again, the division between optimists, who welcome these incursions into the home, and pessimists, who view them with alarm.

TELEVISION

Cable and satellite between them can provide a vast range of TV channels from all parts of the world, which now makes television more akin to the written word, with people receiving a wide range of communication (instead of a narrow handful of channels) and national governments increasingly unable to control or censor material. There will also be enormous problems of copyright, and just as people have for years (illegally) recorded material from radio and record players using domestic tape recorders, so now television material (often costing considerable sums to produce) will become available to all. This will greatly change – both in quantitative and qualitative terms – the style of TV entertainment entering the home, and certainly lead to major restructuring of broadcasting as we know it in Britain. But, overall, will this be for the better?

Cable

As we saw in Chapter 7, the development of cable in Britain has had a chequered history and, by 1990, cable TV had made little headway. Only 27 cable franchises had been awarded (covering some six million homes) and, with the possible exception of Westminster – where 6500 homes and 1000 hotel rooms receive 16 TV offerings, other information, home banking etc. – take-up has remained slow. By the mid-1990s things were little better: only one in five cable subscribers took the TV channels on offer. In the USA, two-thirds of franchised areas take the TV services, but it is thought that 50% penetration is a more realistic figure for the UK, and most cable companies would probably settle for 30%. Interactive services are promised soon, but with competition from satellite, Channel 5 and digital TV – not to mention video and the existing terrestrial channels – cable TV has a fight on its hands to become established.

Satellite

Satellite has been a different story. During the late 1980s, satellite business communications began to develop, and during the 1990s we have witnessed a steady growth in satellite entertainment. The early days were far from easy for satellite TV companies, and many fell by the wayside, including British Satellite Broadcasting (BSB), which was granted the franchise to run the first three direct broadcasting by satellite (DBS) channels. From a stationary satellite 22 000 miles above the equator, DBS made it possible for viewers to receive programmes on a dish antenna only 18 inches in diameter, but BSB proved unprofitable and merged with Rupert Murdoch's Sky (transmitting from the Luxembourg-based Astra satellite) in 1990 to form British Sky Broadcasting (BSkyB). Saddled with billions of pounds debt and continuing to lose over £10 million every week, many predicted an early demise for the new company.

Satellites come in three strengths – low-, medium- and high-powered – and, roughly speaking, the higher the power, the smaller the dish antenna needed to receive the signal. The early low-powered satellites needed a dish over a metre in diameter, and were therefore mainly used by cable companies or techno-freaks with big wallets and gardens. Astra is a *medium*-powered satellite, and, though initial take-up was slow, Murdoch had the financial clout to weather the storm and see things improve. In 1996 BSkyB reported record profits – thanks mainly to securing rights to certain sporting events and Hollywood movies – and cable and satellite channels topped 10% of all TV viewers for the first time, even though they were only available in 20% of homes. This showed the growth of satellite TV and, in October 1995, BSkyB added Disney and Playboy to its existing nine channels. Not that this expansion was universally welcomed: the Methodist and Anglican churches both sold shares in BSkyB in protest at the launch of the 'soft-porn' Playboy channel. But such protests appeared to have little effect on market forces: further 'adult' channels opened on cable and satellite in the mid-1990s.

Thames TV and the BBC set up UK Gold as a joint satellite venture, and Carlton and Granada followed with 'Gold' channels – showing old programmes. The Broadcasting Bill removed the barrier to ITV companies owning non-terrestrial channels outright and, in 1995, Granada revealed plans for four new satellite channels. The satellite world had arrived and seemed a natural one for the BBC and ITV companies to move into.

Digital TV

A major technological development that will have a profound effect is digital broadcasting, which is expected to be in place by the next century. A digital TV (or radio) set receives signals from a transmitter or cable in a series of noughts and ones instead of electrical waves. Turning broadcasting signals from analogue transmission to digital means much greater compression of data, improved screen and sound quality, and a vast range of other services – radio, games, movies, video, interactive services, telephones, business news, the Internet etc. – i.e. multimedia.

The 1990 Broadcasting Act made provision for a new independent TV station, Channel 5, and opportunities for launching hundreds of local radio and TV channels. Accordingly, in 1995 the government awarded the last terrestrial TV channel to Channel 5 Broadcasting, and a White Paper suggested around 20 new terrestrial, digital channels for the UK.

The 1996 Broadcasting Act proposed that the digital frequencies would be grouped together in six 'multiplexes', each capable of offering 3–6 channels. The BBC was awarded its own multiplex and a bundle of digital channels and ITV was guaranteed channels, but anyone is entitled to buy up to three of the six multiplexes, which critics fear will mean Murdoch, Disney etc. further extending their influence over British television. The act effectively launched a 'media ownership free-for-all', allowing an explosion of choice for viewers with the possibility of up to 36 (and eventually 500) new digital channels. The lifting of the two-licence limit means likely takeovers between ITV companies. Newspaper groups are also able to control ITV companies for the first time, but News International and the Mirror Group are barred because they each exceed the threshold of 20% of total national circulation. But they *can* expand their cable and satellite interests and run digital TV services. Many are concerned at the abandonment of universal access, and fear that certain regions may not be offered the new services. Existing channels will continue broadcasting analogue services alongside the digital version, but will be allowed to develop extra channels, widescreen services and pay-TV. BSkyB quickly announced plans for 'pay-per-view', and many feel that the BBC will be pushed in the same direction. The new services are expected by 1998.

The signs are that if the BBC and ITV do not respond swiftly to digital TV BSkyB will dominate the market. Rupert Murdoch – who is thought to be two years ahead in the digital race – has promised over 500 digital channels. Media experts predict a 'box war' over the next few years between a £300–400 digital *satellite* box offering hundreds of different services and a £700 digital *terrestrial* box offering the proposed 18 channels. The general consensus is that, for all their reputation and expertise, the BBC and ITV companies will have their work cut out to compete with the satellite companies. Conversely, some BBC and ITV executives welcome the opportunity to enter the subscription market.

THE THIRD AGE OF BROADCASTING

We are entering what might be termed the 'third age of broadcasting' – from radio, to television, to digitally transmitted satellite and cable channels. This will involve not merely a revolution in a technological sense, but also in terms of deregulation. The USA indicates the direction in which things seem certain to go.

The USA has witnessed considerable upheaval in the broadcasting world – especially since American law now permits TV and film companies to merge – and changes in the 1980s and 1990s suggest the market will increasingly be dominated by a small handful of large companies. Rupert Murdoch bought Twentieth Century Fox to create Fox Network; Disney bought the ABC television network; CBS sold out to Westinghouse; and Time Warner merged with Turner Broadcasting. (By 1996 similar mergers were occurring in Europe.) Such developments are termed *vertical* integration for they allow companies to control production *and* distribution (e.g. Disney can use ABC to distribute its films). Telecommunications companies have been merging with cable companies, and Bill Gates's Microsoft has been in talks with Turner and Murdoch about providing news and other services for the Internet. This shows the considerable pace of technological convergence and the growing concentration of ownership. The American media world is now dominated by fewer than a dozen major companies compared with around 5000 some 50 years ago.

Murdoch again set the pattern. In 1985 Twentieth Century Fox merged with Metromedia, the largest chain of TV stations in the USA, to give Murdoch partial control of stations in seven key American cities. The price he had to pay, however, was taking out American citizenship, for neither Australia nor the USA allowed dual citizenship and the rules of the Federal Communications Commission prevented foreigners from owning more than 20% of a US TV station. They also required that no one can own both a TV station and a newspaper in a single city, and although he was in the clear in Washington, Houston, Dallas and Los Angeles, he had to sell the *New York Post* and *Chicago Sun-Times*. On the Australian side, he had to surrender his TV interests in Adelaide and Melbourne, for the Australian Broadcasting Tribunal insisted that anyone owning more than 15% of a TV station had to be Australian. Such concerns, however, may become irrelevant if, as many predict, the American Congress deregulates cross-media ownership – allowing national networks to buy local stations and newspapers – a move that critics maintain would destroy local diversity.

Meanwhile, in Europe, BSkyB attracts viewers as far apart as Finland and Tunisia, and has proved particularly popular in Holland, where it has over three million subscribers. This is no doubt due to the fact that the 14 million Dutch audience is already considerably fragmented – between two Dutch, three German and a Belgian channel – and is attracted by a commercial, English-speaking station. In 1996 Murdoch launched a joint venture (with other major broadcasting companies) to provide an array of satellite TV channels in South and Latin America. With his News Corporation already offering Star TV in Asia, BSkyB in Europe and Fox TV in America, this agreement means that Murdoch now effectively covers the globe. Such developments are fast making national broadcasting boundaries, network structures and even legal requirements increasingly obsolete. No doubt Kerr and Bell would again argue that this supports their convergence thesis.

The upgrading view
There are optimists who welcome these developments and believe that they are enhancing the quality of home entertainment. They maintain that television provides a rich source of varied material and that if people now have a larger choice this is all to the good. They feel that in Britain especially – with our long tradition of public service broadcasting through the BBC – we have for too long fostered an elitist, exclusive view of broadcasting, and that this should be removed. The possibility that the licence fee – by which we all contribute to a broadcasting elite who then decide what programmes to make for us – might be replaced by either advertising or direct subscription is widely welcomed. The emergence of independent television (so fiercely resisted in 1954) is now widely accepted as having provided a healthy air of competition, and the additional BBC and ITV channels have catered for minority interests, some of which (thanks to television) have become major events (e.g. snooker). Educational initiatives, such as the Open University and the BBC microcomputer programme have been universally acclaimed, and the growth of cable and satellite merely allows this kind of provision to be further extended. A wider range of channels allows people to watch what they want to see, not what network programme controllers decide is good for them, and this removes much of the stuffiness from British broadcasting. Optimists argue that this can only be welcomed in a democratic society. It should also, given the wide choice available, make people more selective in their viewing and less inclined to sit in front of the set gaping at whatever happens to be on.

This view was nowhere more clearly expressed than by Rupert Murdoch in his James McTaggart Memorial Lecture at the 1989 Edinburgh Festival, when he insisted that British public service television was obsessed with class, dominated by anti-commercial attitudes and harked back to the past. 'Much of what passes for quality on British television' he maintained 'is no more than a reflection of the values of the narrow elite which controls it and has always thought that its tastes are synonymous with quality'. Attacking the view that British TV produced 'quality costume dramas' as opposed to 'frothy soaps', he claimed that Britain produced 'costume soap operas in which strangulated English accents dominate dramas which are played out in rigid class-structured settings'. He insisted that such programmes pandered to an international (and particularly American) desire to portray and freeze Britain as a museum, and asked whether it was really healthy for British society to be served up a diet of television which constantly looked backwards.

Murdoch also questioned the notion that journalists have greater freedom in a publicly controlled, as opposed to a privately owned, system. He claimed that British broadcasters surrendered their freedom in exchange for government protection of their monopoly, and that every government, of whatever political complexion, would exact a price for that protection. 'I cannot imagine', he continued, 'a British Watergate or a British Irangate being pursued by the BBC or ITV with the vigour of the American networks.' Government control – in the form of reporting restrictions, vetting of staff by security services, banning of programmes etc. – would, he insisted, become impossible in a multi-channel age. 'The multiplicity of channels means that the government "thought police", in whatever form, whether it be the benign good and great in Britain or the jackboots in the night elsewhere, will find it hard to control more and more channels.'

Finally, he concluded that those who resisted more competition were akin to those who sought to control and censure the printing press. 'Why should television be exempt from these laws of supply and demand any more than newspapers, journals, magazines or books or feature films?', he asked. 'I can see no reason. I believe that a largely market-led television system with viewers choosing from a wide variety of channels financed in various ways will produce a better television system than today's.' He praised American TV, which he said had been disgracefully misrepresented, and dismissed the suggestion that his personal ownership was an unhealthy concentration of media control.

Many also see cable as an opportunity for entrepreneurship, export sales and general economic expansion. Various politicians and proprietors, including Murdoch, take this line, and many independent producers welcome release from the paternalism of the BBC and ITC. Leading names from British entertainment (e.g. Peter Bowles, Jonathan Lynn, David Puttnam, Michael Peacock) have welcomed the government's pay-per-view proposals on the grounds that it will encourage British programme-makers, for people will pay to watch new British material (rather than old movies), but will not pay for a whole *channel* (as proposed by Hunt) of minority British interest programmes. The argument is that this will raise bidding prices for special events and bring the maximum amount of revenue to cable. The greater number of channels, coupled with the fall in technology and production costs, should lead to more low-cost, high-quality programmes.

The major sporting bodies too welcome pay-per-view TV and the growth of competition. BSkyB has shown the popularity of sport, yet the BBC has traditionally chosen to allocate only a small proportion of its revenue to sporting coverage. The sports authorities maintain that the growth of satellite and cable has attracted much needed income and led to modern facilities and top sporting figures coming to Britain. The argument is that if people pay to watch live sporting events, why shouldn't they pay to watch them on television?

Optimists claim that the merging of cable, satellite and telecommunications will liberate viewers from 'appointment television'. Instead of being tied to the schedules of TV programmers, viewers will be able to watch what they like when they like. American telephone companies are scrambling to merge with cable TV operators as they prepare for digital technology and a future in which video pictures, computer data and speech all flow down a single cable.

Some are perturbed by such developments and the fact that satellites can now be used to spread political propaganda across national boundaries, but optimists (such as Ronald Reagan, mentioned in Chapter 2) see this as a positive, democratizing development which allows citizens of every country to obtain a broader perspective on world affairs and not just the one determined by their national government. Many multinational companies also welcome the opportunity to advertise their products over whole continents, particularly in Europe, which does not have a tradition of television advertising. Finally, others are simply excited by the new technology itself and welcome the opportunity it provides for new forms of broadcasting (e.g. involving viewer participation).

The downgrading view

Pessimists believe that the dangers from cable and satellite broadcasting are considerable, particularly in Britain, which has built up a strong international reputation for high broadcasting standards. The response to those who advocate minimum regulation in broadcasting affairs is that some level of control must always exist (e.g. in deciding over the use of the air-waves) and that certain forms of regulation may be no bad thing. The public service tradition, it is argued, has produced some commendable features in that it can provide a 'national consensus' in times of crisis, emphasizing unity rather than division; high-quality, 'impartial' current affairs reporting; high-calibre artistic, educational and cultural programmes; and special interest programmes for 'sizeable minorities'.

In broad terms, the fear over cable and satellite is that public service broadcasting will be replaced by 'private profit narrowcasting': that, far from providing greater diversity, each channel (on limited resources) will aim to capture the largest possible slice of the audience by showing those programmes (soap operas, quiz shows, westerns etc.) with the widest possible appeal. Rather than broadening choice and encouraging minority interest output, this is likely to result in the re-running of old (and thereby cheap) glossy American imports. The argument is that rather than widening and developing tastes and interest, cable and satellite lead to the reinforcement of *existing* tastes, for taking risks and offering surprises are discouraged. The situation becomes akin to that operating in many American cities at present, where one has a 'choice' between numerous channels all showing soap operas or chat shows at the same time in the hope of attracting a particular audience. Pessimists question the notion that more choice equals better broadcasting: after all, many good restaurants offer little choice, while many of the worst offer a lot!

The concerns of the pessimists can be summarized as follows. First, there is a fear of fragmentation – that cable and satellite will break up any semblance of a national audience as wealthy companies 'buy out' big events and deny accessibility to others – and this is a particularly thorny issue in relation to sport. The 1990 Broadcasting Act made *all* sporting events available to *all* channels, but eight national events – the FA and Scottish Cup finals, home cricket test matches, the Wimbledon tennis finals, the Grand National, the Derby, soccer's World Cup and the Olympic Games – were restricted from 'pay-per-view' TV. This, however, did not prevent Rupert Murdoch bidding for exclusive rights to the Football League, Olympic Games, Rugby Union and Rugby League during the mid-1990s, for Sky Sports was classed as a *subscription* channel, not 'pay-per-view'. The turning point came in 1995, when Murdoch obtained exclusive rights to golf's Ryder Cup and refused to allow the BBC to show recorded highlights of a dramatic win for the European team. Pessimists became fearful that Murdoch would incrementally 'take out' major events, move to 'pay-per-view' and eventually monopolize the entire sporting calendar. The International Olympic Committee declined to grant him exclusive rights to the 2008 Olympics and, with a huge majority, the House of Lords defeated the government over the Broadcasting Bill and preserved the eight 'national' sporting events for terrestrial TV. (The Labour party also offered to include the Five Nations Rugby Union Championship, the Ryder Cup and the Open Golf Championship.) It was argued that such events should be accessible (i.e. free at the point of delivery) to *all* viewers, particularly as sporting figures were role models for young people. The BBC was delighted with this outcome, and BSkyB was not too disheartened, as it was still free to bid for listed events even though it was denied *exclusive* coverage. The major sports bodies, however, eager to attract maximum income to their sports, were less enamoured: they did not wish to be shackled by the law and were keen to strike deals with the highest bidders. In the long run it seems likely that technological development will favour BSkyB, even if the BBC remains protected for a decade, and there is still the vexed question of who decides on 'the list'. Many would lament the omission of the British Formula 1 Grand Prix, the Rugby League Cup Final or the Boat Race!

Linked with this is the insistence that 'self-regulation' is unacceptable in a situation dominated by commercial interests. Ownership of the media – TV, radio, newspapers, journals etc. – becomes ever more concentrated, and is highly intertwined with many of the key players part-owning each other. To take some obvious examples at the time of writing: the Mirror newspaper group owns SelecTV and Live TV cable network, is part owner of the French TV station TF1 and has sizeable stakes in Central TV, Border TV, Scottish Television, the *Independent* and various cable TV services; the Guardian & Manchester Evening News group has shareholdings in Anglia TV and the production company Broadcast Communications; Cumbrian Newspapers has a stake in Border Television; the newspaper group D. C. Thomson has holdings in Central TV and the programme making company Trilion (which is also a shareholder in Broadcast Communications); the bookseller W. H. Smith is a shareholder at Yorkshire Television and has moved into satellite TV; Granada TV is a major shareholder in BSkyB; the French TV channel Canal Plus has holdings in TV South; and the Pearson group owns Penguin books, Longman books, HarperCollins, the *Financial Times*, Thames TV, Grundy Worldwide and Madame Tussauds, and has substantial stakes in Channel Five Broadcasting and Yorkshire Television. In turn, and most significant of all, Rupert Murdoch's News International owns 40% of BSkyB and a substantial slice of Pearson, and publishes four UK newspapers (which are used to advertise BSkyB). In 1996 BSkyB entered the European pay-TV market for the first time by acquiring 25% of Germany's Premiere channel and formed an alliance with Bertelsmann and Canal Plus to provide digital pay-TV for Europe. World-wide, Murdoch owns hundreds of newspapers, magazines, TV channels and publishing houses in Australia, the USA and the Pacific basin. Indeed, many politicians are uneasy at taking on Murdoch's BSkyB over TV access to sporting events, because he might turn against them at election time in his newspapers!

Pessimists feel that such developments are highly dangerous for democratic society; that the various Acts provide a get-rich-quick recipe for the media buccaneers and their financial backers; and that technical, cultural and employment prospects will suffer. They question suggestions of 'enhanced competition' and note that media barons seem to work increasingly in collusion against the public interest. Hood (1984) similarly fears that the owners of cable and satellite systems will inevitably control the message their systems transmit, and argues that these should rather meet social needs and be part of a public communications system.

A third concern relates to cultural identities and the fear that, far from creating greater diversity and preserving regional distinctiveness, cable and satellite will smother the world with the same bland (i.e. American) cultural influences. This is clearly seen in Scandinavia, where home output – with its commitment to national and Nordic identities – has been caught flat-footed by the advent of satellite. Channels like BSkyB have proved attractive because most Scandinavians can speak English, and Finland is the only country with any history of TV advertising. But this has created new problems. Parents in Sweden, for instance, have protested at the advertising of war-like toys (which is banned in Sweden) on BSkyB, but appear powerless to do anything about it. The Scandinavian countries planned to beam domestic programmes to each other with Nordsat, but this was torpedoed in 1982 when Denmark withdrew (for fear that their language would be eroded), and Finland and Norway pulled out of Sweden's proposed Tele-X satellite system in 1985, which meant that each small nation became even more subject to the commercial and cultural pressures of the multinational companies.

We are faced with a clash between two freedoms: the free flow of information across national borders and the right of every society to preserve its national and cultural identities. The convergence writers are apt to overstate the gains from the first at the expense of the second, for they suggest that national cultural differences will fade (thanks to world-wide telecommunications) as societies converge towards common values. But true convergence does not occur simply because the whole world is watching *Dallas*! America should be equally prepared to watch television from all other countries and this, of course, does not happen. We have not experienced convergence, but domination – American domination – and many Afro–Asian countries find it impossible, both economically and politically, to develop home-based productions in the wake of cheap, glossy US imports. A 1960s edition of *Perry Mason* is far cheaper (and often more appealing) than a documentary on local farming methods, and even 14% of British television now consists of American programmes.

A fourth concern relates to regional and social provision. New technology will prove far more economic in the large urban areas, and these could come to receive superior provision. The public service tradition has always stressed an adequate service for all – 'the best of everything for everyone', to quote Lord Reith – but cable is likely to represent an 'urban culture' to the 60% of the population able to receive it.

A fifth area of concern is over trans-border transmission and the possible use of cheaper, low-power satellites to issue propaganda, pornography and violence, and poach good-quality, expensive and successful pro-grammes. To pessimists, the whole area becomes ripe for piracy and political intrusion, and consequently they insist on certain minimum levels of national and international regulation, not to inhibit and curtail, but to provide a framework within which reputable and creative programme makers can operate. Otherwise a state of 'broadcasting anarchy' could ensue in which propaganda, 'video nasties' and pornography will dominate the cable and satellite channels at the expense of 'quality' productions in drama, music and current affairs.

In 1993 and 1995 the British government outlawed the supply of decoder equipment in order to prevent the satellite channels Red Hot Dutch and TV Erotica beaming hard-core pornography into Britain. Tech-nically it is not feasible to shut out satellite signals and, in view of this, the EU proposed, in 1986, a 'common market for European TV' to effectively sweep away most national controls on broadcasting. But Britain opposed this (as did France and West Germany) and the EU's broadcasting directive does allow member states to suspend retransmission of a service that could 'manifestly, gravely and seriously' harm children. The signs are, however, that this will become ever more difficult to administer, and open TV access across Europe seems the likely long-term outcome. This will make national broadcasting laws increasingly anachronistic.

In 1996, with many people expressing concern over the ease with which children could see unsuitable programmes, President Clinton announced that all new TV sets in America would be fitted with a V-chip, allowing parents to scramble programmes they judged inappropriate. Sceptics, however, see the V-chip as the most outwittable child-control device since the out-of-reach biscuit jar, for children only have to be old enough to outsmart their parents at programming the chip, clever enough to watch an old set in their bedroom, or able to watch forbidden shows at a friend's house or on video. They also fear that it offers programme makers the opportunity to show even *more* explicit material on the grounds that parents can now protect children from it. For pessimists the V-chip is mainly symbolic – it allows politicians to respond to a widespread concern – but it is doubtful whether it will ever prove effective as a control device.

A sixth concern relates to the British tradition of public service broadcasting, for the BBC and ITV could now be pushed to the margins. The BBC, if it received only a small percentage of the viewing audience, would have difficulty justifying its licence fee, while ITV would find it far harder to attract advertising. With reduced funds, both would be pushed into producing 'instant' programmes – news, sport etc. – rather than major documentary and drama series which take some time to 'mature'. Standards will fall if revenue sources are affected and funds transferred to satellites. Supporters of public service broadcasting maintain that the two great safeguards have been (a) the licence fee, which has allowed the BBC to maintain its standards, and (b) the franchise system, under which the ITV companies operated for set periods if they produced approved programmes. The second safeguard has now been removed, and the first is under constant threat. Critics fear the very series for which British television is most renowned – *The Jewel in the Crown*, *Life on Earth* etc. – will be threatened with extinction. Pessimists dismiss the so-called 'public access' cable programmes, advocated as a way of providing wider public participation, as merely cheap ways of filling air time with astrologers, job opportunities, house sales and music videos. They believe that broadcasting should lead as well as reflect, and fear a severe fall in programme standards.

Linked with this, finally, is the fear that as broadcasting becomes more entwined with commercial interests and increasing convergence takes place between different forms of new technology, so governments will feel more able to intervene in areas from which they have traditionally detached themselves. Critics would maintain that the Conservative government has viewed broadcasting as part of its economic and industrial policy rather than an aspect of the nation's culture. Furthermore, that it has been inconsistent in its position, in that it has encouraged the deregulation of broadcasting in organizational and economic terms but resisted a 'free market in morality'. (Witness the setting up of the Broadcasting Standards Council as a watchdog of taste and decency.) The irony is that with deregulation the government seems to have become *more* involved with broadcasting. Until recently, Britain did not have a Heritage Minister and politicians rarely mentioned 'broadcasting policy': this was left to the 'independent' professional broadcasters. But with government increasingly engaged in the commercial and industrial aspects of information technology, it has entered the territory of programme planning, as in the celebrated cases of *Real Lives*, *Rough Justice*, *Everyman* and *Death on the Rock*.

CONCLUSION

The introduction of satellite and cable allows for greater diversity of information, education and ideas, but also mass propaganda, violence and puerile entertainment. Will the proliferation of choice lead to healthy democratic pluralism or a fragmented society increasingly subject to multinational influences? Will more air time be given to minority interests or will power simply remain where it is, with the multinationals, the media magnates and the USA? Is any form of international control for broadcasting advisable or even feasible? These are the sorts of question we have raised in this chapter, and once again the outcome is largely a matter of choice. We could have cheap, locally based TV systems offering a community service for far wider communication and information-sharing; conversely, under the cover of talk about choice and competition, a handful of companies and individuals could penetrate our lives more deeply than ever before. Opinions differ as to the likely outcome and whether it will prove beneficial, but in focusing on television we have been able to consider the crucial technologies of cable and satellite, which, linked with microelectronics, will markedly affect both work and the home. The debate surrounding television largely centres on whether one believes it should provide people with what they want, or whether it has a role in cultivating tastes and interests: whether it should reflect or lead. The British tradition – stemming from the BBC's first Director General, Lord Reith – has been that broadcasting should 'inform, educate and entertain', and many believe that by refusing to separate these we have avoided the 'Sunday ghetto of serious programming' that exists in America. Reith believed that the function of broadcasting was primarily educative – to train 'character' – and was not there to provide people with what they wanted, for they didn't always know what they wanted. Television's task is therefore to cultivate audiences as well as cater for them, and to introduce people to new interests and views of which they might be unaware. Supporters of this tradition fear that, as a result of cable and satellite, standards will fall and television become clogged with mindless trivia catering for the lowest common denominator.

It is interesting that the main criticism of each side against the other is the same: namely, that of authoritarianism. The optimists see the Reithian view as conservative, arrogant, pompous and elitist. It presumes a homogeneous 'middle class' national culture which does not exist, and prevents market forces discovering what people demand from a broadcasting system. They also argue that these fears have never been confirmed in other branches of the media: commercial radio has not destroyed Radio 3; the *Sun* has not eliminated the *Guardian*; and sales of gangster novels do not appear to have adversely affected the sales or status of Dickens. Opening up the air-waves allows for 'public broadcasting' in a far truer sense – what we might term 'community broadcasting' – in that the public participate to a much greater extent than was ever permissible under the traditional, centralized broadcasting authorities.

The pessimists, on the other hand, maintain that deregulation permits a far more insidious form of control – that of commercial interests – in which any form of public accountability for broadcasting standards is lost. Reith may have been authoritarian, but at least as head of a public corporation he was answerable to the nation. This brings us back to the recurring theme of invention and innovation and the pessimists' emphasis on the latter. Their concern is not with the technology itself so much as with the way it is introduced and controlled. The key innovators in cable and satellite (such as Rupert Murdoch and Ted Turner) are in no sense technologists, and probably haven't the first idea how a satellite works, but are practical businessmen, media entrepreneurs, who possess the vision, cunning and confidence to apply the new forms of technology.

As in the early days of telegraphy and broadcasting, the innovators come from outside the mainstream of communications technology and, apart from being similarly accused of authoritarianism, seem a million miles away from John Reith, a dour Scottish Presbyterian, who believed that the BBC's mission was to provide a public service of excellence. The present-day magnates no doubt see their task as meeting people's wishes, and dislike distinctions between 'high' and 'low' culture. Rupert Murdoch owns both *The Times* and the *Sun*, but does not consider one better than the other; merely different. The signs are that British broadcasting will gradually approximate to the American pattern, with an advertiser-financed sector for mass audiences, minority interest pay-television, and a third sector financed by either private or public subsidy.

Our feelings about new technology in the home are somewhat mixed. We take a fairly optimistic stance towards the improved washing machines and domestic robots, for they remove much of the drudgery of housework, provide considerable advantages for the housebound and handicapped and, most important, will remain under the control of the humans operating them. This *could* also be said for cable, and hopefully remains the aim of those who wish to introduce the various interactive services. But one is left pondering whether it will ever happen and fearful that the introduction of cable will merely result in downgrading effects on television broadcasting. Commercial interests who seek financial gain from cable and satellite television seem unlikely to assist the development of other facilities or to offer TV as a community service. One is reminded of the fact that, at the start of the industrial revolution, the British ruling classes taught the working people to read, but not to write. This allowed them to read instructions, and the Bible for moral improvement, but did not permit them to answer back. The same could happen with cable.

CHAPTER ELEVEN

A New Work Ethic?

We noted in Chapter 3 that pessimists, such as Jenkins and Sherman, and optimists, such as Stonier, all agreed on one thing – that in future, people will spend less time 'at work' (i.e. in employment) than they do at present. Life at work and in the home, and the balance between the two, could change so dramatically that the way we presently think of work and non-work could cease to have any real meaning. It is this broader question, of our whole attitude to work and leisure, that we wish to consider in this chapter.

It is important to remember that work ideologies – by which we mean the collection of values, attitudes, beliefs and opinions that people hold towards work – have not remained static throughout history. The ancient Greeks believed that work brutalized the mind (which is why slaves were used), while the Hebrews saw it as drudgery, a punishment for original sin. With early Catholicism, work became a natural right and duty, but was still subordinate to prayer and contemplation; only with the coming of Protestantism, the effects of which have only been felt in the last few centuries, did we develop the attitude to work that we know today. It was Luther, and particularly Calvin, who stressed that work was natural and commendable, and idleness a sin. It was their teaching that elevated the virtues of hard work, thrift and sobriety, and provided the 'industrial work ethic'.

There is therefore nothing 'natural' about work as we know it. Men and women do not have to work five days a week from nine to five, 48 weeks a year or whatever, and when people talk of the 'problem of increasing leisure', this would in fact be nothing new for Western society. In the 13th century, a feudal peasant worked around 190 days a year, and it was only with the coming of industrialization that men, women and children came to work appallingly long hours in mills, factories and mines. Modern workers enjoy about 1200 hours per year more free time compared with 1890, when the average working week was 62 hours in contrast to the 40 hours we know today. In terms of the total lifespan, we should also remember that workers now enter the labour market later and live longer and, in total, experience considerably more non-work time. During the last century we have seen shorter working weeks, longer holidays, earlier retirement etc., which, if anything, is a return to the working patterns of pre-industrial society.

It is also in the industrial age that most people's work has taken the form of 'jobs', and this too may be coming to an end. Employment became widespread when the enclosures of the 17th and 18th centuries made many dependent on paid work by depriving them of the use of land and the opportunity to provide a living for themselves. The factory system then destroyed cottage industries and removed work from people's homes, while improvements in transport made it possible for people to commute long distances to work. This particularly put women at a disadvantage: whereas in pre-industrial times, men and women shared productive work in the household and village community, it now became customary for the husband to pursue employment while the unpaid work of home and family was left to the wife. Therefore the present increase in women at work can also be seen as a return to former work patterns.

WORK AND NON-WORK

How is work defined? Many see an element of compulsion in work roles – something you have to do – and also an aspect of payment, but the dividing line is thin (e.g. one may feel compelled to paint one's house in non-work time, but do it oneself in order to save money: it is hard to say whether this is work or leisure). We need to distinguish between activity, which we enjoy doing, and labour, which is work done for someone else to earn a living. As we shall see, information technology makes these dividing lines increasingly blurred.

In a useful model, Parker (1983) identifies the different components of 'life space', by which he means all the activities or ways of spending time that people possess (Fig. 11.1).

The model divides the total amount of time available between work and non-work activities, and suggests that some of these approximate to things we 'have to do' (constraint) and others to things we 'choose to

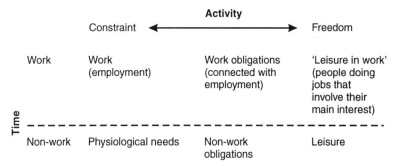

Figure 11.1   Components of life space.

do' (freedom); other activities fall somewhere in between (i.e. various obligations). Work refers to working time, sold time, subsistence time – time spent earning a living – but for some this may contain elements of 'leisure' in that they are doing jobs that involve their main interest (e.g. the actor, sportsperson or business tycoon). For such people there is no sharp divide between work and leisure – they are often workaholics – and their work is what they would choose to do with their time anyway. Similarly, in non-work activities some time is spent on things we have to do (eating, sleeping etc.), while pure leisure includes things we choose to do. Between the extremes of constraint and freedom, much time is now spent on activities we feel *obliged* to undertake, in connection with both work and non-work. For instance, many spend considerable time commuting to work: this may involve leisure aspects (e.g. reading a paper, listening to the radio, having a chat), but one would not make the journey unless one was obliged to go to work. Similarly, at home more time is now spent gardening, taking the dog for a walk, picking the children up from school, DIY etc.: for some these may be chores, while to others they are important interests, but they cannot easily be classed as work or leisure. They are not things we have to do (or conversely choose to do) in a strict sense, and consequently are best termed 'non-work obligations'.

Of course, some of these activities may overlap (eating a meal meets a physiological need but may also be a leisure activity), and people fit on to Parker's grid in various ways. Life for a prisoner or the unemployed is far more constricted in both time and activity dimensions, while for the housewife there is considerable blurring between work, leisure and obligations (which perhaps helps to explain why so many find it unsatisfying). Meantime, the 'idle rich', and those doing jobs involving their main life interest, spend far more time towards the freedom end of the continuum. The question is whether new technology will provide similar opportunities for the rest of the population.

INFORMATION TECHNOLOGY AND LEISURE

Parker also examines how information technology could affect leisure patterns and suggests that there are two main aspects to consider. In the first place, new technology will continue to influence leisure activities directly, as we saw in the last chapter. Just as leisure has been transformed by technologies such as the car and television, so this will continue with home videos, programme libraries, wider travel and IT-related pastimes. For instance, in 1996 the brewing company Bass invested £40 million in ten 'virtual emporia' in Britain which will provide continual entertainment based on the latest technologies. That leisure will continue to be 'technologized' therefore is not in serious dispute. What is contentious is whether such changes will lead to more 'creativity', an upgrading or downgrading of leisure activities. This, of course, is highly subjective, for what is creative to one person may not be so to another, but it raises a similar discussion to the one on television in the previous chapter.

Optimists believe that the release of people from the necessities of employment will enable them to pursue qualitatively superior leisure activities. Martin (1981) predicts that a small proportion of the future leisured class will become far more creative, and draws a parallel with the wealthy, non-employed class of Victorian England, who produced many of the great inventors, writers and musicians. Leisure will increasingly provide greater freedom for individual choice and expression; people will not just passively accept the provisions of mass entertainment. Individuals will instead manipulate and exploit them: accepting some, rejecting some, and modifying others. Networked fifth-generation computers, by making complex techniques available in simplified form, will spawn a new kind of 'Renaissance person' – able to obtain a deep knowledge of science, literature, music etc. – and with increased leisure time people will be more able to 'work' on activities of their choice.

Pessimists, however, such as those of a Marxist persuasion, have long argued that leisure time will not suddenly become meaningful to industrial workers simply because there is more of it if the nature of their work degrades them as human beings. They maintain that it is hard for a five-day slave to suddenly feel free at weekends, for stultifying work leads to stultifying leisure, and if people spend most of their time pulling machine handles on assembly lines it is little surprise if they then spend their leisure time playing one-armed bandits in amusement arcades. Gorz (1985) argues that the worker uses leisure to escape from the alienation at work; therefore leisure is used to *live with* the problem of alienation rather than to solve it. Just as the capitalist system shapes the working day, so it also shapes leisure activities: it creates the passive consumer who merely inhales the products of the manufacturing and entertainment industries. So long as capitalist society survives and the nature of work continues to be deskilled in the ways suggested in Chapters 4–6, extra non-work time will not necessarily result in an upgrading of leisure activities: in capitalist society, people are alienated from both work and leisure. Optimists reject this as a rather elitist view of leisure and argue from a historical viewpoint that working-class culture is qualitatively higher today than it was a century ago. Even if we regard bingo and the *Sun* as hardly representing 'high culture', both require basic numeracy and literacy, which back in Victorian times most of the population simply did not possess. The implication that at that time the population (or even the middle classes) were all immersed in a high culture of theatre, opera etc. is dismissed as a romanticized view. Indeed, the General Household Survey for 1989 showed that, even in an age of ever-increasing television, people are actually reading *more* books than previously, often inspired by the television programmes themselves. Optimists reject the idea that with increasing leisure people become bored and restless; and even a restless spirit may prove an asset, driving them towards as yet undiscovered interests. They perceive a broadening and enriching of leisure activities which will extend further as a result of new technology.

We again see a divide between optimists and pessimists, though each camp agrees that as a result of microtechnology we can expect reductions in working hours which will profoundly affect the work–leisure relationship. Our personal hope is that any inability to cope with increased leisure will only prove a transitional problem and that it will increasingly take on the character of work. If one accepts (as we would) that people are naturally energetic, inquisitive, imaginative and creative, then, if less time is spent in formal employment, more leisure time will be spent on 'chosen work'. Work and leisure become ever more blurred and fade into what is better termed 'activity', for if our mental balance is not to become totally distorted we cannot spend all our new-found leisure time in rest and relaxation. We must discover 'activated' leisure, which could result in a division between:

(a) a basic economy, in which people work on producing goods and services, and

(b) a secondary economy, in which people work on tasks of their own choosing.

Toffler envisages paid work being done in the basic economy for a minimum time with maximum technology, and 'prosuming' – self-directed work in which goods and services are produced for one's own use – in the secondary economy. In similar vein, Gershuny and Miles (1983) talk of a 'self-service economy' in which people do their own laundry, provide their own travel, pursue home-based leisure activities etc. and rely less on outside services. More people buy capital goods (made by fewer workers) to service themselves at home. Robertson (1985) also talks of 'ownwork' in which individuals and local communities work for themselves – perhaps at home, perhaps in part-time conventional jobs – but always setting themselves up, not waiting for others to provide work for them.

All this affects the time–space model (Fig. 10.1) introduced earlier, for less time is now spent in employment, and work obligations become compressed as more people work from home. While pessimists would argue that time at work is increasingly deskilled, there is some hope that with more leisure time available (and technology providing our basic needs) activities towards the freedom end of the continuum may grow. These could well take the form of non-work obligations and lead to a richer life within the home and family.

A NEW WORK ETHIC?

The Western industrialized world thus becomes faced with a curious paradox. For centuries we have lamented the dehumanizing effects of many forms of work, and sought to reduce toil and improve the quality of working life, but now as we approach the opportunity to perhaps do just this – to live to work instead of working to live – we find ourselves so totally immersed in the Protestant work ethic that we are unable to let go of entrenched attitudes and embrace new-found freedoms. Rather like the prisoner who wants to be free but is fearful of the world outside, we are frightened, even if we dislike work, to face a world without it. We welcome the thought of more leisure, but at the same time fear that unemployment could threaten the whole fabric of our society. Increased leisure and unemployment can easily become the same thing unless we are careful. Measures need to be taken to ensure the benefits of the former without the tragic consequences of the latter.

It is not simply an economic question. People do not work just to get paid, but also to pursue activities with and for others. Work is of crucial importance to individuals in a world that tells them that work is commendable, and it is no substitute to pay them to do nothing. It is hard to see enforced leisure ever becoming an acceptable substitute for work, and we have to devise means for

(a) sharing available work, and
(b) inculcating leisure with work-related activities.

This way – by creating a society in which people are no longer primarily paid (or judged) by employment – seems to offer, in the long term, the best hope of avoiding societal breakdown.

The work ethic may therefore be replaced by a 'leisure ethic', in which leisure becomes the central activity in life, with work as a means to that end. Jenkins and Sherman (1981) prefer a 'usefulness ethic', in which work is not abolished but its creative functions are enhanced by greater choice. Similarly, Clarke (1982) suggests a 'contribution ethic', which recognizes more unpaid work and the things people do for each other.

The most important development, however, could be a move away from labels altogether, and any one over-arching ideology, towards a situation in which individual differences are increasingly recognized. The move to new work patterns that we discussed in Chapter 3 could in part encourage this. We may experience a number of *competing* ideologies, none of which is totally dominant, and move to a situation in which work ceases to be 'good' and idleness 'bad'. People clearly vary in their needs for work and leisure, and we could experience a society where those who wish to work may do so, while those who do not can be idle (like the ancient Greeks) with a clear conscience. In pre-industrial society, work, play and jollification went side by side, and perhaps today we spend too little time helping each other enjoy life. Is the idea that 'work is good for you' and must be pursued at all costs (even to the extent of preventing someone else taking a share in it) necessarily virtuous? Perhaps the stigma of 'not working' will be removed and five-day working (not to mention overtime) be made socially unacceptable? In short, maybe we exalt work too much and allocate less time than we should to enjoying life with others. Handy (1984) is optimistic that we are moving, slowly but surely, towards new work patterns, and cites the growth of part-time work, DIY, non-work obligations and the informal economy as manifestations of this. In his later work (1994) he tells us that 'proper jobs' are no longer available – but there are customers if we can find out what they want and deliver it. We must turn ourselves into 'portfolio people' (with a portfolio of customers and products) for uncertainty is the only thing of which we can be certain (Handy, 1995). Like Gershuny and Miles, he believes we are evolving from a materialist, employment-based society to a 'self-service society', in which work is redefined, not by legislation, but by people creating new forms of work for themselves.

If such a move were to occur, and we switched our efforts and resources away from the goal of creating jobs for all to helping people manage without full-time employment, what implications would this have for the way our society is structured? In the first instance, it could mean that work is no longer done predominantly in a factory, office or shop, but in small workshops or from home. The idea that work has to be done five days a week, and between set times, becomes obsolete, and we noted the move towards new work patterns in Chapter 3. There would also be shifts away from formal employment as fewer remain tied to particular firms and more work on contract. People could retire earlier, and the working week be cut (as advocated by the TUC) to allow available work to be spread more evenly. Jenkins and Sherman advocate a 'shorter working lifetime' to create larger blocks of time for people to travel, undertake sabbaticals, enjoy family activities etc.

Job sharing

Much of this sounds attractive, but pessimists would argue that within the confines of capitalism and its prevailing ideologies there is no apparent mechanism for bringing such a transition about. The working wage is still the primary means by which wealth is distributed to the mass population, and work still principally means employment.

It is hard to see how we move away from this. How do we get the 80% in employment to give up part of their work (and presumably their wage) on the promise that society could thereby be made more fulfilling, exciting and peaceful? We noted in Chapter 3 the dangers of a society polarized between those in full-time, highly skilled, highly paid occupations and an unemployed pool of up to seven million, but is this not the direction in which we appear to be inexorably heading? The danger is that we could move into a society in which industrial collapse becomes so extensive that our entire social fabric breaks down. A small technocratic elite could control all forms of information, and a vast backwater economy emerge in which unemployment, menial work, crafts, moonlighting, barter and brigandry become standard features of everyday life. Such a situation was depicted in Kurt Vonnegut's novel *Player Piano*, where a small minority control the available work and wealth and the rest are shiftless drones. How do we avoid this and spread the available work more equitably to provide each worker with a 'smaller job'?

One obvious policy is some form of 'job sharing', which was encouraged in the early 1980s by the then Employment Secretary Norman Tebbitt when he suggested voluntary 'job splitting' whereby grants would be given to companies who split jobs and kept people off the dole. He felt that this could have particular appeal to the elderly and to married women, but it was rejected by the TUC as 'an attempt to disguise the unemployment figures'. Trade unions are naturally cautious about job-sharing schemes as it could lead to a dilution of their control over a larger, dispersed, part-time workforce. Workers too are reluctant to embrace any scheme that might mean a drop in terms of pay, security or responsibility. Not that it should be thought, however, that trade unions are opposed to shorter working hours. On the contrary, they see this as the direction in which things must go, but the call is for a shorter working week and longer holidays (with no drop in pay), rather than job sharing. We still have the longest working week – around 40 hours on average – in Europe and the highest levels of overtime. Moreover, such demands are not confined to Britain. In Germany unions have achieved a 35-hour working week, and in Japan – where the average worker puts in 2152 hours a year compared with 1910 in Britain, 1908 in the USA and 1656 in Germany – the unions are making similar demands.

In many ways, job sharing and shorter working weeks sound like much the same thing, but just as unions are suspicious of job sharing, so employers (especially in Britain) are cool on a shorter working week. In 1984, when the EU tried to introduce shorter working hours to alleviate unemployment, Britain alone among the 10 member states rejected the idea. The government argued that although it was not opposed 'in principle' to shorter hours, competitiveness remained the top priority, and Britain was in no position to reduce working hours if they remained high in Japan and the USA. We therefore reach a position where government, CBI and TUC all support shorter working hours in principle, yet offer not the slightest indication of any mutually agreed mechanism by which this might be achieved. Such changes only seem feasible in an atmosphere of mutual trust, understanding and compromise, and this seems noticeably absent.

A social wage

Even if agreement could be reached on shorter working hours, an even greater problem arises over the question of pay. Work is presently considered as *paid* employment, and the implication of people working in smaller jobs for shorter periods is that the form of remuneration will change. Leach and Wagstaff (1986) propose a 'personal benefit', on the lines of child benefit, payable as a fixed sum to everyone, whether they are in employment or not. In similar vein, Keith Roberts (1982) proposes a national dividend paid to everyone, on top of which people could still earn as much as they like from employment. He assumes that people will need to do less work to achieve their desired standard of living, but this is problematic (for today's luxuries can become tomorrow's necessities) and will only occur if there is a marked change in existing work attitudes. Barry Jones similarly advocates a society in which income should be a right to economic support, not a reward for work, and in which the right to work (and not to work) is guaranteed for all. Meade (1995) proposes a 'citizen's income', which guarantees a given basic income to everyone.

These, and similar proposals, are far more feasible in theory than practice, but they do seem the direction in which we have to go if we are to avoid the social polarization and upheaval mentioned earlier. The implication is that eventually, instead of being rewarded for output and effort, workers will be paid according to need, and issued with a 'social wage' as of a right of citizenship. This may smack of Marx ('from each according to his ability, to each according to his need') but, given that the unemployed are already paid a social wage (unemployment benefit), why should this not be extended to the rest of the population? The emphasis would now be on consumption rather than production; the stigma of not working would be removed; overtime would be outlawed; and greater encouragement given to work-related leisure activities.

Various suggestions have been made as to how, in the short term, we could ease such a transition by adopting certain legislative measures. In the first place, one could offer tax concessions to people prepared to give up some work to others, or the fifth day of work could be more heavily taxed (as in the case of overtime). Employers are presently penalized for employing more people, and this could be eased if firms paid far lower national insurance contributions for part-time workers (and an increased rate for full-time workers). Similarly, employers might even be subsidized for employing *more* workers in part-time jobs. A further measure would be to legally limit the amount of overtime worked: in West Germany, the legal limit is 60 hours and in Belgium 65, but similar restrictions do not operate in Britain. Evidence suggests that the role of the state is vital in initiating and supporting change, and those countries with established tripartite machinery seem at the moment best able to introduce new schemes for working hours, wages and work conditions.

Rustin (1985) makes the point that up to now the 'right to work' has been a *social* right rather than a legal one – as is the case, say, with education, health care and social security. He maintains that the money spent on unemployment benefit could be more effectively used, and calls for a series of regional labour boards to act as 'employers of last resort'. These boards would have a statutory duty to provide work for all who sought it and would adjust their policies to meet demand – much as local education authorities are required to maintain enough places to meet the needs of all eligible children. Regional funds would be measured against regional joblessness, and boards could offer subsidies to private and public concerns. Such proposals may seem radical, even unfeasible, but they address issues that we seem ever more likely to face.

The problem is that our economy is designed to fit the conventional patterns of big business and big government, and work is regarded as embracing employment by large-scale organizations. People are seen as relying either on an employer for a wage or the state for unemployment benefit, and it is difficult for government to break free from this pattern. We have a deep-rooted system of rigidity, embodied in tax, company and employment legislation, which makes change extremely difficult. The whole capitalist system (including various financial allocations from government) encourages capital investment, which inevitably means further automation. The focus is on technological innovation rather than employment creation (though capitalism's defenders would claim that the former assists the latter), and large organizations are not well placed to change their attitudes or develop the small-scale, decentralized, informal, local work patterns that many now advocate. As James Robertson (1983) has noted, in the early 19th century the Whigs and Tories refused to accept that Britain was ceasing to be an agricultural country and, by delaying the repeal of the Corn Laws, put off the introduction of cheap food and caused much unnecessary hardship and distress. We could now be going through an equally profound transition, and politicians may again be similarly unable, or unwilling, to respond to the situation.

THE POLITICAL RESPONSE

Over the past decade the major political parties have taken up the 'work issue', but most of the discussion is still couched in traditional terms. Various reports refer to 'new work patterns', but contain little indication as to how we bring them about. All parties still seem to share the basic ideology of unlimited growth, and see technology as a tool for enhancing efficiency and providing the greater material wealth we all desire. Of course, politicians are psychologically tuned to the short term – the next election – and most of their concern is with the here-and-now rather than the long-term future, but such an approach skirts the issues raised in this chapter. There is little discussion on how we adopt new work patterns; few debates on truly radical policies such as a social wage; and no apparent awareness of the societal dangers that may unfurl. Concern over these questions raises the debate to a higher level and poses the questions over the uses of technology that we raised in the opening chapter. Should we automatically adopt technology just because it happens to be available, cheaper, faster, more reliable or whatever? Perhaps we should question technology's role; ponder its ceaseless development; and ask whether its application is always the 'force for good' that some would have us believe. In short, perhaps we should more closely examine the options before us.

Over the past two decades these sorts of issue have received much greater attention, partly as a result of the emergence of various environmental groups and the Green Party. The heart of the ecology argument is that technological development and economic growth have become gods in our society but that there are environmental limits (e.g. energy) to continued economic expansion. They claim we already have enough to meet people's basic needs and should escape from the treadmill of ever greater production and consumption: the economics of more and more should be replaced with the economics of enough. On new technology the Green Party has argued that 'As the new microchip technology begins to bite, unemployment is going to get dramatically worse, which is why we must find some new way of dividing up the national cake that does not necessarily depend on people having a job.' (election manifesto, 1983). The Greens accept an increase in unemployment as inevitable, and advocate a national income scheme under which everyone (whether in work or not) would get a basic income payment to replace social security benefits and tax allowances, which could lead to a reduction in hours worked, overtime, large-scale working, full-time working etc. We would pay less attention to the quantity of work undertaken and more to the *quality* of work: this should be judged not by its profitability or productivity, but by its usefulness and intrinsic satisfaction to the worker. *New* jobs could be created in such areas as energy conservation, development of alternative energy resources, combined heat and power schemes, small-scale mixed farming, labour-intensive food production, land reclamation, recycling and reuse, housing renovation, rural regeneration, repair and maintenance etc. The Green Party's view – and its view of technology – was summed up in its 1987 manifesto: 'Real wealth is not stocks and shares and money in vaults. It is the planet and the life it supports in all its rich array. The basis of economics is learning how to live within our means, and to Greens that implies living within the means of the planet'.

APPROPRIATE TECHNOLOGY

The ecological viewpoint may have become more prevalent, but it should not be thought of as new: it has in fact a long tradition in the writings of Mumford (1967), Ellul (1973), Illich (1974), Schumacher (1974), Dickson (1974) and Robertson (1983) and also in the New Age movements that have developed in the 1990s. Ellul argues that technology is basically antagonistic to human values, and the danger is that it comes to dominate us. We become obsessed with technique, – which emphasizes means rather than ends – and discussion over *how* something should be done obliterates debate as to whether it *ought* to be done. Because technique dictates, we lose the freedom to choose.

This school is not 'anti-technology', but believes that we must use it to provide tools rather than machines, and should carefully consider the way it is applied. The proposal is that technologies, including information technology, should be used to create a society with devolved structures, limited growth and low energy; in short, they should be used in an 'appropriate' manner. Mumford believes we are obsessed with (a) faster, (b) farther away, (c) bigger and (d) more; the effect of which is to remove limits, hasten the pace of change, smooth out seasonal and regional differences, standardize internationally etc. This brings us back to the concerns raised in Chapter 1. Whereas the 1960s may have been the period of technological optimism, considerable doubts are now raised as to technology's ability to solve human problems such as famine, poverty, pollution and international conflict. The danger is that we develop a fatalist conviction that a technological solution exists for everything, and the more complex a situation is, the less likely debate is to occur. We come to accept that we have no choice but to build nuclear power stations and motorways, and a false dichotomy is forced on us whereby technology equals rationality and progress while resistance is irrational and reactionary. Must we always accept the *highest* technology available, or are there varieties of technologies and choices to be made? Because something is technologically possible (or profitable), does this mean it must be pursued? Are electric carving knives 'rational' when humans are starving in less developed countries? Are sophisticated nuclear weapons 'progress'? Even if we choose a particular technology, there are still further decisions as to how it should be applied. Some cities built freeways to encourage the use of private cars (e.g. Los Angeles) while others concentrated on effective public transport systems (e.g. Stockholm). All these arguments apply to the chip. Technological determinism suggests that technology is a single entity and that its effects are universal; but outcomes are much more a matter of political choice.

Probably the best-known exponent on these lines is E. F. Schumacher (1974) who, in *Small is Beautiful*, argues for reversing economies of scale. Instead of *more* things being produced by fewer people using high technology, we might inflict less damage and violence on society and the environment if more people produced *enough* things with low technology. He argues that small-scale labour-intensive industries serving regional needs should be encouraged instead of being squeezed out by the large capital-intensive firms.

Schumacher's work raises five major concerns:

- Modern production is based on the use of fossil fuels which are 'natural capital' and cannot be replaced. Industrial society therefore consumes the very bases on which it is erected, and treats irreplaceable capital (e.g. oil) as income.
- Pollution is a major problem, as little thought is given to the recycling of products. There are 'tolerance margins of nature', and city smog, river pollution etc. show little sign of abatement. Some of the most advanced industrialized societies have the greatest public squalor and pollution. Why should we assume that further growth will rectify this situation?
- There is a danger of increased specialization and centralization. Small enterprises provide more personal control, more rewarding jobs etc., and are better placed to provide socially useful goods at suitable prices.
- Technology has proved ineffective in solving many of the developing world's problems. The 'green revolution' did not end food shortages;

new high-yield crops have been found to have low resistance to disease; fertilizers and other aids have proved expensive; and generally the quality of food has, if anything, been reduced.

- Technological advance can endanger the planet. Vast amounts are still spent on defence, supersonic aircraft, nuclear power stations etc., and the risks from this are high.

Schumacher advocates the use of natural foods to retain soil fertility; urges the use of small-scale technology so that workers can feel part of an organization; and calls for less emphasis on economic growth and production. Though he does not, of course, refer to information technology (it was not in existence when he wrote his book) his general philosophy would still apply, for he would wish to see it used in an 'appropriate' manner. To repeat, Schumacher is not anti-technology, but is concerned as to its application, organization and control. The *appropriate* use of information technology could prove highly beneficial to humankind, but the danger is that moral and social aspects become secondary to economic considerations. He questions the convergence writers' argument that less-developed countries should necessarily industrialize on the lines of the West. He also suggests that public ownership may be necessary to achieve social rather than economic goals, but private ownership is acceptable if small-scale. The key factor is size rather than ownership, though the two are inevitably interrelated.

Various labels have been used to describe socially useful technologies. Dickson talks of alternative technology, Illich of convivial technology, while terms such as 'people's technology' or 'soft technology' are also used. The theme is essentially the same – that continuous exponential growth is neither inevitable nor desirable and technology should reflect the genuine needs of society. Some emphasize ecological issues, such as pollution (e.g. Clarke), and others political issues, like control (e.g. Dickson), but basically appropriate technology means that it should be intelligible to, and controlled by, the local community; use indigenous resources and skills to provide socially useful products; offer safe, purposeful employment; and be non-pollutant, ecologically sound and (wherever possible) capable of being recycled.

ALTERNATIVE SCENARIOS

A continuing theme of this book has been that we cannot state precisely what will happen, but with regard to work patterns we can now at least summarize a number of alternative scenarios. The first is the optimistic view that nothing much will change or, that, if it does, it will only get better. More work, and more interesting work, can be provided in an increasingly affluent, democratic, open, meritocratic – in short, superior – society. Work has traditionally meant jobs, and there is every reason to think that more of these can be created following the introduction of new technology. This view still finds favour (for different reasons) at both ends of the British political spectrum, for the Conservative government believes that jobs can be created through market forces, while many in the opposition maintain this can be achieved through the state. Personally, we believe that both views underestimate the degree of change we can expect and offer traditional remedies for novel situations. Neither wing talks in terms of alternative scenarios, but rather the restoration of full employment.

This gains little support from those pessimists who maintain that unemployment – high enough already – will only get worse as a result of new technology. They fear that we could simply come to accept unemployment as an inevitable part of modern life, and rationalize its existence as the necessary price for keeping inflation under control and making our society industrially competitive. Unemployment is seen as preferable to international poverty, and if it means some going without work this is unfortunate but unavoidable.

Our society has already gone a long way towards accepting this view. Unemployment of over three million is (or has been) tolerated and, as Handy points out, we often explain away the situation by convincing ourselves that the unemployed either don't want work (i.e. the scroungers); don't need work (e.g. married women); or don't deserve work (e.g. the unskilled). This may clear the consciences of the employed, but, as a long-term recipe for social stability, it seems disastrous. The economic cost will run to many billions and the social cost will be the polarization discussed in Chapter 3.

A third alternative is a 'leisure scenario' in which technology provides all our basic wants and allows us to pursue a life of true leisure. As we have seen, this can be viewed optimistically or pessimistically: people may either pursue considerably enriched leisure-time activities or, alternatively, lead lives of endless boredom broken only by the mindless trivia pumped out by media barons. The key point is that when optimists talk of 'enriched leisure', what they really mean is that leisure takes on work connotations. A society based on idleness – such as the unemployed experience now – is not a serious consideration, for people must be given the opportunity to develop interests and skills. When we talk of the 'leisure classes' of the past, we should recall that they worked hard – at governing, running their estates, patronizing the arts etc. – and never pursued a lifestyle of total leisure.

This brings us to an 'activity scenario', and the one we would broadly advocate. Our need is to re-think work; to extend it beyond merely 'doing a job' to embrace non-work obligations, community services, home crafts, DIY etc. We must escape from the treadmill whereby work means employment and employment means a wage. The problem is, however, that in the market economy we only employ people to make things or provide services that can be sold; and if new technology increasingly takes over the jobs of the factory and office then there will inevitably be unemployment. But there are clearly jobs waiting to be done – in rebuilding our towns, upgrading our hospitals, improving our schools and developing leisure facilities. Surely this is 'wealth creation' (even if it is not 'sold' in the conventional sense), for people are provided with a higher quality of life in which they can, more effectively, pursue the things they really want to do. Thus work and leisure merge into each other to form activity. Such a transition will not be easy (for, as we have seen, it contains important implications for employment legislation, social benefits, income distribution etc.), but it increasingly appears the most sensible way forward. It requires us to appreciate the nature of the debates and to raise our sights to broader issues concerning the whole nature of our society. Most important of all, it requires us to examine our own assumptions and prejudices, for we are blinkered by an industrial culture which makes it difficult for us to consider appropriate choices.

CHAPTER TWELVE

People and Chips

OPTIMISTS AND PESSIMISTS

Many have written of 'people and chips' and how one affects the other. We have suggested that this society/technology interface, particularly as it relates to information technology, can be usefully explored through two main perspectives, which we have labelled optimists and pessimists. The first group starts with the technology; highlights the various benefits it can offer; regards it as a 'fact of industrial life'; and inclines to the view that a predominant form of technology pervades a given epoch. Technology is the independent variable and, in the case of the microchip, it enables us to experience a new industrial revolution and reap the fruits of post-industrial society. Indeed, work organizations (even nations) are faced with a stark choice of 'automate or liquidate', for failing to embrace the new technology will simply mean that they become uncompetitive.

Pessimists, on the other hand, who comprise a more diverse group and can be considered at different levels, tend to see technology as the dependent variable – a social product – and more the result of dominant economic and political forces. They see the continual capitalist search for greater profits and wider control as the driving force behind technological change. From this standpoint automation does not automatically raise the levels of skill and autonomy of the workforce, but instead, jobs are deskilled and management control enhanced. The optimistic view generally finds favour on the political right, and the pessimistic on the political left.

These two approaches (summarized in Table 2.1) adopt different stances towards society, technology, the social structure, the nature of work etc., and we attempted to show how they can be applied to a discussion of

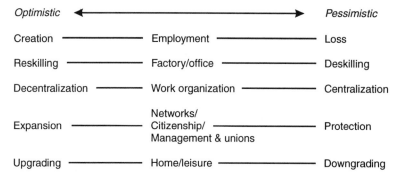

Figure 12.1   Main concerns of the contrasting perspectives.

the human effects of information technology. In each chapter, we argued that the particular concerns of the two camps varied according to context, and indicated this by adopting further labels, as summarized in Fig. 12.1.

We used Bell and Braverman as representative of the different ends of this continuum and, in applying the model to particular issues, branded various writers as either optimists (e.g. Evans, Toffler, Minford, Leontief, Blauner, Guiliano, Tapper) or pessimists (e.g. Reinecke, Dickson, Jenkins and Sherman, Cooley, Downing, Hewitt, Hood, Gorz).

A final word though on labels and, in particular, optimists and pessimists. We stressed at the outset that they must be used with care and always in context, for the pessimists in particular can be considered at different levels, which allows certain writers to be pessimistic in one sense but optimistic in another.

A particular danger is that the labels carry with them certain connotations. The optimist is seen as forward-looking, hopeful and positive, while the pessimist is presented as miserable, downcast and a die-hard reactionary reluctant to change. Technology itself is invariably presented as 'progressive', which provides the optimists with a far better public image, for to oppose it is seen as irrational, old-fashioned and Luddite. This often allows those on the political right, as in the case of employment, to portray themselves as radicals, boldly marching forward into the micro-based, post-industrial society. In short, they present a positive approach to technology through the continuation of existing policies and attitudes: the adoption of conservative means to meet radical ends. Many pessimists on the political left, however, branded by their opponents as timid, unrealistic, obstructive and dogmatic, would reject the accusation of being reactionary and indeed apply it to their critics. They share the vision of a 'better' society and are pessimistic not towards technology, which they concede can provide substantial human benefits, but over its likely use in capitalist society, or particular government policies. No doubt they would prefer to be labelled realists.

The danger over labels can be illustrated in the work of Jenkins and Sherman. In Chapter 3, we termed them pessimists over the employment issue because they foresaw a 'collapse of work' whether we adopt new technology or not; but overall, theirs is not a pessimistic book. As they say:

> It is a prospect at which we should not quail or rush to the nearest bunker. This is an opportunity to rethink our traditional attitudes and to accept boldly the new opportunities. It is an occasion for hope, not despair.

This is an optimistic outlook, accompanied by a radical programme for social transformation which would utilize the higher prosperity and greater leisure time now available to the working population. Conversely, Reay Atkinson (1980), while 'moderately optimistic' that new technology would not lead to considerable labour displacement, doubts whether Britain is prepared for or able to grasp the new opportunities. Whether particular writers are optimistic or pessimistic about a particular issue is therefore not necessarily a reflection of how they see the effects of new technology as a whole, or even on another issue. This is why we cautioned over the use of labels at the outset and have often used them in quotation marks to reflect differences in interpretation.

Despite these dangers, however, we feel that the two approaches provide a useful framework for collating and considering the wide range of discussion on the human implications of information technology. We are aware that there are many important areas we have not covered: the effects of further technological advances, such as biotechnology and artificial intelligence; likely applications in motoring, medicine, education, social services etc.; social issues such as crime; occupational changes in banking, insurance, hospitals, police etc.; and, most important of all, global issues such as nuclear weaponry and the less developed world. The arguments, however, would remain much the same. As we noted in Chapter 1, some regard sophisticated weaponry as the safeguard of civilization (optimists), while others see it as the major threat to life on our planet (pessimists). Similarly, with less developed countries some claim microtechnology will stimulate these economies, while others see it intensifying the existing control of advanced nations. Convergence writers may see new technology as the key to the door of industrialization (and then post-industrialization) for less developed countries, while pessimists foresee a growing polarization between rich and poor as the multinationals control any technological development on their terms (e.g. allowing chip manufacture to be done in less advanced countries by cheap, unskilled labour, while research and development is retained within the advanced economies).

A new industrial revolution? Not necessarily. The chip may be revolutionary in a technological sense – and book titles such as *Micro Revolution* and *Microelectronics Revolution* perfectly justified – but this is not the same as saying that such developments represent a revolution in the broader social, political and economic sense. The new technologies *could* result in a new industrial revolution, but at the moment such predictions seem premature.

We therefore reject an optimistic view which suggests that technological advancement will somehow automatically transform and improve all aspects of social life. This is probably most glowingly presented by Masuda when he writes:

We are moving towards the twenty-first century with the very great goal of building a Computopia on earth, the historical monument of which will be only several chips one inch square in a small box. But that box will store many historical records, including the record of how 4 billion world citizens overcame the energy crisis and the population explosion, achieved the abolition of nuclear weapons and complete disarmament, conquered illiteracy, and created a rich symbiosis of god and man, without the compulsion of power or law, but by the voluntary cooperation of the citizens to put into practice their common global aims.

This seems to us to be 'optimism gone mad', and we see little justification for such a scenario – certainly not in the foreseeable future. But just as we cannot accept that technology will impose a certain form of society, so equally we reject the highly pessimistic view which suggests that technology is wholly implemented and controlled by those holding economic and political power, and we do so on the same grounds: that it is over-deterministic and ignores the importance of choice. Both polar views suggest, for different reasons, that we are powerless in the face of technological change, and that as individuals and groups we have no say over its introduction. Any technology certainly contains societal implications, and those holding power unquestionably influence its application, but the recurring theme of this book has been that, within these parameters, individuals – through political parties, trade unions, community groups etc. – can significantly affect the way it is used. It is like travelling by car on a motorway: we cannot turn back, and the technology of the vehicle imposes certain constraints on us. Similarly, the route and regulations are determined by those with the power to build and control motorways. But within these limits we can exercise choices – over the turns we take, the speed we travel or the extent to which we consider others – and can make demands for changes in speed limits, car design, safety provisions etc.

TECHNOLOGY AND CHOICE

We have come full circle, and we intentionally conclude the book, as we did its opening chapter, with a discussion of choice. Various key words have appeared in our discussion – convergence, innovation, revolution, deskilling – but the most important is choice. Real choices *can* be made, and we must be careful of global predictions (for better or worse), as the outcome is always influenced by why, how, where and when technology is used. We cannot formulate conclusions in simple cause and effect terms, for the wide range of applications can lead to an equally wide range of effects, many of which may be in very different directions. What we have discovered is that so much depends on the *particular* – the particular society, legislative framework, government policies, workplace, management style, household, even individual – and the choices that are made. This provides us, in effect, with a third perspective, – one in which technology is not for better or worse, but *problematic* – for as we explored different facets in each chapter, we discovered wide variations in application, and the deeper we investigated, the more the level of analysis seemed to be pushed down – down to the bottom point of our 'upturned conceptual triangle' (Fig. 2.2), and the issue of choice. (This 'social action' approach is advocated in the work of McLoughlin and Clark, Piercy *et al.* and Child. It can also be found in social constructionist writing (Bijker, Hughes and Pinch etc.), accounts that focus on gender (Webster, Cockburn and Ormrod) and recent work on cybersociety.) From this perspective technical change is seen as a *process of negotiation*, not some sudden 'big bang' event where everything falls into place overnight. There *are* choices to be made: between one machine and another; between removing skills and enhancing them; between hierarchical and democratic systems; between technical and human factors etc. We have included a wide range of opinions as to what various commentators think *likely* to happen; but what *will* happen depends on the outcome of a multitude of various decision-making processes.

In saying this, we are not belittling the contributions of global discussions, for they raise important questions and help us to focus the debate. The contribution of the optimists is to show us the benefits that information technology has the potential to provide. The contribution of the pessimists is to point out that these are by no means certain; to make us aware of threats and dangers; and to help us make informed choices.

In periods of change, there are greater opportunities for making individual choices and yet, paradoxically, at such times we often feel incapable of doing so. New technology deepens and widens all our choices and makes us hesitant: we are better informed than ever before, but the stakes are higher. We can use technology to expand our freedoms in democratic, pluralist society or allow moves towards far greater tyrannical, dictatorial control. We can cure disease and feed the hungry, or pollute the atmosphere and blow ourselves to pieces. This is described by Cooley as a choice between 'architect or bee': human beings can either be reduced to bee-like behaviour in which they react to the technology specified for them, or they can be architects designing the use of technology to enhance human creativity and individual freedoms. Especially important is the fact that the choices we make are greatly constrained by the choices made by those more powerful than ourselves (i.e. our political, industrial and commercial leaders). To take our earlier analogy; the choices we make on the motorway are greatly restricted by the prior decisions taken by those who built it. What then does the future hold? In assessing this we shall start at the global level and then consider the British situation specifically.

ASSESSING THE FUTURE

Talking of motorways, the 'Information Superhighway', as analogies go, is more appropriate than most, and the superhighway seems certain to be as significant for the 21st century as roads were for the 20th, but the metaphor should not be stretched too far. Road networks were constructed by *nations*, while a key feature of the Internet is that it is already international. But if IT networks are to span the planet successfully then some kind of 'highway code' is required, and this seems likely to evolve through the free market, which means that the contest is wide open to all-comers.

In other words, those who get in first will define the rules of the IT game and the rich will get rich while the poor stay poor. The prizes seem likely to be contested by four main power blocks.

The United States of America

The USA has long been at the forefront of IT development, and this situation looks certain to continue. IBM may not hold quite the dominant market share it once did, but it still remains a formidable contestant and, like other American computing giants, has responded to the growth of PCs, reorganized its operations and adjusted to new market developments. Microsoft, Apple, Digital and many others also remain considerable players. The American IT market – business, military, domestic, educational – is vast and greatly boosted by widespread PC purchase and cabling.

Japan

Japan – which terrified the West as it moved so swiftly and successfully into IT development – is certain to remain a major force, but not perhaps to the same extent it once was. It has failed to make much impact outside its home shores in hardware, software or telecommunications. Considerable sums have been spent on flashy, but failed, projects (e.g. high-definition television); software development is weak because it is so much harder to write in Japanese than in English; while cable remains neglected (only 3% of Japanese households subscribe to cable services). The effect of this is that as far as networking goes, and the Internet in particular, Japan has lagged behind. The Internet Society's 1995 figures showed that Japan had 96 632 hosts, compared with 241 191 in Britain, 207 717 in Germany and over 2 million in the USA. While 52% of American PCs are hooked into a network of some kind, the figure for Japan is less than 9%. In-fighting between separate ministries has also held back the development of Japan's infrastructure, while telecommunications remains in the hands of a state-run monopoly. Perhaps most significant of all, at a time when the West is spending less on defence as a result of the end of the Cold War – which releases funds for IT development – Japan is spending *more* because of renewed uncertainty with regard to Russia, North Korea and China.

The Pacific Rim

A new group of countries that have emerged on the IT scene, and cannot be ignored, includes the likes of Malaysia and Singapore. They see the digital highway as a means of establishing themselves: Singapore, for instance, has launched TradeNet and LawNet (IT systems to improve port registration and legal documentation procedures for shipping vessels) and introduced smart transport cards and digitized property transactions. For the moment, however, the Pacific Rim countries are restricted by their size, which is why there are moves afoot to created a united economic block.

The European Union

The EU may not be considered the front runner in the IT race, but it is a more serious contender than many realize. European countries are strong in fields such as software development and telecommunications, and hardware manufacturers (like Olivetti and Siemens) hold respectable market shares. Moreover, the EU, with the exception of the USA, has the greatest spread of cable. As we noted in Chapter 7, provision is uneven but, by 1995, 25% overall coverage had been achieved and this is steadily expanding. Enthusiasts believe that an integrated European grid of optical fibres would do more for the European Union than, say, a single currency.

The EU's Bangemann report, *Europe and the Global Information Society* (1994), argued that Europe needed to create a continent-wide regulatory body to provide an integrated approach for constructing an IT highway. Without this, it was suggested, Europe will waste resources, suffer unnecessary duplication of systems and software, and experience unreliable network links. A central body could determine rules for licensing, network connection and IT resource management; ensure network access; resolve disputes between member states and IT companies; guard against monopolistic market tendencies; establish the interconnection of different national networks; and set common standards to ensure full operability of equipment and software. The report concluded, however, that such developments should not be left to national governments but should be market-led, with the regulatory body aiming to reduce monopolies and restrictions at every level. In other words, the central body would construct the highway and enforce 'the highway code' while the choice of vehicles, passengers and cargo would be left to end users of the network.

The problem, however, is that the EU has been bedevilled by internal rivalries, fragmentation and slow market response. By 1985 the EU was spending only £360 million on IT research programmes out of a total budget of over £17 000 million, and various initiatives received mixed support. Britain's role has generally been low-key and inconsistent: in 1987 we were the only country to oppose a £4.8 billion collaborative programme, but a year later we offered £200 million a year to the ESPRIT programme, even though we had previously been cool on it, complaining of its bureaucracy and big-firm bias. Overall, the various European projects – ESPRIT, EUREKA, RACE etc. – have remained disjointed and precarious.

THE BRITISH RESPONSE

Despite an ideological commitment to 'market forces' the Conservative government was, during the early 1980s, highly interventionist with regard to IT. By 1982 – dubbed 'IT Year' – the government was investing *four times* as much as its Labour predecessor: grants were made available for new investment, awareness campaigns were encouraged, funds were provided for research and education, and training programmes expanded. It spent some £570 million on various programmes for computers in schools, industrial robots, fibre-optic cables, and microchip and software research.

But in 1984 the government ordered a freeze on all programmes, and one is puzzled as to why, if the policy of expansion was so right for 1980, it was wrong four years later. In the event, the government announced its support-for-innovation policy, the main effect of which was to maintain most schemes, but not to expand them. The £350 million five-year Alvey programme – described by Kenneth Baker in 1983 as 'by far the most important research and development programme undertaken in Britain since the war – probably since the jet engine' – tried to create Japanese-style collaboration between academic research and industrial development, but floundered in 1987. Alvey was killed by the very short-termism it sought to cure. The 1986 Bide report had called for £1 billion further funding for Alvey 2, but by 1988 the government had switched high-tech support from big firms to small and from suppliers to users. Innovation grants to companies were effectively ended, and the aim was to encourage small companies and collaboration between firms and universities. Critics pointed out that this meant a new, small company importing Japanese technology would get government assistance, while a company planning to compete with Japanese technology would not. In 1988 the all-party Warren Committee on IT (under Conservative MP Kenneth Warren) called for more IT training, greater government funding, a national electronic grid and greater ministerial responsibility for IT strategy, and this gained further support from the all-party Trade and Industry Committee a year later. In 1996 the government launched its £35 million Information Society Initiative to encourage smaller companies – 40% of whom have no computers – to utilize IT, but critics claim that such initiatives are not introduced as part of an overall strategy. The British government has been criticized for pursuing policies that are inadequate, disjointed, piecemeal, inconsistent and – at times – even contradictory.

Fragmentation

In reviewing the British response – both political and industrial – the key word has to be fragmentation. Britain can feel proud of its developments in schools and its tradition of high-quality research and inventiveness, but an overall, long-term, coherent strategy seems to have been lacking. Enthusiastic bursts seem to occur in isolation; sometimes even in conflict with other initiatives. Whereas Japanese and American industries are adept at organizing with their governments, British proposals invariably appear insular and piecemeal. This can be seen in various areas and at different levels.

● Government policy

There has been little long-term coherence in government strategy. The policy in 1979 was to reduce public spending, but this was reversed in 1982, only to be changed again in 1984. In 1988 there was a further switch from suppliers to users. INMOS, the chip manufacturing company, was left to market forces (and sold in 1989 to the Franco-Italian company SGS-Thomson) while taxpayers' money was spent attracting Japanese and American chip makers to the likes of 'Silicon Glen' in Scotland.

● Government departments

The convergence of different technological areas has also made government structures obsolete and highlighted the outmoded boundaries between government departments. For instance, while the DTI is responsible for publishing, films, aerospace and British Telecom, the Home Office is responsible for broadcasting, cable systems and data protection. (We saw in Chapter 9 that such divisions are increasingly irrelevant). This has resulted in fragmented policies and a lack of coordination between different departments: while the DES cut higher education, the Microelectronics Education Programme (MEP) and subsidies for schools buying computers, the DTI expanded provision for schools and the ITECs; while the Home Office backed satellite the DTI backed cable; while the DTI wanted to encourage cable companies the Treasury cut capital allowances; and so on. In the meantime, three separate departments – education, defence and trade – were each involved with the Alvey programme. Given this situation, it was hardly surprising when the Trade and Industry Committee called for the restoration of an IT minister.

- Research and development

A further problem is that with too many R&D programmes the two separate halves are insufficiently integrated. We, in Britain, are far better at research than development. The transputer, fibre-optic cabling, viewdata – all British inventions – were not sufficiently developed by industry and have been taken up elsewhere. Britain's inventiveness is legendary – a Japanese government report in 1985 claimed that 52% of products developed successfully since 1945 had originated in Britain, compared with 22% in the USA and 6% in Japan – but while we are brilliant in the laboratory we are lousy in the workshop. The situation is compounded by the fact that our concentration on defence research means that, because of security requirements, many projects operate in isolation and potential benefits in other areas are not realized. We are strong at invention but weak on innovation, and all too often fail to integrate theoretical research and practical application. A 1993 government White Paper resulted in the Technology Foresight Programme being set up to advise on research and development and provide links between government, industry and academics.

- Infrastructure

Because the government has, to date, rejected the provision of a publicly funded national electronic grid – incorporating cable TV, telephones, home services etc. – the signs are (as we saw in Chapter 7) we shall end up with a plethora of systems, technologies etc. with different organizations laying different cables in different localities for different purposes. Notwithstanding the 'double digging' in our roads, this could result in very uneven geographical provision as British Telecom installs fibre-optic cable for the new national trunk network while cable TV companies operate independently.

- Industry

There is fragmentation in the industrial sphere, not just in terms of the vast chasm between those companies who are technologically aware and those who are not, but also among companies contributing to IT projects. The Alvey programme, System X and DBS are all examples of projects held back by inter-company wranglings. Similarly, among microchip companies there have been few signs of firms working together. But in Europe, Siemens of Germany and Philips of Holland now share resources, while Thomson of France and SGS in Italy have merged their chip businesses. (These countries also provide considerable backing from central government.) The effect of this is that we have become increasingly dependent on Japanese and American suppliers for IT products and mass-market chips. A lack of strategy has also hit the small personal computer companies, an area where initially we achieved considerable success. The problem is that we rarely think in integrative terms, and find ourselves with different companies providing different products in different ways. The result is that we end up looking for markets for products rather than products for markets. The City has also been part of the problem, with its unwillingness to provide sufficient long-term high-tech capital.

- Education and training

The Microelectronics Education Programme (which provided IT courses for teachers) and the DTI's 'micros in schools' scheme allowed government ministers to boast that Britain had 'the best computer-educated schoolchildren in the world'. But, as we saw, these programmes were fragmented between different departments, and by the mid-1980s were being curtailed. By 1996 Britain was providing greater access to computers for secondary school children than virtually any other developed nation, but had fallen behind in primary schools. We have also witnessed cuts in higher education at a time when Japan is providing up to 40% of its population with a university education. Of particular concern is the low priority we give to industrial training, and studies show 'lack of skilled personnel' as the major reason for companies not investing in IT – way ahead of cost or union resistance. The IT industry still needs 30 000 more skilled workers, with demand rising 7% a year, but there is minimal provision for training workers in the new skills, and the situation could worsen further, with fewer school-leavers coming on to the labour market. We also need to overcome the fragmentation that exists *between* education and industry, for the former should inform the latter. The Alvey programme probably broke down barriers as never before, but, as we noted, it was effectively discontinued after 1987. We appear ineffective at identifying and developing those areas where we could achieve considerable success

– 'picking winners' – in the way countries like Sweden have done. Many companies are 'anti-education', while academics often prefer to remain in their 'ivory towers'. As far back as 1983 ACARD advised the government that £15–30 million more a year should be spent on removing the barriers between higher education and industry, but, despite some notable success stories, there still seems a wider gap between the two than in most other countries.

Government and industry would claim, justifiably, that they have spent many millions on developing new technology, but, because their efforts have been so fragmented, the results have generally been disappointing. Ironically, this fragmentation – between EU members, government departments, research and development, IT companies, industry and education etc. – has occurred at a time of increasing *convergence*. In the first place, there is, as we have seen, growing convergence between the technologies themselves, which has encouraged convergence at the international level through joint European programmes. Cynics would add that this trend also permits a further convergence – in political terms – for it has allowed American and Japanese multinationals a foothold in our high-tech industries. Japan's Technopolis programme for 'technological cities' – which many dismissed as fanciful when it was first launched in 1980 – is now bearing fruit (as we saw in Chapter 7) and has been developed through state financial backing, insurance guarantees and cheap loans. Eventually there should be around 30 research-core cities, each with a 20-year development plan. The programme represents an integrated policy towards IT development, totally different from the British approach.

In many respects, Britain, like the rest of Europe, is well placed to develop IT – it has a well-educated younger generation; more personal computers and videos per head of population than any other nation; a high standing in financial services and technical consultancy; and a notable degree of inventiveness. This was confirmed by the Taylor Nelson report (1986) which argued that we possessed more of the 'new people' (people prepared to abandon the ideologies of the industrial age) than any other nation, bar Holland, and that by the turn of the century Britain could be a 'winner' again, as it was in the first industrial revolution. (Ironically it is the 'peak nations' – USA, Japan, Germany – where the dying industrial ideologies are strongest.) The report concluded that in Britain it is our established *institutions* – government, management, trade unions etc. – that have been trying to 'catch up with the past' (i.e. obsessed with *restoring* industry rather than developing new 'people-related skills'), while the general public possess a firmer vision of the future. (This is a theme that Hutton (1995) examines in some depth.) Indeed, many of the most innovative applications have been at the local level – 'bottom-up' rather than 'top-down' – in individual workplaces, schools and homes. Our supposed inability to change is therefore a myth: the British *people* are very ready to change; it is our entrenched institutions that are not.

A PERSONAL POSTSCRIPT

So where do we stand on information technology? We stated at the outset that our aim was not so much to preach a particular line as to consider and contrast the various lines being preached. For the most part we hope we have done this. We have not tried to offer precise, simple answers – we don't believe they exist – but rather to pose questions, supply information, increase awareness, raise issues, and offer a framework within which the reader can better appreciate the various debates. To repeat: we cannot specify what will happen, for the overriding theme is uncertainty. We are not concerned with predicting the future, so much as with the *options* that face individuals, organizations, communities and societies. However, we have personal views on the matter (and we are sure they have surfaced from time to time), though we would stress that our standpoint is merely one more, and far less important than the idea that the reader should develop his or her own.

In terms of the *potential* that IT offers we are very much optimists. The chip can clearly mean the removal of much alienating work from the factory; the reduction of many repetitive tasks in the office; more widespread decision making throughout the work organization; greater democratic participation among citizens; more effective medical surgery and benefits to the handicapped; enhanced opportunities for education and leisure pursuits; and so on. At the workplace level some companies are indeed using technology to upgrade jobs, and in many homes it has expanded and enriched non-work activities. Both of us appreciate being able to extract money from the bank electronically or to obtain information from the Internet, and the writing of this book was eased considerably thanks to our PCs! Information technology can clearly be a liberating influence in many ways, and there is every reason to feel positive about it.

But, as we have repeated throughout, the fact that technology means that something *might* happen does not mean that it *will* happen. We must not confuse what is possible with what is probable. The key issue is not what the technology can do for us, but what we do with the technology and, as this final chapter has tried to show, our decisions are constrained by those holding power. Consequently, as we survey the British scene, we have to admit to being somewhat pessimistic. Indeed, this pessimism has grown during the 1980s and 1990s, for we feel that, because of our fragmentary policies, we are missing out on many opportunities. For instance, the lack of a national electronic grid means that citizens cannot develop interactive services even if they want to, while our failure to retain an indigenous base for mass-market chips restricts our options and makes us ever more reliant on overseas suppliers. Other nations – France, Sweden, Japan and the USA – have developed more coherent strategies, which permit them, more effectively, to develop the new technology. We therefore share many of the pessimists' forebodings. We are concerned over threats to employment and individual freedoms; further deskilling in many factories and offices; the trivialization of broadcasting; the invasion of privacy; the growth in computer crime; and our ability to make the necessary transition to an 'activity-based' society. We see little indication, certainly in Britain, that the microchip is providing the boost to democracy – either at work or in general – that many optimists predict, and are equally concerned over ecological issues and the dangers from nuclear holocaust. Despite these misgivings, however, it is by increasing awareness and encouraging the exercise of choice that we stand the best chance of avoiding such pitfalls, and that has been the aim of this book. Our own position can be summed up simply: we look forward to what new technology might do *for* us; we dread what it might do *to* us.

Bibliography and Further Reading

Advisory Council for Applied Research and Development (ACARD) (1980) *Technological Change: threats and opportunities for the United Kingdom*, London, HMSO.

Anderson, R. J. (1996a) *Security in Clinical Information Systems*, London, British Medical Association.

Anderson, R. J. (1996b) Clinical systems security, interim guidelines, *British Medical Journal*, Vol. 312.

Atkinson, R. (1980) The employment consequences of computers; a user view, in *The Microelectronics Revolution* (ed. T. Forester), Oxford, Basil Blackwell.

Avner, E. (1993) Trade unions, IT and equal opportunities in Sweden, in *Gendered by Design?* (eds. E. Green, J. Owen and D. Pain), London, Taylor & Francis.

Bamber, G. (1980) Microchips and industrial relations, *Industrial Relations Journal*, **11**(5).

Bangemann, M. *et al.* (1994) *Europe and the Global Information Society*, Brussels, Report to the European Council.

Bell, D. (1974) *The Coming of Post-Industrial Society*, London, Heinemann.

Bell, D. (1979) The social framework of the information society, in *The Computer Age: a Twenty-year View* (eds. M. L. Dertouzos and J. Moses), Cambridge MA, The MIT Press.

Benson, I. and Lloyd, J. (1983) *New Technology and Industrial Change*, London, Kogan Page.

Berg, A. (1995) A gendered socio-technical construction: the smart house, in *Information Technology and Society* (eds. N. Heap, R. Thomas, G.

Einon, R. Mason and H. Mackay), London, Sage in association with the OU.

Bevan, S. *et al.* (1985) *Secretaries and Typists: the Impact of Office Automation*, University of Sussex, Institute of Manpower Studies.

Bibby, A. (1995) *Teleworking: Thirteen Journeys to the Future of Work*, Calouste Gulbenkian Foundation.

Bijker, W., Hughes, T. P. and Pinch, T. (eds.) (1987) *The Social Construction of Technological Systems*, Cambridge MA, MIT Press.

Blau, P. M. and Schoenherr, R. A. (1973) New forms of power, in *People and Organizations* (eds. G. Salaman and K. Thompson), London, Longman.

Blauner, R. (1967) *Alienation and Freedom*, Chicago, University of Chicago Press.

Braverman, H. (1974) *Labour and Monopoly Capital*, New York, Monthly Review Press.

Burns, A. (1981) *The Microchip: Appropriate or Inappropriate Technology?*, Chichester, Ellis Horwood.

Campbell, D. and Connor, S. (1986) *On the Record*, London, Michael Joseph.

Castells, M. (1996) *The Rise of the Network Society*, Oxford, Blackwell.

Checkland, P. (1981) *Systems Thinking, Systems Practice*, New York, Wiley.

Child, J. (1988) *Organization: A Guide to Problems and Practice*, London, Harper & Row.

Clarke, R. (1982) *Work in Crisis: the Dilemma of a Nation*, St Andrew's, St Andrew's Press.

Cockburn, C. and Ormrod, S. (1993) *Gender & Technology in the Making*, London, Sage.

Cohen, R. (1984) *Whose File is it Anyway?*, London, National Council for Civil Liberties.

Confederation of British Industry (CBI) (1980) *Jobs – Facing the Future; a CBI Discussion Document*, London, CBI.

Conference of Socialist Economists (1980) *Microelectronics: Capitalist Technology and the Working Class*, London, CSE Books.

Cooley, M. (1980) *Architect or Bee? The Human/Technology Relationship*, Slough, Langley Technical Services.

Cooley, M. (1984) Computers, politics and unemployment, in *Microchips with Everything; the Consequences of Information Technology* (ed. P. Sieghart), London, Comedia Publishing Group.

Cooper, C. L. and Cox, A. (1985) Occupational stress among word processor operators, *Stress Medicine*, **1**(2), April/June.

Crozier, M. (1983) Implications for the organization, in *New Office Technology: Human and Organizational Aspects* (eds. H. J. Otway and M. Peltu), London, Francis Pinter.

Daniel, W. W. (1987) *Workplace Industrial Relations and Technical Change*, London, Francis Pinter with Policy Studies Institute.

Deane, P. (1980) *The First Industrial Revolution*, Cambridge, Cambridge University Press.

Dickson, D. (1974) *Alternative Technology and the Politics of Technical Change*, London, Fontana.

Dodgson, M. and Martin, R. (1987) Trade union policies on new technology: facing the challenges of the 1980s, *New Technology, Work and Employment*, **2**(1), Spring.

Downing, H. (1980) Word processors and the oppression of women, in *The Microelectronics Revolution* (ed. T. Forester), Oxford, Basil Blackwell.

Ellul, J. (1973) *The Technological Society*, London, Random House.

Evans, C. (1979) *The Mighty Micro*, London, Victor Gollancz.

Featherstone, M. and Burrows, R. (eds.) (1996) *Cyberspace\Cyberbodies\Cyberpunk: Cultures of Technological Embodiment*, London, Sage.

Forester, T. (1978) The microelectronic revolution, *New Society*, 9 November.

Forester, T. (ed.) (1980) *The Microelectronics Revolution*, Oxford, Basil Blackwell.

Forester, T. (ed.) (1985) *The Information Technology Revolution*, Oxford, Basil Blackwell.

Forester, T. (1987) *High-Tech Society*, Oxford, Basil Blackwell.

Francis, A. (1986) *New Technology at Work*, Oxford, Oxford University Press.

Francis, A. and Willman, P. (1980) Microprocessors: impact and response, *Personnel Review*, **9**(2), Spring.

Gann, D. and Senker, P. (1993) Construction robotics: technological change and work organization, *New Technology, Work and Employment*, **8**(1), March.

Gates, W., Myhrvold, N. and Rinearson, P. (1995) *The Road Ahead*, New York, Viking.

Gershuny, J. and Miles, I. (1983) *The New Service Economy: the Transformation of Employment in Industrial Societies*, London, Francis Pinter.

Gilbert, R. (1989) *Employment in the 1990s*, London, Macmillan.

Gorz, A. (1985) *Paths to Paradise; on the Liberation From Work*, London, Pluto Press.

Green, E., Owen, J. and Pain, D. (eds.) (1993) *Gendered by Design?*, London, Taylor & Francis.

Griffiths, P. (ed.) (1987) *The Role of Information Management in Competitive Success*, Oxford, Pergamon Infotech.

Grint, K. and Gill, R. (eds.) (1995) *The Gender–Technology Relation*, London, Taylor & Francis

Guiliano, V. E. (1982) The mechanization of office work, *Scientific American*, September.

Handy, C. (1984) *The Future of Work*, Oxford, Basil Blackwell.

Handy, C. (1989) *The Age of Unreason*, London, Century Hutchinson.

Handy, C. (1994) *The Empty Raincoat: Making Sense of the Future*, London, Hutchinson.

Handy, C. (1995) *Beyond Certainty: The Changing World of Organizations*, London, Hutchinson.

Heap, N., Thomas, R., Einon, G., Mason, R. and Mackay, H., (eds.) (1995) *Information Technology and Society*, London, Sage in association with the OU.

Hewitt, P. (1984) What's in a file?, in *Microchips with Everything; the Consequences of Information Technology* (ed. P. Sieghart), London, Comedia Publishing Group.

Hirst, P. (1989) After Henry, *New Statesman and Society*, July.

Hood, S. (1984) The politics of information power, in *Microchips with Everything: the Consequences of Information Technology* (ed. P. Sieghart), London, Comedia Publishing Group.

Hutton, W. (1995) *The State We're In*, London, Jonathan Cape.

Huws, U. (1982) The chip on whose shoulder? The effects of new technology upon female employment, *Guardian*, 5 November.

Illich, I. (1974) *Tools for Conviviality*, London, Fontana.

Jenkins, C. and Sherman, B. (1979) *The Collapse of Work*, London, Eyre Methuen.

Jenkins, C. and Sherman, B. (1981) *The Leisure Shock*, London, Eyre Methuen.

Jones, B. (1982) *Sleepers Wake*, Brighton, Wheatsheaf Books.

Jones, S. G. (ed.) (1994) *CyberSociety, Computer-Related Communication and Community*, London, Sage.

Jones, T. (ed.) (1980) *Microelectronics and Society*, Milton Keynes, The Open University Press.

Kerr, C. (1984) *The Future of Industrial Societies*, Cambridge MA, Harvard University Press.

Kerr, C., Dunlop, J. T., Harbison, F. and Myers, C. A. (1973) *Industrialism and Industrial Man*, Harmondsworth, Penguin.

Kondratiev, N. (1925) The long waves of economic life, in *Readings in Business Cycle Theory*, American Economic Association (1950).

Labour Party (1995) *Communicating Britain's future*, London, The Labour Party.

Large, P. (1984) *The Micro Revolution Revisited*, London, Francis Pinter.

Leach, D. and Wagstaff, H. (1986) *Future Employment and Technological Change*, London, Kogan Page.

Leontief, W. (1986) *The Future Impact of Automation on Workers*, Oxford, Oxford University Press.

Lindop, Sir N. (Chairman) (1978) *Report of the Committee on Data Protection*, CMND 7341, London, HMSO.

Lobban, P. (1985) *Microelectronics and the Improvement of Working Conditions: a Management View of Developments in the UK*, London, CBI Mimeo.

MacKenzie, D. and Wajcman, J. (eds.) (1985) *The Social Shaping of Technology*, Milton Keynes, Open University Press.

Mansell, R. (ed.) (1994) *Management of Information and Communication Technologies*, London, Aslib.

Martin, J. (1981) *The Wired Society*, Englewood Cliffs NJ, Prentice Hall.

Masuda, Y. (1982) *The Information Society, as Post-industrial Society*, Tokyo, Institute for the Information Society.

McLoughlin, I. and Clark, J. (1988) *Technological Change at Work*, Milton Keynes, Open University Press.

Meade, J. E. (1995) *Full Employment Regained? An Agathotopian Dream*, Cambridge, Cambridge University Press.

Minford, P. (1984) High unemployment is not permanent, *Economic Affairs*, **4**(4), July–September.

Moore, D. (1995) *The Emperor's Virtual Clothes: the Naked Truth About the Internet*, North Carolina, Algonquin Press.

Mulgan, G. (1988) Machines for living in, *New Society*, 4 March.

Mumford, L. (1967) *The Myth of the Machine*, London, Secker & Warburg.

Mumford, E. (1983) *Designing Human Systems*, Manchester, Manchester Business School.

Murray, R. (1985) Benetton Britain: the New Economic Order, *Marxism Today*, November.

National Economic Development Council (NEDC) (1982a) *Technology: the Issues for the Distributive Trades*, London, NEDC.

National Economic Development Council (NEDC) (1982b) *Policy for the UK Electronics Industry*, London, NEDC.

Noble, D. F. (1985) *Forces of Production*, New York, Alfred Knopf.

Northcott, J., Knetsch, W. and de Lestapis, B. (1985) *Microelectronics in Industry: an International Comparison: Britain, France and Germany*, London, Policy Studies Institute.

Northcott, J. *et al.* (1986) *Robots in British Industry: Expectations and Experience*, London, Policy Studies Institute.

Parker, S. (1983) *Leisure and Work*, London, Allen & Unwin.

Piercy, N. (ed.) (1984) *The Management Implications of New Information Technology*, Beckenham, Croom Helm.

Pringle, R. (1989) *Secretaries Talk: Sexuality, Power and Work*, London, Verso Press.

Rajan, A. and Pearson, R. (eds) (1986) *UK Occupations and Employment Trends up to 1990*, London, Butterworth.

Reinecke, I. (1984) *Electronic Illusions*, Harmondsworth, Penguin.

Richardson, R. (1994) Back-officing front office functions – organizational and locational implications of new telemediated services, in *Management of Information and Communication Technologies* (ed. R. Mansell), London, Aslib.

Robbins, K. and Webster, F. (1982) New technology: a survey of trade union response in Britain, *Industrial Relations Journal*, **13**(1).

Roberts, K. (1982) *Automation, Unemployment, and the Redistribution of Income*, European Centre for Work and Society.

Robertson, J. (1983) *The Sane Alternative*, Ironbridge, James Robertson.

Robertson, J. (1985) *Future Work*, Cholsey, Temple Smith/Gower.

Rosenbrock, H. *et al.* (1981) *New Technology: Society, Employment and Skill*, London, The Council for Science and Society.

Rowan, T. (1986) *Managing with Computers*, London, Pan Books.

Rowe, C. (1984a) The break-up of computer services departments: the effects of the micro, *Industrial Management and Data Systems*, MCB University Press, January/February.

Rowe, C. (1984b) How will the new technology affect the office secretary?, *The British Journal of Administrative Management*, **34**(6), October.

Rowe, C. (1984c) The impact of computers on the work organization, *Industrial Management and Data Systems*, MCB University Press, November/December.

Rowe, C. (1987) Reorganizing data processing: towards the information centre, *Office & Information Management International*, **1**(4), September.

Rowe, C. (1988) Computer awareness among functional managers, *Industrial Management and Data Systems*, September/October.

Rustin, M. (1985) *For a Pluralist Socialism*, London, Verso Press.

Scase, R. and Goffee, R. (1989) *Managers: Their Work and Lifestyles*, London, Unwin-Hyman.

Schumacher, E. F. (1974) *Small is Beautiful; A Study of Economics As If People Mattered*, London, Abacus.

Sewell, G. and Wilkinson, B. (1992) Someone to watch over me: surveillance, discipline and the just-in-time labour process, *Sociology*, **26**(2).

Shaiken, H. (1985) *Work Transformed: Automation and Labour in the Computer Age*, New York, Holt, Rinehart & Winston.

Sieghart, P. (ed.) (1984) *Microchips with Everything; the Consequences of Information Technology*, London, Comedia Publishing Group.

Simons, G. (1985) *Silicon Shock; The Menace of the Computer Invasion*, Oxford, Basil Blackwell.

Sleigh, J., Boatwright, B., Irwin, P. and Stangon, R. (Department of Employment Manpower Study Group) (1979) *The Manpower Implications of Microelectronic Technology*, London, HMSO.

Stoll, C. (1995) *Silicon snake oil: second thoughts on the Information Highway*, New York, Doubleday.

Stonier, T. (1979) *The Third Industrial Revolution, Microprocessors and Robots*, IMF Central Committee Meeting, Vienna.

Stonier, T. (1983) *The Wealth of Information: A Profile of the Post-industrial Society*, London, Methuen.

Stonier, T. (1984) Learning a hard lesson about living with hitech, *Guardian*, 28 March.

Sylge, C. (1995) Wired Women, Information Technology, the Workplace and the Gender Debate, *Managing Information*, **2**(10).

Tapper, C. (1983) *Computer Law*, London, Longman.

Taylor, F. W. (1980) *The Principles of Scientific Management*, London, W. W. Norton.

Taylor Nelson Monitor (1986) *Taylor Nelson report* (unpublished), London, National Economic Development Office.

Thomas, R. (1995) Access and inequality, in *Information Technology and Society* (eds. N. Heap, R. Thomas, G. Einon, R. Mason and H. Mackay), London, Sage.

Thompson, L. (1989) *New Office Technology and the Changing Role of Secretaries*, ACAS report.

Thompson, J. and McGivern, J. (1996) Parody, process and practice: perspectives for management education?, *Management Learning*, **27**(1), March.

Thompson, P. and McHugh, D. (1989) *The Nature of Work: An Introduction to Debates on the Labour Process*, London, Macmillan.

Thompson, P. and McHugh, D. (1990) *Work Organisations: A Critical Introduction*, London, Macmillan.

Toffler, A. (1973) *Future Shock*, London, Pan Books.

Toffler, A. (1981) *The Third Wave*, London, Pan Books.

Trades Union Congress (TUC) (1979) *Employment and Technology*, London, TUC.

Trades Union Congress (TUC) (1996) *New Information Technologies at Work – a TUC Discussion Document*, London, TUC.

Trist, E. L. and Bamforth, K. W. (1951), Some social and psychological consequences of the longwall method of coal-getting, *Human Relations*, **4**(1).

Watson, T. (1987) *Sociology, Work and Industry*, London, Routledge & Kegan Paul.

Webster, F. and Robbins, K. (1986) *Information Technology: a Luddite Analysis*, Norwood NJ, Ablex.

Webster, J. (1986) Word processing and the secretarial labour process, in *The Changing Experience of Employment: Restructuring and Recession* (eds. K. Purcell, S. Wood, A. Waton and S. Allen), Basingstoke, Macmillan.

Webster, J. (1993) From the word processor to the micro: gender issues in the development of information technology in the office, in *Gendered by Design?* (eds. E. Green, J. Owen and D. Pain), London, Taylor & Francis.

Werneke, D. (1983) *Microelectronics and Office Jobs*, Geneva, International Labour Office.

Willcocks, L. and Mason, D. (1987) *Computerizing Work*, London, Blackwell Scientific.

Williams, N. (1990) Security, Privacy and Control, in Williams, N. and Hartley, P. (eds.) *Technology in Human Communication*, London, Pinter Publications.

Williams, R. and Steward, F. (1985) Technology agreements in Great Britain: a survey 1977–83, *Industrial Relations Journal*, **16**(3), Autumn.

Williams, V. (1984) Employment implications of new technology, *Employment Gazette*, May.

Zorkoczy, P. and Heap, N. (1995) *Information Technology; an Introduction*, London, Pitman.

Index